MAKING MISS INDIA MISS WORLD

Gender and Globalization

Susan S. Wadley, *Series Editor*

*Diana Hayden's homecoming.*

# Making
## *Miss*
## *India* *Miss*
# WORLD

*Constructing Gender,*

*Power, and the Nation*

*in Postliberalization India*

S U S A N   D E W E Y

 Syracuse University Press

For a listing of books published and distributed by Syracuse University Press,
visit our Web site at SyracuseUniversityPress.syr.edu

ISBN-13: 978-0-8156-3176-7       ISBN-10: 0-8156-3176-6

**Library of Congress Cataloging-in-Publication Data**

Dewey, Susan.
   Making Miss India Miss World : constructing gender, power, and the nation in
postliberalization India / Susan Dewey. — 1st ed.
       p. cm. — (Gender and globalization)
   Includes bibliographical references and index.
   ISBN 978-0-8156-3176-7 (cloth : alk. paper)
  1. Women—India—Social conditions.   2. Women in development—India.   3. Miss
World Pageant.   4. Beauty contests—India.   5. Beauty contestants—India.   6. National
characteristics, East Indian.   7. Ethnicity—India.   8. India—Social conditions.   I. Title.
   HQ1743.D49 2008
   306.4'613—dc22
   2007037079

*Manufactured in the United States of America*

To Susan and Robert

*Dil Se*

SUSAN DEWEY is a cultural anthropologist with a specialization in India. She received her doctorate in anthropology from Syracuse University in 2004. Dr. Dewey has worked as consultant on gender and counter-trafficking for the International Organization for Migration in Yerevan, Armenia, and Sarajevo, Bosnia-Herzegovina. Her broader research interests lie in how changes in macro-economic policies at the state level impact individuals, particularly women. She is the author of the upcoming *Hollow Bodies: Institutional Responses to Sex Trafficking in Armenia, Bosnia-Herzegovina, and India* (to be published by Kumarian Press), and she is a contributor to *Ethnography and Education Quarterly, South Asian Popular Culture, Labrys,* and *Manushi.* She has also been a contributing writer for several years for the Mumbai-based women's magazine *Gurlz.* She is currently the principal investigator for a National Science Foundation–funded project in Fiji entitled "Learning Difference: The Politicization of Ethnic Identity in Educational Institutions in Viti Levu," which examines conceptions of cultural autonomy among Indo-Fijians and indigenous Fijians in the wake of four coups in Fiji.

# Contents

# Illustrations

# Acknowledgments

$\mathcal{T}$his book would not have been written if not for the encouragement and mentoring I received from anthropologist Dr. Susan Snow Wadley, my doctoral dissertation advisor, and words are not adequate to express the depth of my gratitude for her continued support of my work. My research was made possible by funds from a twelve-month Fulbright-Hays Doctoral Dissertation Research Abroad Grant and four months of a Foreign Languages and Area Studies (FLAS) fellowship. I am deeply grateful to sociologist Dr. Julia Loughlin for an independent study she conducted with me on the social construction of the body; it informed research for this book in innumerable ways. Linguist Dr. Tej Bhatia not only provided me with an understanding of advertising in rural India, which helped me to grasp the dynamics of sponsorship and commodity culture at Miss India, but also gave me the priceless gift of fluency in Hindi. Anthropologist Dr. Hans Buechler's depth of knowledge on the dynamics of neoliberalism in Latin America and focus on life histories and reflexivity greatly informed the theoretical and methodological stances taken in this book.

I can never repay the generosity that has consistently been shown to me by the people of India, a country for which I have a deep and abiding love, and it would be impossible to list all of the wonderful individuals who helped me throughout the course of my research. A. P. Parigi, the managing director and CEO of the event management company 360 Degrees, and Pradeep Guha, former president of the Times of India Group, were exceedingly generous in allowing me unrestricted access to the Miss India pageant, and I am deeply grateful to both of them. Former *Femina* editor Vimla Patel provided me with background on the history of the magazine, and Sathya Saran was gracious enough to tolerate my presence as a temporary part of her editorial staff (and kind enough to help facilitate the publication of my first novel, *Penumbra*, published by Haranand, Delhi). Publisher and editor of *Gurlz* magazine Urmilla Talyarkhan was extremely helpful by providing me with firsthand experience with what I think is the most vibrant and dynamic women's magazine in India. Shilpa Rane, Sangeeta Wadhwani, and Ninaz Khodaiji were always there for me in Mumbai with friendship and advice, and Lucia, Joseph, and Lawrence Fernandes in Candolim, Goa, gave me a space in their guesthouse to write the first draft of my novel in addition to their lifelong friendship.

I must also thank my husband for his love, support, and continued willingness to listen to my Mumbai stories.

MAKING MISS INDIA MISS WORLD

# 1

## Beauty as Cultural Performance

You must remember that you are onstage twenty-four hours a day," intoned instructor Rukhshana Eisa to the twenty-six Miss India contestants as she guided them through a session on dinner etiquette. "You will all be ambassadors of your country someday, whether or not you make it to the Miss Universe pageant, and you must learn to do so graciously, because our culture does not teach these things. You should be able to handle any social situation gracefully, with people from cultures different from your own." As she held up a glass of red wine in front of the contestants in a poised manner and asked rhetorically, "Now, is this ladylike?" Eisa smiled at the cameras that were circulating throughout the room as part of the meticulous documentation of the lives of contestants at the pageant's training program.

The contestants sat at tables facing one another as the cameras filmed each young woman's studied imitation of Eisa's elegant mannerisms. As she guided them through a seven-course French dinner designed to teach them Western European table manners, she reminded them not to eat anything. "I know it's tempting," she said, "but remember that this is simply instructional. I don't have to remind you not to overindulge." The contestants had all been on an extremely strict diet and exercise regimen for the past three weeks as part of the intense residential training program that transforms young women into slender beauty queens prior to the Miss India pageant, and so Eisa's comments provoked quiet sighs as plates of exquisite desserts and glasses of wine were placed in front of the contestants. In an almost obvious moment of surveillance, one of the cameras focused on a contestant's untouched plate as if to document her self-control. This, I thought to myself, was Foucault's concept of the panopticon writ on an almost comical scale.

Contestants at the Miss India training program are under scrutiny twenty-four hours a day by chaperones as well as by a panel of experts appointed by pageant officials. After pageant organizers complete the selection rounds in three Indian cities, twenty-six contestants are invited to Mumbai (Bombay) for one month of intensive instruction, which involves extensive physical, emotional, and cultural transformations designed to improve their chances of winning at the Miss Universe or Miss World pageants. The contestants are allowed to leave the five-star hotel in which they are housed only a few times under close supervision during the course of the training program and are otherwise ensconced in a Foucauldian total institution with the sole purpose of making them into slim, fair, and relatively articulate young women who fit the Miss India mold.

Young women enter the pageant fully expecting to change not only their bodies but also to emerge several months later as fundamentally altered human beings. Individual women try their best under the gaze of the experts at the training program to embody the qualities that Miss India is associated with both in India and at the Miss Universe and Miss World pageants, which include fluent, British-accented English, a superficial espousing of women's empowerment and simultaneous affirmation of gender roles, fair skin, extraordinary height, and a great deal of cultural knowledge about the United States and Western Europe. What is most notable about the training program is that all of these qualities (with the exception of height) are created with the assistance of a group of media professionals known as "the experts."

The Miss India training program highlights a number of similarities between the creation of beauty queens and ways of thinking about the body as a machine with parts to be repaired and replaced that characterize many industrialized societies with vibrant consumer cultures. More than one individual at the training program referred to contestants' bodies as "in need of work" or "not up to standard" as part of a broader discourse that separated the mechanics of beauty into distinct categories with room for improvement. The construction of twenty-six potential Miss Indias from a group of relatively ordinary young women points to ways in which the body is both "cultural plastic" (Davis 1995) and a space for the performance of gendered identity (Butler 1993).

This was made increasingly clear to me as I looked through the archives of *Femina* magazine, which has been directly associated with the pageant since its inception in the late 1950s. I could hardly recognize photographs of the teenager in these files who was identified as former Miss Universe Sushmita Sen, now famous in India for her voluptuous figure; to my eyes, Sen as Miss India contestant bore almost no resemblance to the actress who featured prominently in Hindi films at the time of my research. Similarly, I found my way through the *Femina* archives to images of former Miss World and current Hindi film star Aishwarya Rai's photograph, in which she was a blue-eyed young woman wearing a sash that read, as an advertisement for an Indian brand of refrigerator, "Kelvinator Miss Perfect Ten." The irony of an individual who is now routinely referred to in India as "the most beautiful woman in the world" advertising kitchen appliances seemed to underscore the transformational progression from ordinary young woman to emblem of beauty for which Miss India is so renowned. I remember just a few weeks later watching Aishwarya dart dramatically out of a fashion show in highly stylized fear designed to elicit maximum attention from paparazzi when she realized that her former boyfriend, the muscular Hindi film actor Salman Khan, was also in attendance. As I struggled to reconcile these two spectacularly different images, I marveled at the flexibility of both identity and the body that being Miss India entails.

Beauty pageants have not been a focus of popular culture in the United States since mid-century and perhaps have never been accorded the same amount of cultural capital that they have in India. Most North Americans associate them with kitschy parades of elaborately coiffed women in evening gowns, and yet beauty pageants are often criticized as "Western" by Indian religious conservatives. Indian English uses "Western" to indicate a constellation of behaviors and beliefs related to the individual choice and independence associated with a place culturally and historically marked as "the West," generally considered to be located in Western Europe and North America. In India, Western behaviors and beliefs include a (superficial) sense of male-female equality, English language education, and the acceptance of the right to individual choice and pleasure. Because Miss India is primarily about individual women seeking to make contacts in the media industry to advance their film and modeling careers, it is, in this use of the word, indeed a Western event.

Yet given the extreme popularity of the urban cultural phenomenon that is Miss India, I contend that beauty pageants are also uniquely Indian and that it is important that the access young women are granted to wealth and power via their participation be explored as part of a broader effort at understanding what it means to be female in urban India. As an intrinsic part of a culture that often values young women only as decorative objects, the pageant serves as an excellent site within which to examine the complex connections between femininity, beauty, and power in India.

As a feminist and ambivalent viewer of events such as Miss India, I choose to separate beauty as an oppressive and hegemonic concept from beauty as empowering practice as well as to recognize that pageants are simply manifestations of gender inequality rather than causal agents. It is precisely because of the institutionalized sexism that women have to negotiate in everyday life that it is extraordinarily easy for certain groups in India to blame beauty pageants for the subjugation of women. Women throughout the world are forced to contend with deeply flawed systems that position them as inferior beings, and yet sometimes these systems allow certain types of women opportunities for social mobility and self-esteem. This book is about how young women who fit a very narrow set of institutional criteria defined by the Miss India pageant are granted career and life opportunities that are beyond the reach of the vast majority of their peers.

Young women choose to participate in Miss India because beauty pageants as a misogynist concept are very different from beauty pageants as empowering practice. Although I started research for this book with a perspective that considered beauty pageants were guilty of both classism and sexism, watching twenty-six young women work so hard to win made it extremely difficult not to have some degree of respect for what

Miss India means to them, and to large parts of India, as an institution. As such, although beauty pageants as a concept are fundamentally flawed in the way they commodify women, the Miss India pageant in practice is a space of social mobility like no other.

## Lymaraina D'Souza's Wedding Gown:
## Toward a Real World Feminist Theory and Methodology

No matter where I went in India, Miss India was never far away. From a remote beach in the Eastern Indian state of Orissa, where a tea vendor questioned me about my work with the pageant, to eager phone calls from a friend in Delhi inquiring how a contestant was doing in the training program in Mumbai, being an active participant allowed me access to a fascinating world in which everyone seemed to be connected to Miss India in some way or another. Without a doubt, however, the most memorable Miss India story that I heard came from a woman in a small town in the Western Indian state of Goa who had been a neighbor to former Miss India contestant Lymaraina D'Souza. The woman spoke in awed tones of how D'Souza had been transformed from an ordinary Goan teenager into a glamorous woman of the world. She spent nearly half an hour telling me about how expensive and beautiful D'Souza's wedding gown had been and described D'Souza's life as a fairy tale not unlike the English language romance novels many urban Indian women read.

"'Mills and Boon', I said to myself when I saw her husband, because he looked just like a hero from one of the romance novels we used to read," she said, describing in detail D'Souza's wedding to an Irish man she met while in college in Hawaii. To the woman telling the story, D'Souza and her fantasy wedding gown represented a life of social mobility made possible by Miss India. In order to understand just how accessible D'Souza's dream-like existence was made to seem to a woman in small-town Goa, a new way of thinking about beauty and, indeed, feminism, is necessary.

As Ruth Behar (1995, 45) observed, "Feminist revision is always about a new way of looking at all categories." What is lacking in contemporary feminist approaches is an understanding of the ways in which women manipulate patriarchal social structures to their own advantage by actively

1. *The life of Goan Lymaraina D'Souza is often described by many women from her ethnic group as "a fairy tale" because of her participation in the Miss India pageant.*

participating in them. The Miss India pageant is certainly an instrument of male domination at a structural level and yet it can also be seen as a space of female empowerment and social mobility for women like Lymaraina D'Souza. It is thus useful to come to an understanding of a real world feminism that pays as much attention to individual women's motivations for participating in patriarchy as it does to the flawed institutions that patriarchy perpetuates.

This book employs three key themes as a way of thinking about Miss India and the complex nexus of beauty, power, and class that surround it: the power of the gaze, gender, and globalization. The central question that this book seeks to address is, How is gender and globalization performed at Miss India and how has this changed following the implementation of the International Monetary Fund's structural adjustment policies, also known as economic liberalization, in 1991? The first key theme of the power of the gaze is the subject of chapters 2 and 3, which detail the connections between visual media's veritable postliberalization explosion and dramatic changes to Miss India. The magazine and film production that are central to so many elements of Miss India increased considerably following structural adjustment, when Indian media sought to compete with the seductive international images that had become available.

The book's discussion of the gaze draws upon an anthropological tradition of examining the impacts of class, power, and colonialism on specific social groups. Much has been written about the gaze and its power within a colonial or neocolonial context (e.g., di Leonardo 2000; Gill 1995; Pels 1997) or within a framework that considers class or politico-economic dominance (Bryan 2000; Fisher 1997; Gledhill 2000; Wolf 1999) and yet very little has served to document understandings of the gaze within a specific cultural group outside of Europe or the United States. Anthropology is by its very nature an extremely visual discipline, which makes it even more crucial to explore what it means to "see" both within and across cultural groups. The power of the gaze is paramount at Miss India, and discussions of how young women construct themselves vis-à-vis Indian ideas about "international standards" serve to illustrate how the gaze can be a force that profoundly shapes young women's lives.

Chapter 2 analyzes interviews with six young women, including a Mumbai local pageant winner and a former Miss Universe, to examine how performing gender at beauty pageants has altered the course of their lives. To fully appreciate the broad spectrum of different types of pageant experiences, chapter 2 also features a narrative from a young woman who experienced a period of severe depression after she did not win Miss India, although she went on to become a film star because of the contacts she made at the pageant's training program. Chapter 2 also details the differences in background and preparedness between the twenty-six contestants at the Miss India training program and how each saw herself vis-à-vis the other contestants.

Chapter 3 discusses how contestants at the Miss India training program, a month-long intensive seminar held inside a five-star hotel that the contestants are seldom allowed to leave, negotiate extreme surveillance and attempt to manipulate social networks to their advantage. Foucault's description of power as omnipresent because it is situated at once inside and outside situations via complex processes of positioning (1980, 93) informs this chapter's discussion of the way in which young women at the pageant construct elaborate hierarchies of beauty and nationality at the training program. Chapter 3 also discusses how the gaze is central to Miss India. Although film stars and business tycoons have always been venerated throughout urban India—a phenomenon that mirrors similar patterns of social behavior in India, including the feudal system of Rajasthan and the guru system—economic liberalization's concomitant media explosion has created a culture of celebrity that positions individuals who work in highly visible, media-related professions as authorities on everything from fashion to politics.

Walker (2003) asserts that popular culture has intersected with institutions and everyday life to such a degree that it is no longer possible to make a distinction between "real" experience and artifice, not unlike the very real results of postindependence efforts by Indian media in the form of *Femina* magazine and Miss India to create a homogenous national identity. Virilio (1994) and Buck-Morss (1996) have similarly illustrated how concepts of seeing and remembering have changed dramatically following the introduction of visual technologies such as the camera into mainstream social life. The culture of celebrity as it exists at Miss India and in urban India is directly dependent on such technologies so that one's visibility in such a culture reflects one's position within it: the more one is seen, the more powerful one is. Miss India serves as a direct path to stardom for many young women, because being under the gaze of those who are already celebrities provides an opportunity for accelerated upward mobility.

The second theme, gender, frames chapter 4, which is grounded in feminist theory's concept of power as enacted through gender. Theories of feminism are often rooted in the body as a classed and gendered site from which individuals experience reality. This reality is compounded by Davis's conception of the body as an identity project, which Davis finds to be a crucial part of "the cultural landscape of late modernity" (1995, 2). Davis's use of the term "identity project" refers to the construction and manipulation of the female body as an act central to the creation of a gendered self. Davis's conception follows that of Haraway (1999), who suggests that "bodies are not born but made," as well as Grosz, who argues that "bodies do not simply move through spaces, geographies and cities, but constitute and are constituted by them, at both a local and global level" (1999, 79).

Chapter 4 discusses how women's bodies become representations of the nation via a process that involves femininity as cultural performance. By positioning the pageant as an organization that works toward *strī śakti,* which loosely translates from Hindi as "woman power," organizers are able to stage an event that would otherwise be seen as violating cultural norms in its display of young women's bodies. This chapter also employs a feminist theoretical framework that draws upon Bordo (1993), Butler (1993), Brumberg (1988) and Hammonds (1999) to address how women at the Miss India training program use their bodies as vehicles to advance their sense of self-worth and class status.

Feminist theory is couched in a framework that emphasizes the effect of instruments of domination in a world in which gender is a central organizing principle through which individuals negotiate the course of their everyday lived experience. Beauty pageants such as Miss India are certainly instruments of male domination at a structural level, and yet they can also be spaces of female empowerment and social mobility, as the case of Lymaraina D'Souza's wedding gown demonstrates.

It has long been self-evident that women are embodied subjects (Butler 1993), and yet there is a dearth of literature that addresses how women successfully transform their bodies and selves into culture-bound visions of beauty that can empower them in a number of ways. It is dangerous to label such women mere victims of male domination and thus deny them recognition of the agency and intelligence to negotiate their social worlds. Following Cole's (1991) discussion of Portuguese fisherwomen who aspired to be stay-at-home mothers rather than income earners, it is important to remember that power (and empowerment) are constructed in vastly different ways by individual women.

The literature that surrounds beauty pageants largely focuses on critiques of popular culture (e.g., Banet-Weiser 1999; Handelman 1990; Jewell

1993; Riverol 1992; Segalen and Chamarat 1983), the antifeminist nature of such events (Faludi 1988; Freedman 1988; Perlmutter 2000), or globalization (Cannell 1993; Cohen, Wilk, and Stoeltje 1995; Johnson 1997; Kobkidsuksakul 1988; Maayang 1990). Scholarly work on the performance of beauty at salons and in media tends to similarly deal with the artificial nature of such beauty (e.g., Kuhn 1985) or the unrealistic standards that such spaces impose on women (e.g., Furman 1997; Mulvey 1989). Recognizing that such standards of beauty must be negotiated by most women in the course of their lives serves to help us not only to understand what pageants as a cultural phenomenon mean but also to provide a clearer picture of the complexities of gendered experience.

The fact remains that although most feminist scholarship does not acknowledge it, the vast majority of women would choose to embody culturally prevailing standards of beauty if they could for the simple reason that being beautiful makes life easier. As my discussion of the Miss India pageant process and what it meant to the twenty-six contestants who participated in it will repeatedly illustrate, standards of beauty are created and constructed by specific sociopolitical forces that serve to affect everyone who is exposed to them. Just as the image of the Hollywood blonde (Pitman 2004) and forces of colonialism combine to make certain white European features "beautiful" in both North and South America, there are equal numbers of forces at work that deem other beauties less so.

Beauty is eminently political, as was evidenced by the riots surrounding the 2002 Miss World pageant during which 215 Nigerians were killed and 12,000 left homeless, the politicization of Miss Afghanistan at the Miss World 2003 pageant, and the social construction of fair skin as desirable. Power dynamics are deeply and inseparably embedded in standards of beauty everywhere, and as a single specific site from which to examine what such standards mean to the individual women who meet them as well as to popular culture at large, Miss India is a locus for debates about what it means to be Indian, female, and, above all, a member of an increasingly interconnected world.

The third major theme is globalization, which I define as a never-ending process of cross-cultural interaction that is contextual and enacted on a situational basis in the course of everyday lived experience.

The anthropology of globalization has tended until fairly recently to frame discussions around two poles of orientation without significant middle ground between them. On one side, the concept of "Coca-colonization" gained a great deal of popularity as scholars struggled to make sense of the changes brought by the temporal and spatial compression of images and commodities, and on the other side, scholars attempted to analyze this phenomenon via interdisciplinary discussions that recognized that beyond being positive or negative, globalization is an inescapable reality.

Appadurai asserted as late as 1996 that "the central problem in today's global interactions is tensions between cultural homogenization and cultural heterogenization" (1996, 32). This notion of two extremes pitted against one another has been challenged by more nuanced ethnographies that examine the wide variety of factors that influence how individual social actors contend with the changes that globalization has brought to their lives (Burke 1996; Dickey 1993; Dwyer 2000; Liechty 2002). Others, such as Orlove (1997), contend that commodity fetishism is not at all a new historical phenomenon, and Mathews (2000) argues that individuals are relatively free to pick and choose from identities and images on display in the cultural supermarket.

Numerous ethnographies that focus on media and television (Ganti 2000; Gillespie 2001; Goodwin 1992; Gupta 1998; Hutnyk 2000; Mankekar 1999) underscore the way in which identity is much more malleable and situational than scholars had originally thought. Chapter 5 discusses how the popularity of implementing what are often referred to in India as "international standards" followed the introduction of economic liberalization policies in 1991, when Indian products and the individuals who consume them were further incorporated into the global marketplace. Analyses of advertising in South Asia (Bhatia 2000; Kemper 2001) speak to the way in which "need" is often created via a consumer's sense of identification with a product in a way that mirrors both India's warm reception of Western European and American beauty culture and the incorporation of "international standards" at the Miss India pageant.

Chapter 6 highlights the manifold nature of globalization via discussions of how Sunsilk shampoo, sponsor of the 2003 Miss India pageant, positioned itself as a marker of modernity. This serves to illustrate how these changes are embedded in Indian social values, particularly those surrounding the primacy of the gaze, gender hierarchies, and ideas about male honor and prestige. This chapter's discussion of the creation of national identity via a commodity-driven pageant draws upon an ethnographic literature on consumption (e.g., Gerke 2000) and fashion (Douglas 2003; Jones 2003; Tarlo 1996) that has emerged as part of a focus on how objects are used to define the self.

This literature complements Baudrillard's (1998) discussion of the social meanings of consumption, as well as works by Appadurai (1988) and Gell (1998) that speak to the social nature of commodities in general. In the case of the beauty industry that sponsors the pageant, we see that the products used to advertise and support Miss India are a crucial element in defining both the pageant itself and the way it is presented to an Indian audience. A final body of literature that the theme of globalization incorporates is on behavioral consumption, which is unfortunately a bit more limited in nature, such as Allison's (1994) *Nightwork* and Farquhar's (2002) *Appetites*. Behavioral consumption is a crucial part of both the training program and the pageant itself in the way in which Miss India contestants seek to embody a form of womanhood that is seen as simultaneously international and uniquely "Indian."

Viewing the Miss India pageant through a lens that focuses on globalization, chapters 5 and 6 illustrate how the overly simplistic dichotomies of first/third world and development/underdevelopment have perhaps outlived their usefulness. India is primarily a country of villages that has been plagued by socioeconomic problems resulting at least in part from its former status as a British colony, and yet it is also home to a significant number of individuals who identify far more with the images they see on Hong Kong–based satellite television than the larger rural reality of life on the subcontinent. By addressing how the power of the gaze, gender, and globalization are interconnected in the course of contestants' everyday lived experience at Miss India, a clearer picture will emerge of what it means to live in contemporary India.

Since at least the time of former Prime Minister Nehru's postindependence "temples of modernization" in the forms of dams and factories, urban India as a whole has been caught up in efforts to make it what is often described in India as "on par" with the rest of the world. The "rest of the world" that is most often viewed as worth emulating includes former colonial powers in Western Europe as well as former colonies such as the United States. This project of referencing involves the replication of lifestyle and fashion and does not make use of, for example, commodities or cultural elements drawn from Nigeria or Pakistan. This process has been accelerated and exponentially expanded in scope since the implementation of structural adjustment policies in 1991 and impacts people at all socioeconomic levels, although those who are privileged enough to be able to participate in institutions such as Miss India are obviously more positively affected. The changes involved in such institutions are so similar to broader cultural changes ongoing throughout the subcontinent that it is clear Miss India is not simply a beauty pageant but rather a symbol of the vast socioeconomic shifts that urban India has experienced since liberalization.

*Methodology*

I began research for this book with the knowledge that it would force me to interrogate my own feelings about beauty, and it did exactly that. My clearest childhood memory of interpreting mixed cultural messages about gendered beauty is of watching a soap opera in which an attractive man carrying a pizza visited the home of a beautiful young woman, and he apologetically said, "I know that women won't eat unless someone makes them, because you women are always on a diet so you'll stay beautiful." I remember being extremely puzzled by this statement, wondering why anyone would refuse pizza and what eating (or not eating) had to do with beauty. Yet, as I reached my early twenties I also found myself constantly on a diet, just like the woman on the soap opera. I had, like many other American women, become similar to the televised image that had so perplexed the seven-year-old me. All of the adult women I knew throughout my childhood were perpetually on a diet, or talking about going on one, and people seemed to use the adjectives "fat" and "unattractive" as interchangeable synonyms. Watching women in my family jump from diet to diet, as well as using food as an emotional support system, the message I clearly received was that women are defined by their bodies. I began to believe that it was normal and natural for women to base their sense of self-worth on how closely they approximated the images of women in magazines at the supermarket checkout counter. Curiously, as I spent much of my adult life in and out of India, I began to notice the same gendered phenomenon taking place. What, I wondered, was making women feel so deeply dissatisfied with their bodies and, by extension, themselves?

This book is about the women who are considered the most beautiful in India because they fit a particular set of standards that influence women throughout South Asia. An analysis of what beauty means to them and how it is constructed and performed at Miss India serves to illustrate how standards of beauty are set, maintained, and spread in one particular geographical region. I could not have written this book had it not been for the gracious consent and generous support of the Times of India Group, which owns the Miss India pageant. I began research in October 2002 as a writer for *Femina*, the most widely circulated women's magazine in India and the pageant's parent publication, in order to determine how the pageant had changed since its inception in the 1950s. As the vehicle through which young women learn about how to enter the pageant as well as read about the lives of its contestants and winners, the magazine proved to be a valuable source of information and experience before I began work on the 2003 pageant.

Miss India 2003 was unique in that it was the first year the Times of India Group sought to make the public at large aware of the processes involved in selecting Miss India. I am fairly certain that my participation in the pageant was part of the organizers' goal of making it what they often referred to as "transparent," by which they meant it involved standards and procedures that were fair and democratic, and I was given access to all aspects of the four-month-long Miss India process. The entry forms for the pageant were due at the end of October, soon after which I went through the complete collection in neat white binders with judges' comments on them. I then traveled to Delhi and Bangalore, as well my primary research and residence site in Mumbai, for the initial selection rounds of the pageant in November. This was followed by the month-long training program, in which I stayed with contestants in one of the most luxurious five-star hotels in Mumbai and observed as they were prepared for the pageant. Next, I traveled to Bangalore with Miss India officials for the semifinals of the pageant, followed by a return to Mumbai for the final pageant on January 31.

I had the opportunity to become acquainted with contestants and organizers from a fairly wide range of backgrounds, which allowed me to truly understand what Miss India means to a cross-section of urban Indian society in the poststructural adjustment era. Not much older than many of the contestants when I conducted this research, I had to consciously decide not to compete with other young women. Once the contestants were comfortable with me, they often commented on how strange it was that I had never entered Miss America. I was mistaken for a contestant (usually of Parsi origin) several times by reporters throughout the course of the pageant, and when I informed them that I was a researcher and PhD candidate writing a book on Miss India, many of them were reluctant to believe me. Sadly, the perceived fact remains that beauty is not intelligent.

I was both an active participant and an anthropologist in the 2003 pageant process, which resulted in a sometimes uncomfortable combination of roles. Anthropologists and the degree to which they are accepted by the groups they work with, whether they are beauty queens or nomadic hunter-gatherers, depends largely on their positionality within the community, and it was made absolutely clear to me several times throughout the course of my research by both pageant officials and critics of Miss India that I would not have been provided with such access had I not been a young, fair-skinned, and attractive foreigner. One of my female friends in Mumbai was particularly critical of this reality in her characteristically forthright style when she moaned, "Oh, come on, none of these people would have looked your way twice if you weren't beautiful yourself." I would like to think that my fluency in several South Asian languages, decade of experience with the subcontinent, and familiarity with Indian popular culture also worked in my favor.

I am not convinced that anthropologists can ever simply function as "researchers" separate from the communities in which they work, and would argue that our positions as scholars of human behavior in universities more often resemble roles in the field including friend, fictive kin and, sometimes, beloved. There are numerous examples where contestants confided to me about the unwelcome sexual pressure they experienced from older men with powerful positions in media that I have chosen not to include here in the interests of protecting the privacy of young women who presumably gave me this information as peers and friends rather than with the understanding that it would later appear in a reputation-destroying book. Sometimes such stories were provided to me as cautionary tales about who and what to avoid as a young single woman who frequently interviewed much older Hindi film producers and directors who were, quite frankly, used to getting their way.

Organizers of the Miss India pageant were very much in support of my research and were extremely generous in their provision of flights to the selection rounds in Bangalore and Delhi and meals and accommodation during the training program. No academic grant I had access to as a graduate student would have paid for such luxuries, and I am deeply grateful to the Times of India Group for subsidizing my work. I tried my best to provide services as repayment for this beneficence by providing feedback on the "transparency" of the pageant, writing questions for contestants to answer, and occasionally serving as a liaison to the press. Pageant officials were always very clear that this assistance was nothing more than a way to facilitate what should be a balanced and nuanced analysis of Miss India. Although it is true that my position of relative power may have initially impacted the contestants' responses, this changed so much within just a few weeks of close contact that I have had to omit some of the more private and sensitive pieces of information they shared with me.

The pageant made everyone participating in it in any capacity more conscious of and reflective about beauty. From an organizer who candidly stated, "I know I'm ugly, I never doubted that," to an overweight chaperone in her late teens who noted, "I never knew that beauty queens would be nice to me," the practice of evaluating beauty affected everyone at some level and often informed the subjects of conversation individuals pursued with me. The receptionist at 360 Degrees, the office that handled

Miss India 2003, said over lunch, "I don't want to be a beauty queen, but I do hope I never gain weight. Even if I don't always wear clothes like these, it would be awful to lose the option to wear them." Dressed in her usual ensemble of tight-fitting trousers and a sleeveless blouse, her statement underscored the way in which everyone has ideas about beauty, even if they would never think of participating in a beauty pageant.

What beauty pageants do, then, is to exemplify in a sometimes comical format the hidden cultural constructs that surround beauty. Looking at pageants provides a means by which to analyze these constructs more closely, and there is no better site in urban India than the Miss India pageant from which to examine the prevailing standards of beauty and the institutional structures that have the power to create them. As this book will repeatedly illustrate, yes, beauty is in the eye of the beholder, but some have more power to behold than others.

## Making Modernity? *Femina* Magazine, Miss India, and Structural Adjustment

No discussion of the Miss India pageant would be complete without mention of *Femina* magazine, its parent publication. *Femina* is something of an institution in India; it has been in circulation since 1959 and its subscription rates have consistently been the highest of any women's magazine. Published by the Times of India Group, it is also Indian-owned, as opposed to more recently arrived women's magazines such as *Cosmopolitan* and *Glamour*. Its target readership has always been primarily composed of urban and English-language educated upper-middle-class women who can afford the fifty rupees (about one U.S. dollar) charged per issue. The magazine has consistently marketed itself by its slogan "for the woman of substance" and today looks quite similar to its peer publications in the United States and Western Europe with high quality, glossy images that constitute a considerable change from its original black-and-white newsprint format. The most notable shifts in *Femina*'s orientation and appearance as a magazine are directly tied to structural adjustment, the economic reforms imposed by the International Monetary Fund (IMF) and implemented in 1991.

Structural adjustment programs have been employed in over seventy countries around the world with significant debt to the IMF and consist of two phases, both of which are aimed at reducing account deficits: short-term macroeconomic stabilization and the implementation of structural reforms deemed necessary by the IMF (Rangarajan 1994). Most notably for *Femina,* structural adjustment policies encouraged foreign investment, thus bringing in a vast array of new media and commodity choices from the United States and Western Europe. These reforms specifically amounted to the devaluation of the rupee by 23 percent, the institution of a new industrial policy that was more conducive to foreign investment, government disinvestment in potentially profitable public sector areas, the introduction of private banks, a liberalized import/export regime, cuts in social spending to reduce fiscal deficits, and amendments to laws to support all of these reforms (Chopra et al. 1995). Although these policies did little to help the poor, they vastly altered the commodity and consumption choices available to those with disposable income as part of a pattern that mirrors the further marginalization of already disadvantaged groups throughout the world following the implementation of structural adjustment programs.

Such policies also allowed major media corporations including the Hong Kong–based Star TV to enter India as part of an essential focus on foreign investment. Structural adjustment facilitated the expansion of an already prolific media industry in India, as the changes brought about by the introduction of international media and nearly 60,000 Indian-run cable networks were vast and overarching. After 1991, individuals began to routinely use media-centric metaphors in order to describe ways of being and thinking, such as the expression "MTV culture," to concisely sum up a philosophy of life whose main tenets included individuality, the right to self-expression, and conspicuous consumption. Such media-related language is not surprising given the enormous change in scope that television, film, and even radio have undergone since 1991.

The 1990s also introduced the idea of the beauty queen as a global ambassador with the simultaneous victories of Miss India winners Sushmita Sen and Aishwarya Rai at Miss Universe and Miss World in 1994. *Femina* magazine was an active participant in the representation of these women to Indian audiences by featuring them in a wide variety of fashion layouts and interviews. In the pages of the magazine throughout the 1990s, both Sen and Rai were consistently made emblematic of *Femina*'s "woman of substance" through their beauty and achievement as international pageant winners. Beautiful, glamorous, and relatively articulate, Miss India contestants are often seen as embodiments of the ideal of urban Indian femininity. Yet these role models are also salespeople, and it is rare that their images appear without a product beside them, as Miss India is also a broker extraordinaire who sells everything from Mont Blanc pens to European-style toilets.

The first Miss India pageant was held in 1959, a little over a decade after independence, and was designed to create young and attractive female ambassadors to showcase Indian textiles throughout the world. It is not incidental that cloth and its production are inextricably tied to the Indian independence movement and Gandhian strategies of passive resistance, specifically the refusal to buy British-produced cloth manufactured with Indian cotton. The most potent symbol of the Indian independence movement is Gandhi's spinning wheel, from which he produced his own homespun cotton, known as *khadī*, in order to avoid buying British-produced finished cotton. The pageant was originally designed not only as a way to present a relatively newly independent India to the world, but also as a means of national integration. Vimla Patel, the editor of *Femina* from 1959 to 1993, described the role that the pageant and the magazine had to play in the creation of national identity:

When India became independent, there were, because of the various states in India, different kinds of women. There was a Maharashtrian woman, there was a Punjabi woman, but nobody had identified what was an Indian woman. There was a question mark there. Who is the Indian woman? Nobody knew. Who was going to put all these threads together and make one fabric? That was the question. And the answer to that was *Femina* and Miss India.

Although there are certainly other factors at work in the formation of national identity in India, it is notable that independence and the notion of creating a nation of "one fabric" are linked in the above passage. The Miss India pageant proceeded in much the same way until the implementation of structural adjustment policies in 1991, when Pradeep Guha, head of the Miss India pageant between 1991 and 2002, shifted the focus to what he described as "creating a Miss World or a Miss Universe who is incidentally an Indian." Guha describes India's first serious foray into producing an international pageant winner as something of an accident. In 1992, Miss India Madhu Sapre earned the title of first runner-up at the Miss World pageant with no training at all. When she returned to India, Guha spent a great deal of time with Sapre in order to determine what could have improved her chances of winning. It was this experience that led to the creation of the Miss India training program that was first implemented in 1993, the year before the victories of Sushmita Sen and Aishwarya Rai at Miss Universe and Miss World.

The amount of attention paid to the pageant has exponentially increased since the dual win in 1994. I could not help but notice as I went through the files on the pageant at the *Femina* office that all the years prior to 1994 are consolidated to a rather sad little file of inexpensive newsprint that stands in sharp contrast to the color glossy extravaganzas that subsequent years received. Indeed, when I interviewed former Miss India winners from the years before economic liberalization, their observations on how different the pageant is today were extremely consistent. As Miss India 1972 Roopa Satyam noted in comparing the contemporary pageant, which she would like her daughter to enter, with the Miss India she participated in, "You can't just do this for fun anymore. My life wouldn't have been any different if I hadn't entered." Satyam's statement underscores how what is now a means to attain social mobility did not have much of an impact on the lives of contestants in her era.

Institutions such as *Femina* and Miss India do not exist in a vacuum; they affect and are affected by socioeconomic changes at both the international and state levels. It is self-evident that the Miss India pageant as Roopa Satyam experienced it in 1972 was a different cultural event than the media extravaganza of the 2003 pageant because each existed in a different India: the first still rooted in the postindependence protectionist economic policies that heavily restricted foreign investment and media, and the second that embraced the neoliberal economic regime advocated by the IMF.

The 2003 pageant was unlike any other that had preceded it in that the media and public relations firm 360 Degrees worked incredibly hard to make the Miss India selection process be what they referred to as "transparent" to the public. This focus on transparency, or fairness as a result of processes that are known to all, mirrored the use of similar language across all fields of Indian life following structural adjustment, ranging from government financial policy to lending stipulations imposed on the government of India by the IMF. 360 Degrees had been chosen by Pradeep Guha when he decided to move on to other responsibilities after a decade of organizing the pageant, and so with ample references to Six Sigma management strategies, maximum sponsor exposure, and branding, Miss India 2003 maintained the post-1991 focus on "international standards" while adding language and policies that had become institutionalized in the Indian economy just over ten years after the implementation of IMF reforms.

Although Miss India was essentially the same in its scope, focus, and process in 2003, it was much more media-oriented than previous pageants, most notably in allowing publications and agencies not directly associated with the Times of India Group to have access to the selection process for the first time. This is very much in keeping with a neoliberal economic philosophy, in which all participants are ideally equal players in competition with one another. The 2003 pageant also drew on the decade of experience that preceded it, making it an excellent site from which to examine both how urban India has changed following economic liberalization and the ways in which certain neoliberal ideologies have become embedded in institutions not directly related to structural adjustment.

The process of becoming Miss India begins every year in September, when *Femina* prints entry forms in both its magazine and in the pages of the *Times of India,* which is owned by the same company. Several hundred young women from urban areas all over India submit applications along with two photographs of themselves, one a full body shot and the other a close-up of the face. Based on these photographs, fewer than one hundred are summoned to the next round of the pageant, from which

2. *The Miss India pageant is a media extravaganza involving dance performances by contestants on elaborately designed sets and guest appearances by Hindi film stars and other celebrities.*

twenty-six contestants are selected to participate in a month-long training program that is entirely paid for by the pageant's corporate sponsors. From the submission of entry forms to the announcement of the winners at the final pageant after the training program, the entire process takes four months.

Opportunities to maximize media attention were of paramount importance throughout the 2003 pageant and were organized long before the entry forms appeared in *Femina*. From the preliminary rounds in late November to the final pageant on January 31, media as diverse as the *New York Times*, Star TV, the *Asian Age*, msn.com, and dozens of Indian language presses were invited to interview pageant organizers and observe elements of the pageant process. The training program between December 5, 2002, and January 6, 2003, was a premiere site for media activity in the form of interviews with contestants and organizers, as were the semifinals on January 24 one week before the final pageant.

All of this was designed as a part of a larger, three-part goal of making Miss India into a brand that would be internationally recognizable. The first task was to build credibility for Miss India by attempting to ensure the presence of powerful political and cultural figures, including the prime minister of India, at the final pageant. Organizers also sent out invitations to a curious assortment of American and Western European celebrities, including Gerald Ford; Al Gore; Peg Jordan, fitness expert; Anita Roddick, CEO of the Body Shop; and Hilka Klinkenberg, the managing director of the organization Etiquette International (none of whom actually attended). Second, organizers sought to institutionalize Miss India via the creation of the Miss India Foundation, designed to help underprivileged girls have access to education. The third task was to enhance the brand equity of Miss India in order to, as organizers put it, "proactively promote India Incorporated" via the production of limited editions of handicrafts, jewelry, fabrics, handmade paper, and other products typically associated with the subcontinent.

The slogan of the 2003 pageant was "beauty with a purpose," which comprised a fourfold strategy that sought to address the question of what a Miss India should be. This served to reinforce the way in which the pageant has historically served as a medium through which national identity is both created and negotiated. Pageant literature featured questions asked by a hypothetical Miss India, such as "Who Am I?" and "What Role Am I Expected to Play?" in response to which four facets of "beauty with a purpose" at Miss India emerged:

> 1. I am a proud Indian. I shall devote fifteen days this year to promote domestic tourism, Indian heritage, and Indian jewelry and handicrafts.
> 2. I am expected to be successful in all that I undertake. I will help the Government of India promote the textiles and handicrafts of India.
> 3. I am a person who will use my strengths to help others.
> 4. I am a role model for others. I will conduct workshops at colleges on career options, grooming, AIDS awareness and fashion counseling.

In marked similarity to the pageants of the early 1960s, these four points emphasized the role that Miss India had to play not only in serving as a mentor to others but also as an ambassador to the rest of the world, most notably in the fields of tourism and marketable commodities.

It is not coincidental, then, that Miss India 2003 was presented to potential sponsors as an event that, in the words of organizers, "offers an exclusive opportunity to present Indian culture, beauty, talent and intellect on a global platform." Bangalore, known in India as a center for software and technology corporations, was chosen for the semifinals of the pageant because, as one organizer described, it is "the one city in the country which market research has shown to be a city of innovation." Pageant organizers sought to simultaneously widen the scope of the pageant so that rural areas would eventually become part of the Miss India audience. As a pageant public relations official succinctly said, "We want to gradually broad base Miss India, so that everyone will identify with and support her." The message, then, was that while Miss India is an event and an institution that is part of an international India, it also sought to reach a broader national audience, a goal that was enormously appealing to sponsors who desired to reach new markets in rural areas.

The first stage of the pageant began when all of the application forms were submitted by potential Miss India contestants to *Femina*'s office in Mumbai. The 2003 pageant received 332 applications, out of which seventy-eight young women were invited to Mumbai, Delhi, and Bangalore for interviews with pageant organizers. I spent several days going through all of the applications, which had been annotated with comments by pageant officials, including former Miss World Yukta Mookhey, in order to ascertain what types of young women wanted to be Miss India. Each judge had been given a form that detailed how the evaluation process should work that included a rating scale between one and ten, with one described as "applicant has no chance of making it to the finals of the pageant" and ten indicating "applicant will definitely make it to the finals of the pageant." The form also included a section titled "Objectivity," which mentioned that judges should not evaluate the quality of the photograph but rather the beauty of the woman featured in it, and that they should refrain from comparing applicants to each other when making their selections.

Before listing the criteria on which judges should base their decisions, the form included the line: "The final winner will go on to represent your country in international pageants," as if to emphasize the importance of choosing applicants who had the best chance of winning at Miss Universe or Miss World. The following factors were considered by judges in determining which applicants would be selected for interviews in Bangalore, Delhi, and Mumbai:

| Criteria | Description/Factors to Consider | Rating Scale |
|----------|--------------------------------|--------------|
| Face/Natural Beauty | Smile | 1–10 |
| | Expressiveness | |
| | Complexion | |
| | Radiance | |
| Figure | Attractiveness/Magnetism | |
| | Proportion | |
| | Poise | |
| | Confidence | |

These criteria were measured based upon the evaluation of two photographs and a list of each applicant's height, weight, and measurements, from which names had been removed in order to reduce the possibility of a judge exercising bias based upon ethnic, regional, or religious identity. In some ways, it was only in the applications to Miss India, in which all markers of ethnic identity had been erased, that the pageant's ideal of the Indian woman with no religious or ethnic affiliation actually existed. It was surreal to see the Indian independence movement's ultimate goal of a completely integrated India in this capacity, evaluated on a one to ten scale ideally free of biases based upon ethnic or religious allegiances.

Examining the photographs was a fascinating illustration of the class backgrounds from which young women applied to Miss India, as they were sharply divided between those who had submitted costly professional photographs and those who had mailed in snapshots taken by friends or family members at home. There was a marked difference between the two, as the nonprofessional photographs consistently showed young women who were fully clothed with more demure expressions. One snapshot showed an extremely rural version of beauty with a young woman wearing a garland of flowers, as if at her wedding, her hair discreetly veiled by the upper half of her plain brown sari.

While the occasional photograph revealed this conservative rural ideal, the vast majority showed applicants in their middle-class approximations of fashionable garments. The most notable of the nonprofessional images showed a seductive young woman in a white tube top reclining in a dark room surrounded by all the accoutrements of middle-class Indian life, including trophies from school competitions framed in a glass case, a cassette player, and thin synthetic curtains. Her expression was the most notable element of the photograph, as it was a studied imitation of the slightly lowered eyes and half-smile that she would have seen on the Miss India contestants in *Femina* magazine.

There was little variation in height among the entrants, because all applications that did not meet the minimum height requirement of five feet and six inches had already been covered with a white sheet that had the word "invalid" typed in large black letters. Despite a note on the judges' evaluation form that specifically mentioned that height was not to be considered in decisions about which applicants would advance to the next stage of the pageant, several extraordinarily tall young women who were a bit overweight or had skin problems such as acne managed to meet the judges' approval. Height is the one physical characteristic that cannot be created at the Miss India training program, but changes to weight, skin tone, and hair texture can all be made with the guidance of the experts.

Although there was some variation in body types, many of the applicants were underweight, such as the aspiring contestant who was five feet and six inches tall, weighed ninety-four pounds, and had measurements of 30-23-32. Many of the young women already had Miss India proportions in their photographs, such as an applicant whose professionally taken photograph showed her posing in a red bikini by a pool and listed her height as five feet and seven inches, her weight at one hundred and ten, and her measurements at 33-24-34. Juxtaposed with the next applicant, whose snapshot showed a plain girl in a polyester sari standing in front of a red synthetic curtain at five feet and six inches tall with measurements of 33-27-36, the woman in the bikini by the pool seemed like an entirely different creature.

The dramatic changes that urban Indian beauty culture has undergone since the opening of the economy to foreign investment were unmistakable when going through the photographs of applicants, more than half of which had been taken by professional photographers. Applicants wore a variety of revealing outfits in their professional photographs, which indicated their familiarity with Indian print media and films. One of the applicants wore a leopard-print bustier, black hot pants, blue contacts, and professionally applied makeup in her photograph, a set of visual cues to judges that the applicant was fully prepared to adjust to the cultural norms at Miss India, some of which are quite different than the reality of life for the applicant who wore a flowered garland and shielded her hair from the lens of the camera. The message in many of the professional photographs was that modernity does not wear many clothes.

Judges spent a day in isolation with the 332 applications and were not allowed to discuss the candidates with one another. As part of the focus on professionalizing the pageant in 2003, judges signed legal disclaimers in which they promised not to present unfair bias or discuss the quality of the applicants with anyone in the outside world. Out of the 332 applicants, a total of seventy-eight young women were invited for further meetings with judges in Bangalore (ten), Delhi (thirty-five), and Mumbai (thirty-three). It was from this number that the final twenty-six contestants were selected to participate in the training program.

Miss India contestants have historically come from urban areas, which is largely due to fact that the majority of media in India is concentrated in cities. The result of this is that young women who live in rural areas do not have the same kind of access to media images or personal freedoms that their urban counterparts do, which means that their knowledge base is quite different from those who grow up in places such as Mumbai or Delhi. The pageant has very clear motives for avoiding smaller cities, including the South Indian town of Coimbatore, in favor of larger metropolitan areas, as former Miss India director Pradeep Guha noted when asked why the vast majority of Miss India contestants come from Mumbai and Delhi:

What we found was that the best from Coimbatore—I'm just using Coimbatore as an example—was not even close to the last from Bombay

[Mumbai] or Delhi. It is just an unfortunate accident that someone is brought up in Bombay and someone is brought up in a small town. It is precisely because we looked at the smaller towns that we never won an international title ten years ago, so we decided that we're not looking for a Miss Coimbatore, we're looking for a Miss Universe or a Miss World. We decided that all we want is a girl who has an Indian passport, and that's enough.

In describing the birth of a girl in small-town India as "an unfortunate accident" in that she will not grow up with the same cultural knowledge and attitudes that a girl in Mumbai or Delhi would, Guha underscored the urban-centric nature of the pageant. As difficult as it is to make generalizations about the diversity that is India, there is an enormous and consistent difference between individuals who are raised in urban areas and those who are not. By restricting its search to a few urban areas, the Miss India pageant seeks to find a certain type of homogenized beauty that, as Guha's statement implies, cannot be found in rural areas or even in small towns like Coimbatore.

In keeping with this philosophy, the city of Bangalore in the central southern region of India best known for its software and technology corporations was the first visited by the Miss India judges as part of the 2003 selection process. The judges consisted of a panel of five: A. P. Parigi, CEO of 360 Degrees, the event management company handling the 2003 Miss India pageant; Yukta Mookhey, former Miss World; Nafisa Joseph, former Miss India and Miss Universe contestant; Boman Irani, theater actor; and Reshma Ghosh, television producer. All had direct ties to the media world that most of the applicants sought to enter. The rationale behind the choice in judges was that two former beauty queens would know how to evaluate the chance each young woman had to win an international pageant, the actor and the producer would be able to judge stage presence, and the CEO, of course, was required as part of his responsibilities to the pageant.

We traveled to Bangalore from the head office of 360 Degrees in Mumbai on an early morning flight on November 20 and checked into Le Meridien, a five-star hotel that had provided a conference room in which the applicants could be evaluated. As the judges settled behind a long table with notebooks ready to record their impressions of the young women, I chose a chair in the corner of the room in order to be less conspicuous. Meanwhile, the applicants were measured by pageant officials in a room out of the judges' view; their bust, waist, and hip measurements were provided to the judges soon after. Parigi tried hard to ensure that no outsiders entered the room and forbade the applicants from making phone calls from the hotel. This sensitivity was also partly due to the events surrounding the 1996 Miss World pageant in Bangalore, which was disrupted as a result of riots and violence led by antipageant protestors.

The process for evaluation of applicants in Bangalore was essentially similar to the way it was conducted in Delhi and Mumbai. After being measured by pageant officials, each applicant was required to submit an Applicant Declaration Form that listed her name, date of birth, her status as what the form referred to as "a natural born female," height, weight, measurements, future plans, present occupation, and personal concept of beauty. The judges examined each sheet of paper prior to the announcement of the individual applicant's number, and then watched her sashay down a makeshift catwalk in a bathing suit in front of the judges to determine if the thirty-day training program could potentially transform her into a Miss India. Next, each applicant appeared in a formal dress, some of which had obviously been borrowed from relatives and friends, whereas others had clearly been tailored at great cost to the applicant. Suitably attired, each applicant then sat for a ten-minute interview with the judges in which each was questioned on topics ranging from her reasons for wanting to become Miss India to the whereabouts of al-Qaeda leader Osama bin Laden. A broader discussion of the types of questions asked, judges' interactions with applicants, and differences between applicants based upon their ethnicity, religion, and place of origin are provided in chapter 5.

By late November, twenty-six young of these young women were invited to participate in the Miss India training program held at the luxurious Grand Maratha Sheraton Hotel in suburban Mumbai. Contestants had all of their needs provided for during the thirty-day training program, during which they had a rigorous schedule designed to transform each of them into a slender potential Miss World or Miss Universe. Pradeep

Guha, former director of the pageant, positioned the training program as something that is not only essential to cultivate the confidence required to succeed in media but also as gateway to other opportunities in life. Interestingly, he did so vis-à-vis what he perceived to be the wider array of options available to women in the United States:

> In a country like the United States, a beauty pageant is slightly déclassé, and I can understand that, because there you don't need a beauty pageant to come out of your shell. The environment there has enough and more to liberate young women. In the Indian context, there is very little which allows for a girl to come out and say, "Hello, I have arrived!" There are almost no opportunities. If you look at the so-called glamour industry, there's so much to do in the West. There's almost nothing here except movies. As I see it, the pageant each year plays a positive role as much as it provides a springboard for a few girls, each year, to achieve something.

Guha noted that while the concept of a pageant is not held in high esteem "in a country like the United States" in India it is accorded importance because of the way it is seen to provide career opportunities for young women. Yet this illustration also employs deeply rooted gender biases that situate young women in a "shell" from which they need to be coaxed.

The Miss India training program takes place over thirty days in the month prior to the pageant itself, during which twenty-six contestants are housed, trained, and made beautiful in a Foucauldian total institution with one goal in mind: to create a Miss World or a Miss Universe. For thirty days, Miss India contestants attend fitness classes and have all of their meals designed by a well-known nutritionist. All aspects of the pageant employ the best-known people from what is known in India as "the glamour industry" to perform necessary services that help to construct an image of the pageant as larger than life. Having the opportunity to meet with the extremely well-connected and media-savvy individuals who train them gives young women who compete in the pageant the chance to create social networks that will later allow them to build careers in media-related fields.

The month-long training program extends beyond fitness and diet regimens to include a focus on modeling, fashion, and cinema, as these are the fields into which most Miss India contestants enter after the pageant is over. Portfolio shoots and meetings with Hindi film directors and producers for a month allow contestants to create a new identity for themselves in Mumbai's media industry, and so simply being able to make it into the pageant's training program can function as a life-changing experience for many young women. Pradeep Guha commented on how the pageant's training program serves as "a quick route to careers in glamour and almost instant recognition" before adding, in reference to the contestants, "We don't make them, we chisel them." The concept of chiseling that Guha mentions is particularly salient, as it implies the cultivation of beauty pageant contestants from a template that is already in place, thus underscoring both the agency of contestants in terms of substance and the importance of the training program in developing that substance.

*A Day in the Life of the Miss India Training Program*

Each day of the 2003 training program began early in the morning, was extremely tightly scheduled with only two brief breaks for meals, and ended late at night. Contestants woke up at six-thirty A.M. and then had two hours of fitness classes between seven and nine A.M. followed by an hour or two in which they were able to shower, dress for the day, and quickly eat breakfast. Between eleven A.M. and one P.M., contestants were lectured and questioned by an expert, such as a beauty specialist, etiquette expert, photographer, dermatologist, nutritionist, or filmmaker, followed by an hour for lunch. Contestants then spent an hour with a speech and diction coach whose main goals were to discuss elements of successful stage presence and to cultivate the British-accented English that is an indicator of privileged class status in India. Participants then spent two hours practicing on a catwalk in preparation for the pageant, as well as for future work in the field of media. This was followed by another two-hour session from five to seven P.M. by an expert from the field of media and an hour for dinner. Contestants usually ended the day by engaging in question and answer sessions or by watching DVDs of previous Miss India, Miss World, and Miss Universe pageants that were the subject of detailed commentary by pageant choreographers.

Every morning, twenty-six contestants filtered onto the gated hotel lawns for fitness classes led by personal trainer Mickey Mehta, who insisted that the young women exercise on the grass in order to be closer to nature. Mehta followed a quasi-Hindu line of thought in holding that this would improve their spiritual well-being, an essential component of a good Miss India. The young women who had pulled muscles in previous fitness sessions did yoga on the lawns with Mehta's assistant, while Mehta himself observed the young women running laps. "Breathe in, breathe out!" he exhorted, "If you don't breathe, you can't oxygenate fat! Remember that only the girls who keep working hard are the ones who win!" all the while making sure that each of the young women tried her best to perform. By the middle of the training program, some of them were so exhausted that they would fall asleep on the lawns before beginning their workout.

Mehta's main role was not only to ensure weight loss and toning of the contestants' bodies but also to convey a certain sense of spirituality. At the conclusion of each session, he sat like a yogi in the center of a circle formed by the young women, who sat cross-legged in the grass in the lotus position as he explained his philosophy of the pageant. "Spirituality with intent is not spirituality," he said during one lecture. "If you meditate only on winning the crown, you will not look in the mirror and see yourself, but only an illusion." Although contestants responded privately to these messages in ways which ranged from dismissive to extremely humbled, the Hindu elements of Mehta's conception of the pageant were but one piece of the broader construction of national identity. Mehta concluded each of his speeches to the contestants with a brief discussion of the difference between illusion and reality, as well as the notion of karma, or destiny, all key principles in Hindu canonical thought. During one particularly moving postworkout monologue, Mehta discussed the importance of not valuing the physical over the spiritual and then exhorted the contestants to repeat the phrase, "What I ought to do, I will do, because that is my karma." The message of Miss India having clearly been written into at least one young women's fate was unmistakable.

Contestants then had an hour or two to shower, dress for the day, and eat breakfast, which, like lunch and dinner, was often rushed because it was the only free time that young women had during the day. A nutritionist planned each of the contestants' meals throughout the training program, but the young women alone were responsible for choosing the appropriate assigned foods from a buffet-style selection of three large tureens at each meal. For breakfast, contestants generally had cereal or fruit, then soup and two vegetables for lunch, followed by a protein-based dish and rice for dinner. Meals were often the site of obsessive discussions over consumption between contestants, whether in the form of preferences that could not be met during the training program, complaints about restrictions to one another, or debates on the relative merits of different foods for weight loss or maintenance.

Next, contestants spent two hours from eleven A.M. to one P.M. with a specialist from a media-related field as part of sessions that were designed to be both instructional and instrumental in the creation of a network of media contacts for the young women. An excellent example of how this typically functioned was a simulated fashion shoot conducted by former Miss India contestant and successful model Carol Gracia, who pretended to pose for photographers while giving instructions and career advice to the contestants. Gracia advised them to quickly learn how to deal with the press and handle fame in order to not be personally affected by the negative stereotypes that the Indian media sometimes perpetuates about well-known women. "You must keep your value system in place," she noted as she tilted her head seductively to pose for the camera, "because if fame and money go to your head, the *naśā* [intoxication] is really bad."

Contestants watched intently as Gracia posed for the camera, all the while taking detailed notes in the spiral notebooks that the pageant had provided to them for that purpose. As Gracia spoke about how to deal with photographers who invade personal space, some of the young women who were professional models prior to entering Miss India nodded at her suggestion that body language was an adequate tool to deal with an invasive masculine presence. This was part of the broader vocabulary of "professionalism" at the pageant, which generally referred to the practice of attempting to negotiate a notable bias against women in a male-dominated industry. Gracia cited self-confidence as the best weapon women could have against unfair treatment in the media world, where physical flaws are often highlighted with regularity. Contestants uttered muffled expressions of disbelief when Gracia, who has appeared on several magazine covers, described how she felt one side of her face was lower than the other and that her nose was too large. The twenty-six potential Miss Indias simply did not see the same things that Gracia did when she looked in the mirror, and a few young women spoke up to reassure Gracia that she was indeed very beautiful. Gracia waved her hand dismissively and concluded her session by reminding the young women to have faith in themselves and their beauty, noting, "I used to think about all the flaws in my face all the time, and I was the only loser because of that."

The next hour and most of the hour set aside for lunch was occupied by Sabira Merchant, a speech and diction coach who often had the contestants pretend to be in a situation involving an interview with the media. One particular session began with Merchant's introduction of the guidelines for behavior on television, with the oft-repeated reminder to contestants that "everyone will be watching you." One by one, the contestants went to a podium to talk briefly about their likes and dislikes, the assignment presented to them by Merchant. The first contestant, an extremely articulate young woman from Delhi, managed half a sentence before Merchant interrupted her. "Do something interesting! Say, 'Hi, I'm Deepica, which starts with a 'D', same as the place I come from, Delhi!'" Nodding her head, the contestant began again, in a decidedly more spirited tone, "My nickname is Di, because it's short and sweet! I love simplicity and frankness, and I don't like hypocrisy." Merchant motioned for the next young woman to assume the podium, before reminding the contestant from Delhi that she had to work on her self-presentation, without being "too fast, slow or serious."

When the next contestant paused in response to Merchant's question of which world leader she most admired, Merchant was quick to remind her not to be too serious when she did not know the answer to something. "Be prepared to recover from your mistakes," Merchant advised, citing the example of Miss Greece at a previous Miss World pageant, who was in the final five before being asked the all-important question that would determine the winner of the pageant. The room filled with laughter as Merchant dramatically detailed the story of Miss Greece's response to the question of where she would be in seven years as "I will be twenty-seven!" Part of a larger project at work at the Miss India training program of positioning Miss India as far more intelligent than other candidates at Miss World and Miss Universe, this anecdote helped to reassure some young women that they were more articulate (and fluent in English) than they initially thought.

Immediately following Merchant's session, contestants spent two hours with pageant choreographers Hemant Trevedi and Anu Ahuja during which they practiced walking on a ramp in order to improve the performance of the young women who did not have modeling experience prior to the pageant. These sessions were the most fraught with tension of the entire day, as they were the time when individual contestants' bodies and composure were under the most scrutiny by both the twenty-five other young women and the choreographers, who could be quite acerbic in their comments. This was multiplied by the seating of contestants around the peripheries of the catwalk, so that each young woman's every move was the subject of intense focus. The choreographers were consistently frustrated in their attempts to get the young women to walk the ramp wearing saris, which none of them had ever done. As individual contestants struggled on the catwalk by alternately stumbling over the floor-length hems of their saris and failing to support the upper half adequately, Ahuja and Trevedi would sigh audibly before launching into a detailed assessment of how each individual had failed.

"Where's your confidence gone? You're not walking on eggshells," Trevedi said to one young woman who was clearly on the verge of tears at her inability to carry off a sari in an elegant manner, before adding, "If you don't learn this now, there is absolutely no hope for you." Even those who had been ramp models before coming to Miss India struggled during these sessions because they had grown professionally accustomed to not smiling as part of a mode of femininity that is extremely different from the beauty queen, who needs to look approachable as the idealized representation of India. Although ramp models are expected to behave like the garments they exhibit, rather than displaying the characteristics of individual women, beauty queens at Miss India are expected to evince warmth, purity, and a number of other positive stereotypes typically associated with India.

Sessions with Trevedi and Ahuja often included discussions of how young women could negotiate the male-dominated media industry without compromising what was often glossed as their "integrity" or "morals." This was a topic that was never far below the surface throughout the training program, which demonstrates the tightrope that the vast majority of women who work in media-related professions in urban India have to walk in order to be considered simultaneously respectable and desirable, an almost-impossible equation to master. One such incident took the form of a discussion of then-popular Hindi film actress Kareena Kapoor. "Kareena acts cold and unapproachable so that no one will act funny with her," Ahuja observed, before adding, "People really try to take advantage of you when they think you are weak." Ahuja's suggestion that young women adopt an uncharacteristically tough persona in dealing with the media world outside of Miss India indicates that while the networks cultivated at the pageant do help young women, by no means do they alleviate the unique set of challenges they face in the male-dominated media industry in Mumbai.

The next two-hour session from five to seven P.M. often dealt with similar issues, again by bringing a successful media professional to lecture and interact with the contestants. One session entitled "Cinema as Profession" was led by Hindi film director Karan Johar, who explained the various options that one could explore in the Hindi film industry. As soon as Johar opened the discussion to questions from contestants, a young woman from Mumbai immediately asked how she could best deal with an industry notorious for its exploitation of women, most notably through the "godfather system" of patronage in which younger women attach themselves as companions and sexual partners to older, more powerful men who secure film roles for them in return. Johar responded by reassuring her that the film industry was not a bad place when one knew how to handle herself properly, adding, "If you're going to be a weak person who is swayed by silly people, then that's your weakness." Johar was unfortunately fairly typical of media professionals who assisted at the training program in placing the onus of responsibility for their own fate (and sexual harassment) squarely on the contestants.

Contestants were reminded by a pageant organizer at least once a day throughout the training program of how fortunate they were to have such authorities speak to them. This reminder, notably, often took place in the presence of the expert him or herself. Pageant director Parigi had observed the Johar session and informed the contestants at the end of it that he had been watching them quite closely to observe their reactions. "These ideas provoke thought in you," he noted, "because you're listening to the masters. A Zen master always lives in the present, and you must aspire to be like this also." In an expression of spirituality akin to that of personal trainer Mickey Mehta, Parigi drew upon very ancient religious traditions that have roots in India in order to emphasize the role of the contestants as apprentices of sorts at the pageant.

Contestants then had one hour for dinner, followed by a nightly question and answer session with Trevedi and Ahuja from eight to ten P.M., after which they would go to bed for the night. This session alternated nightly with a screening of DVDs of past Miss India, Miss World, and Miss Universe pageants that were interrupted numerous times throughout for commentary by the choreographers. This was also the only time that contestants were allowed to have chaperoned visits with family members in the hotel coffee shop. Afraid of missing important information that could potentially improve their chances of winning, many young women chose not to see their families at all.

Question-and-answer sessions began with Trevedi and Ahuja seated at a table with a microphone opposite them as they waited for individual contestants to practice articulately answering questions as they would later have to at the pageant. Questions were typically relatively benign, such as who a contestant admired the most and why. In response to this, one contestant cited Rekha, a Hindi film star renowned for her beauty and seductive dances. "No." Trevedi said in response, "You should mention that for an average-looking girl, she's reinvented herself to become a diva. When she walks into a room, everyone says 'wow', because she has all the qualities of a star. This is what you all have to strive for." The young woman nodded and sat down to watch the next young woman in line to take the microphone. It was striking how silent the contestants were in front of the experts, as they would simply nod, do as they were told, and then take detailed notes on how to improve their performance. Like the "average-looking girl" turned celebrated actress of Trevedi's response to the contestant, they were all trying their absolute best at reinvention.

The twenty-six young women who worked so hard at this process of self-reinvention throughout the training program all had individual goals in mind when they entered Miss India but were similar in a number of ways: all were between nineteen and twenty-three years of age, the vast majority were of North Indian descent, most lived in Mumbai or Delhi, half had some modeling or acting experience and all came from families that supported their decision to enter Miss India. Chapter 2 divides the contestants into the three broad categories of those who came from small towns (four), were resident abroad (four), or were professional models or actresses (thirteen) and discusses the four other contestants who were doing voluntary work or nothing at all, as well as the eight who were simultaneously enrolled in university courses of study in addition to the other categories to which they belonged. It is unfortunately impossible to describe in accurate detail what the pageant experience meant to each individual participant in the space of a single book, but as the twenty-six contestants were demographically very similar to past participants, they can be considered representative of the type of young women who enter Miss India.

While their first names and stories are interspersed throughout the rest of the book, it is useful to present a brief (and, not unlike the format at Miss India, alphabetical) introduction to the young women whose experiences at the training program make up a fair percentage of the chapters that follow. Nikita Anand won a total of four pageants before coming to Miss India, the first of which she participated in when she was only thirteen years old. Nikita was well-versed in the kind of preparation needed for the training program and felt that she was not ready for Miss India because she "only had two days to shop" before leaving her study of fashion design in Delhi for the pageant. "I wear the skimpiest of clothes but I'm a good Indian girl and so think twice before I do anything wrong," said Delhi model Shruti Chauhan, who was already familiar with the need to negotiate the fine line between being sufficiently "modern" and adequately "Indian" at the pageant. Anurithi Chikkerur from Bangalore loved to travel and had modeled in New Zealand, the United States, Singapore, and Malaysia before submitting her application to study journalism at the University of California at Berkeley. Anurithi saw Miss India as a way to see the world and earn an income simultaneously and was optimistic that what she called "the confidence" she gained at the training program would benefit her as a serious reporter later in life.

Mumbai-based Diana Delvadavada worked at her mother's travel agency, had no experience in media, and saw the pageant as "a chance to do something different before marriage." Nalini Dutta from Mumbai described the training program as "just beautiful" and often sought me out to insist that certain procedures, such as skin lightening, were "not really all that bad." From the small Western Indian town of Nasik, Kaveri Jha called the notification of her selection for Miss India "the happiest day of my life," although she struggled throughout the training program to compete with the young women from large cities who had more modeling experience and knowledge of the world. I found it sad that Kaveri internalized this to such a degree that she described her status as a contestant "only because Miss India looks for raw material to be molded instead of the finished product."

The athletic Mumbai-based actress Parmita Katkar voiced similar sentiments in reference to social class when she described Miss India as an equalizing force in her life because of which "there is no need to feel lesser than anyone else." Parmita was by far the most professionally ambitious contestant and was the only young woman who had participated in Miss India the previous year as part of a broader effort to advance her Hindi film career. Harsimrat Kaur from Chennai was strikingly different from the others in describing her participation as her father's dream, although other members of her family were concerned that the pageant would encourage what she paraphrased as "nudity, smoking and drinking." Harsimrat also struggled to relate to the more focused and mature contestants from Mumbai and Delhi who were familiar with media professions, such as Mumbai model Anjali Lavania, who often provided me with unrepeatable gossip that can best be summarized in her oft-repeated insistence in reference to other contestants that "some girls will do absolutely any-thing to be in the media, and I mean anything." Perhaps seeking to avoid this predicament, Saloni Luthra from Mumbai entered because she did not want to do what she termed "small-time modeling work" in order to succeed in her chosen profession. Saloni positioned herself in marked contrast to her mother, who had experienced familial reservations similar to Harsimrat's a generation before when her dream of becoming a flight attendant was rejected by family members as "a dishonorable profession for women."

The issue of morality came up again in reference to Nupur Mehta, who was raised in Delhi by her Punjabi father and Cambodian mother but had worked as a model in Milan for two years before coming to Miss India. Nupur was easily the most controversial figure in 2003 because her claims of fabulous success in Italy were privately disputed by chaperones and organizers who felt that Nupur's East Asian features and what they termed her "princess attitude" were not sufficiently Indian enough to al-low her to win. The issue of "attitude" was also raised among chaperones and pageant officials in regard to Purva Merchant, a dental student from Pune. "I am the only one here with a strong professional background," Purva often said in response to questions about why she should win the title of Miss India. This sort of self-confidence was the target of comments by organizers and chaperones who felt that she should be more modest about her achievements.

Shonali Nagrani from Delhi was often the recipient of praise for her twenty-five-pound weight loss prior to entering Miss India. Hers was a striking transformation that perhaps led to her becoming the most suc-cessful in media of all the contestants following the pageant. This sort of assessment was definitely not an issue for quiet Poonam Patil from Mumbai, who was pronounced fifteen pounds underweight by a nutri-tionist at the beginning of the training program and promptly placed on a high-fat, calorie-rich diet. Poonam was not particularly concerned with the outcome of the pageant and noted, "If I win, I'll do something in media, otherwise I'll be an engineer." Mumbai-based Mareesha Parikh, who modeled in addition to her work on a master's in management, af-firmed this sort of sentiment in defining Miss India as "something that can make or break an ordinary girl." Model Hemangi Parte from Mumbai echoed this statement and described her transformation from her old to new self as "amazing" before meticulously detailing to me the way she perceived that the training program had improved every single element of her physical appearance.

Model Shonal Rawat from Calcutta, who had just finished a degree in chemistry, saw Miss India as "a gateway to other opportunities" and jokingly described her love of what she called "partying and odd hours" as something that a career in the sciences might not provide. Delhi-born soap opera actress Deepica Sharma also characterized the pageant as a vehicle for social and professional mobility and often spoke of her personal struggles in media as a darker skinned woman in a country that associates beauty with fairness. Ever ambitious and motivated, Deepica cited black supermodel Naomi Campbell as evidence that fair skin did not have to remain the prevailing standard of beauty in India forever. Purvi Shah from Mumbai, however, insisted that what she called "international norms" were what informed the preference for fair skin in the advertisements she had modeled for before entering Miss India. Sharayu Supenekar from the smaller Western Indian city of Pune was less familiar with these norms than with the idea that Miss India could transform her from what she described as "a tomboy who loves adventure sports" to a beauty queen. Sharayu stood out as the only contestant with short hair and often regretted her decision to cut it prior to entering the pageant, but was consistently adamant that the training program "changed my life in the sense that it brought out my femininity, which has been subdued for so long."

Former flight attendant Sunaina Tandon from Delhi fit perfectly into the Miss India mold of being fair, tall, and slim with long, straight hair, but credited her grandmother with pushing her to enter. "She tries to live her life through me" Sunaina said, "because in her time women couldn't do anything." Payal Thakkar was a first-year computer programming student in Mumbai who had spent her entire life prior to 2003 in Zambia, where Miss India was a point of interest among the Indian diaspora population. Payal described Zambia in direct opposition to India by noting that "we have to be like guys because our life in the bush is hard, but here in India, life is so easy because of servants, so we have to try to be ladies." Payal often found herself in culturally unfamiliar terrain at the training program in which she had to work hard to negotiate the very real differences between the Indian diaspora in which she had been raised and the postliberalization India of the pageant. Payal was by no means the only contestant whose life was in transition at the time of the pageant. "I've learned that expectations reduce joy and surprises increase it," said the ever-eloquent Parvati Thampi from Delhi, who had postponed beginning her MBA to participate in Miss India. American-born Ami Vashi had just finished college in the United States and relocated to India to begin work for a nongovernmental organization when she decided to enter Miss India.

Singer Swetha Vijay from Dubai was by far the most extroverted contestant in 2003 and deserves credit for reaching out to several young women who were clearly struggling with eating disorders. As the most independent and worldly participant at the training program, she often joked with me about what she perceived to be the silliness of the intense surveillance the contestants were under. Delhi-based Gopika Virmani had been a model for two years and was in her final year of a master's in graphic design with plans to open her own studio in the future. The twenty-six young women together formed a group of individuals with a great deal in common who were also cross-cut by class, ethnicity, and skin tone, differences that were pushed to the fore more strongly for contestants who were middle class, of non-North Indian descent, or darker skinned than those who were not.

Two of the contestants seemed to wither away throughout the training program because of their struggles with anorexia, an issue that was largely unaddressed by chaperones and pageant organizers. There is still very little awareness about eating disorders in India, and so it is entirely possible that these young women were simply seen as making an extra effort to achieve a beauty queen body that did not come naturally to them. One of these contestants dieted until her hunger made her so confrontational that I stopped asking her the kinds of questions I routinely posed to other contestants. Chaperones unfortunately chose to label behavior that was clearly the outcome of her struggle with anorexia as "cattiness," leading to avoidance of (rather than help for) this young woman. Both of these contestants went on to successful careers in media and so in retrospect I wonder if I did the right thing in ignoring nagging doubts I had throughout the training program as to whether I had an ethnographic and feminist responsibility to intervene as each lost more weight. I never did answer those questions for myself and really only began to confront the results of the training program once the pageant was over.

*The Miss India Pageant*

The contestants had a two-week break in early January before the semi-finals in Bangalore. The function of the semifinals was to award titles, which often bear the names of their corporate sponsors, based upon particular characteristics of the young women. All twenty-six of the young women at that point in the pageant process began to look almost eerily identical with the same height, body type, and long, straight black hair with highlights in gold or red; in fact, it was almost impossible for me to distinguish between some of them from the back. The training program had instilled a new sense of identity in the contestants, and many young women began wearing their sashes that listed their first name and contestant number in large letters at all times.

The judges for the semifinals included an advertising executive, three models, a female Hindi film director, a Hindi film actor, a South Indian actress, and a doctor known for facilitating the first assisted conception in India. All were given an instructional session on how to best evaluate the young women by pageant officials before the judging began to award the titles of Miss Ten, Miss Beautiful Skin, Miss Beautiful Hair, Miss Beautiful Smile, Miss Talent, and Miss Photogenic. The judging for the semifinals was held in a conference room at the Bangalore Sheraton Hotel, where the contestants first stood together, then walked toward the judges on a ramp one by one before going backstage, and returned individually for a brief interview with the judges. "We want this process to be internationally credible," a pageant official said to the judges in order to stress the work that had been put into the selection and training of the contestants throughout the pageant process.

The judges were slightly overwhelmed with the process that pageant officials insisted on and exclaimed, "This is a contest for us!" on several occasions. As part of their effort at attaining "international standards," it seemed that pageant officials had alienated judges who were used to a much more informal style of evaluation from years past. In an hour-long PowerPoint presentation prior to the evaluation of the contestants, the judges were given detailed instructions on how to assign numbers between one and ten to particular physical characteristics. Judges were reminded to begin their scoring at four or five, as all of the contestants were at least at that level by the end of the training program.

As outlined in the PowerPoint presentation to judges, the criteria to be considered for the Miss Ten title included physical fitness, shape and length of legs, symmetry, and tonal quality of the body. Miss Beautiful Skin was to be evaluated based on the absence of blemishes, including marks, wrinkles, or scars, texture of the skin, radiance and tone, and Miss Beautiful Hair was judged based on shine, length, bounce, and body. Miss Beautiful Smile was to be determined by the evenness of her teeth, the shape of her lips, as well as the warmth and radiance of her smile, and Miss Talent was evaluated based upon the depth of her mastery over her skill and her choice of performance. Miss Photogenic was the only title that did not require interactions between contestants and judges and was evaluated based upon the expressiveness of her features in photographs provided to the judges.

After signing a form that assured pageant organizers that they had no bias toward any particular contestant, the judges selected the winners of the titles to be announced at the semifinals that night in front of a crowd of several thousand people. The performance that night was later nationally televised on Republic Day and began with each contestant giving a short speech on *strī śakti* (woman power). The contestant who eventually won the title of Miss India–World ended her speech to resounding applause when she proclaimed, "Tonight, *bhārat mātā* [Mother India] stands proud, *jay hind* [long live India]!" This was followed by a song competition in Kannada, the language indigenous to Bangalore, and Hindi, the national language, as well as performances by a British dance troupe and several actresses from the Kannada and Hindi film industries.

The final pageant was held in suburban Mumbai and announced the three winners who would go on to the Miss Universe, Miss World, and Miss Earth pageants. The three-hour pageant was televised live throughout India and began with an Indian classical dance troupe that performed as the twenty-six contestants stood in the background. The young women were dressed in saris that had been specially designed for the occasion and stepped forward to take the place of the classical dancers and perform to the sort of Euro-techno that is popular in nightclubs in urban India before returning backstage. This was followed by the introduction of the judges, who included a Hindi film producer, an actress, a professional tennis player, and a prominent figure in Indian finance.

Pageant officials who had waited backstage then informed the fifteen young women who had been previously selected for the next round of the pageant that they were to put on swimsuits and prepare to go onstage again. Each contestant who had been selected as part of the final fifteen appeared individually onstage in her swimsuit as soon as her name was announced and a short video about her life was played on a giant screen mounted above the stage. The judges then reduced the number of swimsuit-clad contestants from fifteen to nine based on their appearance, and the nine who had been chosen changed into evening gowns to answer questions posed by the judges in order to reduce the number of contestants to five. Before the final five contestants were announced, the nine remaining young women posed in elaborately designed saris for the audience while preparing for the end of the pageant. This was followed by the final question, the responses to which were used to select three winners: Miss India–Universe, Miss India–World, and Miss India–Earth, each of whom went on to represent India at the international pageant mentioned in her title.

Miss Universe is by far the most prestigious of the three titles and is jointly owned and managed along with Miss USA and Miss Teen USA as an American corporation by Donald Trump and NBC. All three of the pageants emerged following the refusal of the Miss America 1951 to wear what she termed "demeaning" swimwear manufactured by Catalina, the sponsor of the original Miss America pageant, thus prompting the company to found Miss USA the following year in order to more effectively advertise its products on contestants who would actually agree to wear them. Sponsors are critical for any beauty pageant (including Miss India) and companies such as Mikimoto and Cover Girl have subsidized Miss Universe in recent years. The pageant is held annually in May in locations throughout the world, with approximately eighty participants between the ages of eighteen and twenty-seven who are predominantly from countries in Europe, Latin America and the Caribbean, and North America and are selected via national searches such as Miss India in their home countries.

Despite such diversity, the vast majority of Miss Universe titleholders have been light-skinned and of at least partial European descent: white American contestants have won the pageant most frequently (a total of seven times), followed by blonde Miss Venezuela contestants (four times), and light-skinned women from Puerto Rico (four times). Miss Botswana 1999 was the first and only black African woman to be crowned Miss Universe, although a white South African and white Namibian had preceded her by several decades. In over fifty years of existence, Miss Universe has also had a total of seven winners from the Asian countries of Japan, India, the Philippines, and Thailand, three from Australia and New Zealand, nineteen from Latin America and the Caribbean, nine from North America, and two from the Middle East. The Miss Universe pageant is seen as particularly desirable for Miss India contestants to enter because of its enormous scale in comparison to other pageants, the wide array of access it gives to media and modeling agencies in the United States, and the opportunity to live in New York City for a year as the guest of some of the most powerful corporations in the country. Miss India–Universe is chosen almost exclusively for her physical beauty and height as a result of the perception that intelligence is not a major factor in success at Miss Universe.

The Miss World pageant began in the United Kingdom as a mid-century advertisement for swimwear at the 1951 Festival of Britain by Eric Morley, whose wife Julia Morley continues to manage the pageant. Miss World is held annually in September in different cities throughout the world and features approximately one hundred contestants between the ages of eighteen and twenty-four who have been selected by pageant officials in their home countries, which are more numerous than Miss

Universe but are predominantly in Europe, Latin America and the Caribbean, and North America. Winners of Miss World resemble Miss Universe in that most are fair-skinned and come from either Europe or Latin America. India and Venezuela have each won Miss World five times, and although India is the only Asian country to ever win at all, the twenty total Latina and Caribbean Miss Worlds have come from Argentina (twice), Bermuda, Brazil, the Dominican Republic, Grenada, Peru (twice), Puerto Rico, and Trinidad. Following Miss Universe's unfortunate example, Miss Nigeria became the first and only black African woman to be Miss World in 2001, although two white women from South Africa preceded her by several decades as the only two other African Miss World winners. Miss World has also had a total of twenty-two winners from Europe, three from Australia, New Zealand and the Pacific Islands, three from the Middle East, and two from the United States.

Sponsors of Miss World are generally corporations based in the country that is hosting the event rather than the major multinational companies that pay for Miss Universe, and yet Miss World has donated substantially more money (over four hundred million dollars since its inception) to charitable causes in the past fifty years. This is part of the pageant's slogan of "beauty with a purpose," which distinguishes it from Miss Universe via its supposed greater focus on communication skills and humanitarianism. Miss India–World is chosen primarily for her speaking abilities as a result of the perception (in direct opposition to Miss Universe) that Miss World places a higher value on elements other than pure physical beauty and height, which is why the pageant is seen as less prestigious than Miss Universe by Miss India officials.

Miss Earth was founded in 2001 by Carousel Productions, a Filipino company that had sponsored beauty pageants such as Miss Philippines for a number of years. The pageant is held annually in Manila with contestants between the ages of eighteen and twenty-six from approximately eighty countries that are quite similar to those at the Miss World and Miss Universe pageants. Its slogan of "beauties for a cause" is similar to that of Miss World, although it uses environmental preservation as its theme. Winners of Miss Earth have been from Brazil, Denmark, Honduras, Kenya, and Venezuela. Miss India began sending a contestant to Miss Earth in 2001 in lieu of the Miss Asia-Pacific pageant because, as one pageant organizer put it, "It's more prestigious, because it's much bigger than just Asia." Miss Asia-Pacific was founded in 1968 and has had between fifty and eighty countries participate each year. The winner of the title of Miss India–Asia Pacific or, later, Miss India–Earth, is always a third Miss India contestant who is considered not quite good enough for the two other major international pageants but still worthy of competing at an international level.

While Miss India pageant officials began organizing plans to send the three contestants on to these international pageants, I left Mumbai for the Western Indian state of Goa in order to begin writing this book. I felt a sense of enormous relief when the pageant was over after the grueling schedule that it had presented me with as a researcher and a participant and greatly looked forward to moving on to other areas of life that did not involve long conversations about food consumption, weight, or skin color. I was looking forward to packing as I took a taxi home to my apartment in the southern part of Mumbai, where lighted billboards on the side of the road tower over the Arabian Sea. It was a typical sultry Mumbai night, and the smoke from my cigarette hung in the salty air as the taxi stood immobile in traffic, fingerless lepers occasionally approaching my window to beg for spare change. It was impossible to avoid looking at the most prominent of the billboards displayed along Marine Drive, that elegant curve of a road so often shown in Hindi films, as it featured all twenty-six of the Miss India contestants, some of whom were unrecognizable to me because their skin had been artificially lightened by the photographer to give them what one pageant organizer had referred to as "a nice honey gloss." "*Dekhō, bahinjī,*" the taxi driver simultaneously observed, laughing a bit, "*sab ek-hī lagatī hain- koī farq nahi* [Hey Sister, they all look the same, there's no difference between them!]" In a strangely ironic statement, however, the English sentence below the retouched images of the contestants held a message that was quite different. It read: "I'm not just another face in the crowd."

PART ONE | *The Power of the Gaze*

# 2

# Women of Substance?

## *Situating Self under the Gaze*

> Femininity is donned, draped, hung and painted on the body. It is also something spoken, embodied in gestures, expressed in movements and seen in the things a woman carries. In short, it is a way of being, and it involves meticulous attention to the details of self-presentation. This concern symbolizes the training of the total person, not just what one thinks or knows inside, but how one appears to others on the outside. (McVeigh 1995, 35)

Being a beauty queen means embodying all that is desirably feminine, a difficult exercise that is both learned and performed via complex cultural processes. Academic studies on the construction and cultivation of femininity, such as McVeigh's (1995) analysis of training programs for Japanese secretaries, have illustrated how individual women model themselves upon established ideals of beauty and grace, thereby situating themselves vis-à-vis that which is physically and emotionally possible for them as individuals. The focus that individual women at Miss India and elsewhere share is on attainability, and so while it is acknowledged that not every woman will be Miss India, it is assumed that each of the contestants will try to approximate past winners in appearance and behavior. This closely follows Bartky's (1990) discussion of American women's internalization of the panopticon, in which she contends that women engage in a process of self-identification with culturally constructed models of idealized femininity, so that it becomes difficult to distinguish between object and subject in the hegemony that is inherent in all notions of beauty. This was very much the case at Miss India, where young women consciously mimicked the behavior of past winners in order to improve their chances of winning as part of a larger process of being observed not only by the experts but also by themselves.

Identity is mediated not only via processes of positioning oneself vis-à-vis others but also under the direction of institutional processes and authorities as part of a complex process that broadly speaks to what it means to self-identify as a beauty queen. This chapter discusses how participants in beauty pageants that range from small-scale local events to multimillion dollar productions view themselves as part of a larger system that they must negotiate in order to win. Silenced by a system that insists that they mouth quick platitudes and smile, beauty queens are at best figureheads for social causes. Each Miss India is required to have a "platform issue" that she will at least cursorily address throughout her reign, but these issues overwhelmingly center on care for either children or the sick, such as increasing AIDS awareness, universal literacy, or education for children from marginalized groups. This is part of an unspoken discourse that positions femininity as maternal and uncontroversial, and thus unacceptable platforms might deal with contemporary politics, sexuality, or any cause with even a tinge of militancy attached to it. Such platforms do little more than to reinforce a dominant cultural view of women as apolitical, selfless caretakers with little interest in making real, structural changes to society. Miss Universe and Miss World are no different, as both ally themselves with "causes" and charities that deal almost exclusively with children or those with terminal illnesses.

Beauty queens are positioned as idealized versions of femininity and physically perfect paragons of selfless virtue who are rarely given the opportunity to speak about their experiences beyond a narrowly circumscribed version of what their title means to them, usually (in the case of Miss India) as part of a promotional campaign for Miss India, *Femina,* or a sponsor of the pageant itself. Constantly in the public eye, Miss India contestants must reiterate the rhetoric of "making a difference" while doing very little to actually change anything. One of the aspiring contestants at the Mumbai selection round of the pageant who was not chosen to participate in the training program provided pageant officials with a prepared statement about how as Miss India she would serve as a spokesperson for international harmony and then later whispered to me, "None of us care a damn about world peace, we just want to be famous." It is partly because of the broader cultural recognition that beauty queens engage in such doublespeak, combined with the fact that beauty is synonymous with pride in India, that Miss Indias are often regarded as vain, pampered women despite their best efforts to embody *Femina* magazine's and the pageant's former slogan of "the woman of substance."

During one editorial meeting I attended at *Femina,* editor Sathya Saran related the story of how she shouted at Miss India 2002 Celina Jaitley, who had what Saran described as "the audacity" to ask fashion designer Ritu Kumar how long a fitting would take. The *Femina* writers were astounded at Jaitley's impudence in questioning Kumar, who is among India's most respected designers, and were impressed when Saran described her chastisement of Jaitley in front of the designer:

> I was so mortified at her behavior with Ritu that I scolded Celina and asked her, "Do you realize how honored you are? Ritu Kumar would ordinarily not even look at a person of your caliber! How dare you insult her by asking how much time she will take?"

What I originally perceived to be Saran's gross overreaction to Jaitley's simple question seemed perfectly reasonable to the *Femina* writers, one of whom asked, somewhat rhetorically, "How do they get this way?" to which another replied, "A crown and a sash, dear." A discussion then ensued that ended with one writer's sarcastic description of Miss India as "a monster factory" from which beauty queens with enormous egos emerged. If there is some truth to this, the women being criticized can hardly be blamed. As the focus of constant media attention for several months, it would be very difficult for a Miss India not to cultivate an overinflated image of herself. What Saran's story reveals is the way in which Miss Indias are supposed to be grateful for their title and to behave as the very real commodities that they are. The message inherent in Saran's chastisement of Jaitley was that someone like Ritu Kumar was a person of true merit, whose actions could not be questioned. Jaitley, on the other hand, was supposed to consider herself a person much less accomplished: a commodity disposable after one year of use.

Being Miss India is a temporary role that offers no real form of support for the future, not unlike so many other roles that are deemed feminine, including child care provider, housekeeper, or cook. As young women describe how pageants have shaped their lives in the stories that follow, what it means to be under the constant gaze of both the self and the outside world will be contextualized within the frame of their lived experience.

### Miss Monsoon

Several months before I was actively involved with *Femina* and Miss India, I attended a beauty pageant titled "Miss Monsoon." I was then living in a Mumbai suburb called Malad that was prone to flooding in the monsoon rains, which caused many of the poorly constructed concrete apartment blocks my neighbors and I lived in to sprout bright green mold on our walls. I associate that year's monsoon with the black muck of indiscernible origin and substance that steadily filled the yard surrounding my building and the enormous, yellow-toothed rats that found ways into my closet to escape the rain. The Miss Monsoon pageant was a particularly interesting event because all of the contestants lived in the exact same kind of deteriorating concrete apartment blocks that I did and were equally affected by the flooding that was endemic in my suburban neighborhood.

As fourteen scantily clad suburban girls paraded onto the worn red carpet of the Miss Monsoon stage in the thick, mosquito-filled humidity of August in Mumbai, each declared her unbridled ambition to be Miss Universe. Mumbai's suburbs are culturally and geographically distinct from the more affluent southern portion of the city, which was notably the seat of British imperial rule in Western India prior to independence. Mumbai is similar to most other cities in the world in that its neighborhoods are sharply demarcated by social class and its associated cultural differences, so while South Mumbai is home to the owners of corporations who might consider using Miss Monsoon as an advertising venue, the suburbs are populated by the families of young women who may think of a beauty pageant as a very real opportunity for social mobility. The suburbs are also considerably more conservative than South Mumbai, and this is evident in the kinds of clothing that young women wear. Although a typical South Mumbai ensemble for someone in her early twenties might include a sleeveless blouse and snug-fitting jeans, her suburban counterpart is much more likely to dress in looser garments that do not highlight her figure and attract unwanted attention.

I struggled to cover my own body as much as I could by draping long scarves over my conservative clothing every morning to avoid the stares and unwelcome comments of strange men at the suburban train station, where I also started to experience the same fantasies that sustain the Miss Universe dreams of young women at Miss Monsoon. "Wouldn't it be wonderful," I asked myself at the train station one morning as I commuted to my job at a fashion magazine in South Mumbai, "to be beautiful again?" The reality that space in India is aggressively male prevents women from cultivating their beauty in public; female beauty is something that needs to be carefully hidden, almost as if it were currency or property of a future or current male partner that exists only for his consumption. I grew so incredibly sick of burying myself under yards of heavy cloth in order to avoid the suburban male gaze that I started spending unhealthy amounts of time looking longingly at pictures of young women in Indian fashion magazines who wore the same high heels and miniskirts that I had worn in New York. My own understanding of beauty, it turned out, had become close to that of the women who were my neighbors in suburban Mumbai and especially those who chose to participate in Miss Monsoon.

The Miss Monsoon pageant had copied the format of Miss India and yet it promised little in the way of social mobility, providing instead an opportunity for women to be the focus of what they perceived to be an appreciative rather than degrading gaze that prized their approximation of postliberalization beauty. The contestants at Miss Monsoon indulged in fantasies in which they did not have to hide themselves from the world as if there was something intrinsically wrong with being a beautiful woman. One of the reasons why pageants at multiple levels of organization and prestige have blossomed throughout Mumbai is that they can serve as a space in which one is not socially sanctioned for being beautiful, young, and female.

I spent an afternoon with sixteen-year-old Miss Monsoon 2002 Karishma Acharya discussing her opinions about pageants and beauty in general. A typical suburban Mumbai girl with a profound love of American popular culture, Acharya was a college student and aspiring Hindi film director. Miss Monsoon was her second pageant, and she had heard about it from a judge who remembered her from her experience at a pageant the year before, which had been sponsored by a cloth manufacturer.

Acharya was emphatic that pageants were a profound force in helping to shape her personality, and in the following passage she describes the sense of empowerment she gained from participating in events such as Miss Monsoon.

> Pageants let you learn more about yourself and about the world. Looking beautiful is something everyone and anyone can do, but not everyone can win. Like in this pageant, I was the shortest and the youngest, but my presence is strong, and so I won. Pageants enhance me. Every time, there are new people around me, and participating with the other girls makes me feel better. It's a platform for success, especially for girls who want to model, because you get to know everyone in the industry. Getting work isn't easy for models, you really have to know people, and pageants let you do that.

Her observation points to the social network that participating in pageants allows young women to create in order to "get to know everyone." Participation in pageants in India can be as much about seriously advancing one's career in a country in which access overwhelmingly revolves around social contacts as it is about looking beautiful. This serves to underscore how the pageant as cultural performance differs profoundly from site to site; although it is unfair that while her male counterpart may not have to parade onstage in a short skirt in order to get access to a social network in the film industry, it is also worth mentioning that Acharya's adept negotiation of a deeply flawed system of gender in the film industry may provide her with more access to social networks in media than her middle-class male counterpart would ever have.

Families that are supportive of young women's aspirations for a career in media often recognize that pageants can provide a conduit to the social networks necessary for success. Miss India contestants were adamant that their families had to approve of their decision, which underscores just how many types of relationships young women like Acharya have to negotiate. Acharya highlighted how her mother served as a supportive force:

> My mom designs my stuff for me, and helps me put outfits together, because you can't buy new stuff every time. She gives me advice, like "you were nice, but you have to improve on your walk." She always tells me what is bad, because what is good remains. My mother used to model, so she encouraged me to take this up.

Acharya's mother effectively served as a critic who helped her daughter come closer to embodying the beauty queen ideal. Acharya's mother used her prestructural adjustment experiences to assist her daughter in the creation of pageant-appropriate clothing, which highlights how social class is a powerful element at work even in small-scale events like Miss Monsoon. Her admission of "you can't buy new stuff every time" underscores the amount of economic investment and time that pageant participation requires, as well as the familial financial support that must be set aside to facilitate this activity.

Acharya cited the competitive aspect of beauty pageants as the aspect that interested her almost as much as the opportunities they provide to cultivate valuable contacts in media who may later help her to get modeling work. "The envy part of it motivates me," she said conspiratorially, "not jealousy, but envy." Drawing a curious distinction between "jealousy," which she described as a feeling of longing for something unattainable, and "envy," which she described as a sort of motivated admiration for what another woman may have, Acharya seemed to draw enormous pleasure from placing herself within an evaluative hierarchy of beauty.

Acharya was certainly not alone in this sentiment, as seeing oneself in the mirror of others is unfortunately the only way most women know how to evaluate beauty. Beauty is a construct that is created from outside and imposed upon the self through internal monitoring and careful attention to external detail. This need to approximate a certain set of characteristics one needs to possess in order to be considered beautiful was a consistent theme throughout all of the discussions I had with women ranging from Miss Monsoon to Miss Universe.

## Miss India

Neha Dhupia was a twenty-one-year-old model from Delhi who won the title of Miss India–Universe in 2002 and was preparing to leave for the Miss Universe pageant as we spoke about what Miss India meant to her. Like many other Miss India contestants, she described her victory at the pageant as the culmination of a postliberalization childhood dream. Many young women who saw Miss India contestants win both Miss World and Miss Universe in 1994 described that moment as the recognition of immense possibilities for themselves, because media is the only field in which young women may look for female role models who are economically independent and highly visible. Dhupia described how she calculatedly evaluated her chances of cultivating herself into the kind of beauty queen she saw on the television screen during her childhood.

> I thought, "They're glamorous, they're smart, they're good-looking, intelligent, and that's what it takes to be onstage." I was really young then, and I thought to myself, "The only thing you have in common with them is that they're women and you're also a woman, so if they can do it, why can't you?" There was this hunger for the crown. That was it, I wanted that crown.

Dhupia described herself as a young girl watching the Miss India pageant and engaging in a process of internalizing the images of womanhood and femininity presented within the passage. When she asked herself, as she sat in front of the television watching the pageant for the first time, if she could someday be Miss India, she embarked upon the beginning of a cultivation of a new identity by deciding that she too could transform herself into the kind of woman she saw on the screen. It is notable that Dhupia used the visceral physical metaphor of hunger to characterize just how much she wanted to be Miss India, as the process of becoming a beauty queen is itself so closely connected to discourses of deprivation. She went on to detail her life until the preparations for the Miss Universe pageant as part of a single trajectory toward the pageant, beginning in her late teens when she began to model, which "really helped to develop my stage presence." Dhupia deliberately sought out areas that would improve her chances of competing at the pageant, which illustrates just how much of their emotional and physical selves young women invest in Miss India.

Like most other contestants, however, her decision to enter the Miss India pageant and thus make the leap from model to potential beauty queen was fraught with insecurity. This demonstrates how the process of approximating beauty is never easy and inherently involves a constant gaze into the mirror of the other in hopes of gauging the self. The numerous stages of the Miss India pageant are designed by default to encourage young women to alter themselves in order to become the beauty queen self that the rhetoric of the pageant insists exists inside every woman. This difficult blend of official insistence that "anyone" can be Miss India combined with the requirement that young women alter their bodies in order to do so is a dangerous combination that produces a deep sense of insecurity for many women.

It is perhaps as a result of this insecurity that Dhupia described Miss India as a progression through a difficult series of steps, each of which made her feel unsure whether she would make it to the next level. For example, she noted that the number of initial applicants was 60,000, which is unreasonably high given the 332 entries in 2003, yet Dhupia's extreme overestimation of the number of contestants may simply be indicative of how overwhelming the competition felt to her. She said that at each successive stage of the pageant, she "just was waiting, waiting, on my toes to get selected for the next level." As a series of steps toward a single goal, then, Dhupia's progression toward the Miss India and Miss Universe crowns was fundamentally a project of self-improvement in which the self is never quite good enough. Because it necessitates meeting certain standards that are set by international pageants in terms of height, weight, and other physical characteristics as well as an ability to present oneself in a certain way onstage, the process of cultivating a Miss India within oneself is also an educative process that entails fitting into a predetermined mold to the best of one's abilities.

All aspiring Miss India contestants prior to the 2003 pageant began the entrance process at the regional level by meeting with one individual: *Femina* publisher Pradeep Guha, who alone decided which women fit the standards of international pageants as part of a process that was never quite clear to anyone except himself. In fact, the main goal of the 2003 pageant was to bring a degree of what officials called "transparency" to Miss India in order to avoid the kind of confusion about standards and judging procedures that existed during Guha's tenure as head of the pageant.

Dhupia described the process of being evaluated by Guha as a very impersonal one that sounded much like a visit to the doctor:

> There's an interview where he tries to understand why you want to be in the contest, what your plan for life is, the way you look, the way your body is, the way your skin type is. He very clinically checks you up. . . . The competition keeps getting tougher and tougher each year, because of his strict standards.

It was Guha's "strict standards" alone that previously determined who got the chance to compete at an international level via the Miss India pageant, and yet Dhupia described the process as a very fair one, in which the seemingly impossible task of narrowing a list of applicants was done according to a set of prescribed standards set by Guha himself. Dhupia's choice of vocabulary in outlining this process reflected this perception, as the use of words such as "clinical" and "strict standards" underscored her belief in the unbiased nature of the process by which Miss India contestants were chosen.

Once the young women were selected by Guha, they were given advice on how to improve their chances of winning the title prior to the training program. Dhupia was advised to lose weight and reduced her measurements by four inches in ten days through an extreme diet and exercise regime in order to maximize her potential to win. She described exercising "every day, all day" to lose the requisite amount of weight necessary to compete not as a sacrifice that she had to make in order to fit a set of standards, but rather as an expression of her dedication to the pageant:

> I had to do it, you know? That's how driven I was toward the crown. That I lost all that weight is one of the things that helped me out, because they really got to know that I was really driven toward that crown.

Dhupia felt that her weight loss allowed her to show pageant officials that she would go to great lengths to demonstrate her dedication to the possibility of becoming Miss India. This effort was well worth it in her view, as it resulted in her being crowned Miss India–Universe, a title she had aspired to since her childhood, and thus marked the achievement of Dhupia's life goal that necessitated that she cultivate herself in ways that she otherwise may not have.

She described the training process as "very tough, but lovely" and was characteristic of most young women who go through the training in that she was full of praise for the organization and opportunities that the program provides:

> They thought of every aspect of it, from hair and makeup to body, diet, skincare, making us aware of our country, our past, everything! They covered every aspect, yoga, anything you can think of. And there was no cattiness, all the girls were so friendly that the *Femina* people had to say, "Look, you guys are supposed to be competing—you're not here to make friends."

Dhupia's comment on the friendly atmosphere she felt at the training program is contrary to what one would expect in an environment in which women are competitors against each other for four weeks with the full knowledge that most will not win. Contestants at the 2003 training program certainly did make an effort to appear that they had cultivated close friendships as part of the performance of self-sacrificing kindness beauty queens must evince, yet a subtext of competition and dislike was also clear in side comments, disapproving glances, and other less-noticeable forms.

Dhupia gently alluded to this atmosphere of competition in mentioning that some of the goodwill she experienced at the training program may not have been genuine, as the notebook that contained all of the information she had recorded to help her win was stolen the night before the pageant. In a rather powerful statement about preparation and competition, she noted, "I felt like half of my mind was taken away." Although she was unsure who stole her notebook, she insisted that it was the result of certain contestants getting too nervous about winning. The divisive nature of competition at the 2003 pageant made young women who had appeared to have established extremely close relationships with one another during the training program suddenly pretend not to know each other when the final pageant began. I was amazed to watch how groups formed and then gradually narrowed down until the final day of the pageant when all of the contestants were individually isolated in front of their makeup mirrors backstage, completely immersed in self-evaluations of how well they had managed to inscribe the vision of Miss India onto themselves.

Dhupia described being judged as rather harrowing and using language that emphasized the potential for humiliation in being publicly questioned, she illustrated her feelings about the judging process:

> It's better when you're one-on-one with the judges, because when they ask you questions onstage, and your peers are all standing next to you, you get extremely nervous. I'd rather get really self-conscious in front of just a few people than a whole number of people I don't know, because on the final day you have to focus.

Dhupia found being questioned in front of the other contestants to be exceptionally difficult, presumably because it brought to the fore the level of competition and self-scrutiny involved in Miss India. Dhupia's life changed dramatically after winning the Miss India crown. She moved to Mumbai from Delhi and made herself available for all *Femina*-related events, but her biggest responsibility was to prepare for the Miss Universe pageant that takes place three months after Miss India winners are announced. She was preparing for the Miss Universe pageant at the time of our interview by being personally trained and taking diction classes, and it was clear that her efforts had transcended to another level; mentioning that "the standards are so much higher," Dhupia voiced what she perceived to be a need to further improve herself as she balanced her preparations for the Miss Universe pageant with her role as Miss India.

Dhupia was emphatic that the title of Miss India carried with it a number of responsibilities and privileges that made her both an ambassador and a role model:

> Being Miss India means the world to me. First, being able to have a voice, being able to make a difference, being in front of people, being able to live up to people's expectations and making them my own responsibilities in order to become a better role model for them. And, it also helps me to become a better person, because I'm trying to perfect myself every single day, because at the Miss Universe contest, I'll have more people watching me than any other girl there.

By catapulting her into the spotlight, then, the Miss India title gave Dhupia a set of privileges and responsibilities that must be negotiated during the course of her everyday lived experience. The privileges include almost constant public attention, particularly in the form of media, and the responsibilities largely center on the preparations to compete at Miss Universe in May of the same year. Dhupia notably mentioned having the gaze of the entire nation upon her at the Miss Universe pageant only after having described the project of trying to improve herself "every single day," which hints at the pressure that the title of Miss India, and potential international title of Miss Universe, brings to winners. As the next section will illustrate, the pressure to be perfect only increases as the level of perceived "standards" are raised even higher.

## Miss World

Nearly six feet tall and very outspoken, Miss World 1999 Yukta Mookhey grew up in the Mumbai suburb of Mulund, a fact the Indian media often mentioned in a rather incredulous tone. Mookhey was consistently described both in popular culture and by pageant officials as an unlikely

winner and was often held up as an example of the radically transformative powers of the training program. The press typically described her
as a "gawky, awkward teenager from a far-flung suburb no one has ever
heard of." I found this sort of language insidious, as it effectively robbed
Mookhey of all the credit in becoming Miss World. To hear pageant officials tell it, Mookhey had been a gauche suburban nobody who had been
sculpted into a vision of perfection by the training program.

The way in which Mookhey was stripped of agency by the press and
pageant officials is sadly symptomatic of the entire Miss India process,
which puts far greater emphasis on the production of a specific *type* of
woman in the form of an idealized Miss India rather than accepting individual human beings with a range of physical characteristics. Whenever
articles appeared that celebrated the ability of the training program to
physically alter contestants, Mookhey was always used as the example.
Personal trainer Mickey Mehta, who designed fitness programs for Miss
India contestants for over a decade, described the pretraining program
Mookhey as "so huge people just wrote her off completely."

This kind of cruel language is unfortunately relatively common.
When Mehta described Mookhey's twenty-six-pound weight loss during
the course of the training program, followed by more as she prepared
for Miss World, I felt a kind of anger at standards that were so obviously
unfair. Yet, because I had read and heard so much about Mookhey before
I met her, even I had begun to think of her as more of a pageant-produced
commodity than a human being. Mookhey served as a consultant throughout the 2003 pageant, and I had a number of opportunities to speak with
her informally about her views on and experiences with the Miss India
process. She never expressed negative sentiments about the deprivation
she had to undergo in order to win but did voice her conviction that her
own example proved that anyone could be Miss India.

Mookhey dreamed of participating in Miss India from the time she
was in her early teens, but her low self-esteem held her back until much
later. "I used to think I was not so pretty," she said with disturbing conviction when I asked her why she had previously thought that her chances
of winning Miss India were slim. Contestants often detailed their progression from "ordinary" to beauty queen in similar terms, implying

that beauty is a static category into which young women need to squeeze themselves. This serves to underscore how almost no one is a beauty queen; figures such as Miss India are simply representations of women at a specific moment in time, a kind of photogenic transience that is impossible to maintain for very long.

Mookhey's parents were not happy with her decision to enter Miss India, and in fact refused to allow her to participate for a full five years because of the temporary nature of the kind of fame that the pageant brings. "They thought I was too smart for this kind of career," she noted, "and that I should do something in advertising instead." Although her parents were eventually convinced that winning Miss India could provide Mookhey with an opportunity to do something exceptionally different with her life, the underlying message from both popular culture and Mookhey's parents remains clear: intelligent women do not participate in beauty pageants.

Like most other contestants, Mookhey described being intimidated by the selection procedures and clearly felt the difference between herself as a suburban young woman without previous modeling experience and the other contestants during the initial selection round in Mumbai. "I was so intimidated there" she said, "because all the models had put on beautiful makeup that no one could even see because it was so perfect. Being made up isn't fair to girls like me who aren't professional models." Participating in a beauty pageant is always about placing oneself in a hierarchy of beauty; who measures up, and who does not, becomes a point of pride for young women as they become more and more like the image of Miss India they seek to be. For young women like Mookhey, however, the initial shock of being so far removed from that ideal can be overwhelming.

Mookhey responded to this challenge by becoming obsessed with winning Miss World, and after the Miss India pageant, she spent sixteen hours a day for several months in preparation to travel to London for the competition. She read about current events in order to answer questions more articulately, exercised compulsively to lose even more weight, and practiced walking on the ramp in very high heels in order to mold herself into an image of Miss World. Mookhey described this process as part of her philosophy of life rather than situating it within a discourse of deprivation:

> I always stood first in my class and if I lost out on one mark in math, I would stay up all night and read so I could get ten marks ahead next time. For me, Question and Answer wasn't a problem because I'd done a lot of elocution, but physical grooming was a problem. I had never walked the ramp and everyone else had and so I had to learn how to sit in a short skirt and walk in heels.

Mookhey remembers preparing for Miss World as part of her competitive personality: the same characteristics that made her study obsessively in order to be the best student in her class were those that, in her mind, enabled her to rapidly lose a large amount of weight and focus single-mindedly on winning the Miss World pageant.

Mookhey described her arrival at the Miss World pageant as something of a shock, both culturally and in terms of the competition. She repeatedly emphasized the moral danger she perceived herself to be in at the pageant and how the unfamiliarity of it all was rather overwhelming:

> It takes seven to ten days to adjust at Miss World, because you're in a foreign country. Some girls at Miss World would go out with their boyfriends and spend four hundred pounds a night! You have to make the girls you send strong. I made myself strong before I went, so that I knew I was only going there to compete.

Mookhey seemed uncomfortable with both the wealth and the implicit lack of focus on winning that the other contestants seemed to have. Many other former Miss India contestants who participated in Miss World or Miss Universe informally told me how surprised they had been that not everyone was as serious about winning as they were.

Miss World travels a great deal for her work from her base in London, where she is provided with an apartment for one year in addition to $100,000 in prize money. The first activity Miss World undertakes is a return visit known as a "homecoming" to her country of origin, during the course of which she meets prominent politicians and leaders in business.

Miss World is not as brand-oriented or as effective at self-promotion as the Miss Universe pageant, although it does do a great deal of fund-raising and charity work for social issues related to children. Miss World travels throughout the year both for fund-raising events such as telethons and charity balls and to present the financial results of these activities to hospitals, orphanages, and schools as part of its broader association with its slogan "beauty with a purpose."

Constantly onstage throughout her year as Miss World, Mookhey was always escorted wherever she went and also brought a male member of her family with her to every Miss India event that involved her traveling outside of Mumbai. When I asked her why this was the case, as it certainly marked her as unusual in a world of at least superficially independent young women, she said that she had found it especially helpful to always have someone with her when she was Miss World:

> Miss World always travels with an escort. That way she doesn't have to deal with certain situations. Miss World cannot be directly approachable by just anyone. Her escort can say things that are not appropriate for her to say, because she can't speak to just anyone and everyone, only to the top people. And now that I'm a celebrity, there are always crowds wherever I go, so I need someone with me. Of course, security will be there if it's a big event, but there will always be men trying to push through, and that's where my Dad or my uncle comes in, because they're both strong so then I don't have to worry.

Mookhey's reasoning is redolent with the fear of an anonymous threatening male presence, and although this was the only time I heard such a view so clearly expressed throughout the course of the research for this book, it is nonetheless notable. When Mookhey described "men trying to push through" as something of a matter of course, the vision it creates is particularly vivid and disturbing. Her description of having been Miss World sounds remarkably like an experience of danger in which a persistent male threat needed to be negotiated.

Mookhey spent several hours speaking to contestants at the training program in order to prepare them for the possibility of competing at Miss World. She was emphatic that being labeled professionally beautiful via

Miss India was a life-changing experience that made romantic relationships with men exceedingly difficult. After announcing that she would never get married and planned to adopt a baby in a few years, she told contestants that, "It's difficult for a man to deal with your fame and success, their ego that is. So don't get married unless you want to have someone's baby. Find someone who helps you grow." Men, in Mookhey's view, find it difficult to deal with the pressures of female achievement, even if it is success in terms of Miss India or Miss World. Mookhey may simply be honest and outspoken about emotions others remained silent about, but her experience reveals that some are not able to adapt to the role of the beauty queen, whereas others positively excel in their role as the face of a nation.

## Miss Universe

Miss Universe 2000 Lara Dutta was at work on her first Hindi film when we spoke about her experiences at the Miss Universe pageant. Known in India as "the most professional Miss Universe," her focus on winning the international title from the moment she decided to enter Miss India was striking. Dutta was already an established professional model when she entered Miss India and was adamant about her ambitions, noting that, "I never did Miss India saying I wanted to be Miss India, I did Miss India saying I want to be Miss Universe." Dutta was a reluctant entrant to the Miss India pageant who hesitated as a result of her winning the *Gladrags* magazine Supermodel pageant the year before. *Gladrags* and *Femina* are rival magazines, and so she was concerned that this would work against her, because "they would want to choose someone who was a younger, fresher face and market her as their *Femina* girl." When the Times of India Group contacted her while she was still in college in Bangalore, she felt that the time was right to pursue her dream. The Miss Universe pageant is fantasy material for a period of time for most young middle class Indian women, and Dutta's rather sharp assertion that "everybody dreams of being Miss Universe" highlights this in a matter-of-fact way.

Miss Universe has a rigorous schedule that begins when she wins the pageant in May and ends when she surrenders her crown twelve months later. Her title and celebrity are used for the promotion of beauty products, fashion designers, and the Miss Universe pageant itself as well as social service activities related to HIV/AIDS. Miss Universe serves as a kind of walking advertisement for the pageant and the sponsors who pay for it throughout her tenure by traveling to various countries throughout the world in conjunction with visits to national beauty pageants. During her travels she meets with heads of state, United Nations officials, and business leaders in order to raise awareness about HIV/AIDS among young people and is affiliated with advocacy organizations in the United States such as the Global Health Council and the Gay Men's Health Crisis. Miss Universe is especially active in HIV/AIDS related social service activities in her country of origin, but her schedule necessitates international travel at least twice a month in order to attend hundreds of promotional events in combination with humanitarian work. A typical year for Miss Universe includes travel to attend pageants in countries as diverse as Brazil, Canada, Nicaragua, Puerto Rico, Thailand, and Ukraine in conjunction with voluntary work. When she is not traveling, she serves as a representative of the Miss Universe Corporation and lives in an apartment that is provided for her in New York City.

It is the desirable nature of being a beauty queen with access to such privilege that contributes most to the discourse of fantasy surrounding it. Although I heard similar language in various forms from all the contestants I spoke to, Dutta far surpassed anyone else in her use of dream-like phrases to describe the pageant. She emphasized the whirlwind nature of her year as Miss Universe, relying time and again on a kind of language that could just as easily been culled from a romance novel:

> The transition actually was a bit of a shock. I left Cyprus two days after I won and headed straight to New York and was whisked away to one of these big buildings in the heart of Manhattan and all of a sudden you have people coming at you from all directions, saying, "I'm your manager" and, "I'll be representing you." People saying, "do this, do that" and, "don't say this, don't say that" and once that's done then it becomes routine. You don't really get much time to let it sink in and think, "Oh, this is great!"

3. *Beauty pageants are cultural performances in which the fantasy of idealized feminin-ity is highly prized, such as this image of an announcer dressed as a helpless mermaid stranded on rocks.*

Dutta chronicled both the magical experience of becoming someone called Miss Universe and the highly supervised life that she led, high-lighting the transformation in identity beauty queens must undergo via their associations with institutions. As a young woman with a dubious skill set, a manager, and a glamorous lifestyle in Manhattan, being Miss Universe requires a certain degree of presumptuousness. To be taken se-riously, or to take oneself seriously, in such a role necessitates that one wholeheartedly subscribe to the fantasy of femininity that the pageant system espouses, and Miss India winners are chosen based on how well they are able to flesh out that fantasy.

From romance novels to sex work to fairy tales, women are irrevoca-bly tied to notions of fantasy, both in their own minds and in the minds of men. In practice this is evident in the way in which women strive to embody ways of being that are considered beautiful and in how many women still choose to neglect long-term planning for their own lives in favor of relying on hopes of a male savior to rescue them. To be Miss Universe, perhaps above all things, is to embody all that is fairy tale feminine: a woman who does not reveal any suspicions about the inequality inherent in such beliefs and their supporting institutions. Utilizing the language of fantasy once again, Dutta described being Miss Universe as a completely dream-like experience that will never be surpassed in her lifetime:

> It's turned my life upside down! It's a gift, a charming and wonderful gift that is given to you for one year. I know that there are lots of wonderful things that will happen to me in my life and I look forward to them, but I don't think anything will ever be quite as amazing as that year. It's a very short span of time in which you go through, see and are exposed to so much that it's almost an intensive course that shows you the whole world at once—the glamour, the glitz, as well as the very gritty realities of the issues you work and deal with.

Her use of adjectives is especially notable throughout this passage: "glamour," "charming and wonderful gift," and "glitz" are almost overpowering in their intensity. This is the essence of the Miss Universe fantasy that has at its core the belief in a world in which all the lies that popular culture tells women are possible actually become true for one woman.

The "gritty realities" that Dutta referred to center mostly on working with HIV/AIDS-related issues with the United Nations, although this "work" is largely done in a very superficial context that involves more posing for photographs than it does actual advocacy. That Miss Universe does charity work that is suitably feminine is self-evident: if she works with HIV/AIDS-related issues, she does so by visiting hospitals and afflicted children, not, for example, by distributing condoms on the street to gay male sex workers. Even the slightest political affiliation would serve to disrupt the Miss Universe fantasy, much as knowing the painful realities of a nude dancer's life in the fantasy space of a strip club disrupts the male fantasy of willing female servitude.

Women are uniquely able to embody even the nation itself as part of the link between fantasy and the feminine cross-culturally. Part of living out the fantasy of the feminine as Miss Universe entails maintaining the perceived characteristics of one's country, which are described in greater detail in chapter 6. The geopolitics of Miss Universe were a subject of great interest to Dutta, who described the self-segregation that took place during the 1997 pageant by complaining that "the Hispanic girls form their little group, the Caribbean girls form their little group." This grouping is part of pageant lore in which the Americas, particularly Venezuela and the United States, and India are part of a beauty queen rivalry at Miss Universe and Miss World. Dutta felt that this competition focused attention on contestants from these countries:

> India is the most looked for, along with USA and Venezuela because of the winners they've had in the past. I think that what sets us apart is the clothing we bring, because everyone else comes with beautiful ball gowns, but not everyone can carry off a sari with the entire paraphernalia and bangles too. I remember the first event we were supposed to dress up for, everyone kept saying, "Is she down yet? Is she down yet?" and I felt like the belle of the ball, because everyone just wanted to see what I had on!

Dutta was performing India at Miss Universe, although she does not explicitly mention it, and as the exotic focus of every camera's lens, she "felt like the belle of the ball." Pageant officials repeatedly mentioned just how good India is at performing national identity, and with a vast and rich textile tradition, the distinctive and elaborate clothing that the Miss India pageant provides to contestants at Miss Universe is, as Dutta mentioned, the focus of an enormous amount of attention.

Implicit within the performance of national identity in the scope of the international pageant is also the inequality that such a situation presents. Not all Miss Universe contestants have the same (or any) fluency in English or comparable amounts of exposure to the world. Many do not come from pageant cultures such as India or Venezuela and are thus not as prepared for the experience. Dutta felt that as Miss India she was uniquely able to adapt to the situation that Miss Universe presented her with. "In India," she noted, "we live with other cultures all the time. Your neighbors could be Bengali or Punjabi or Muslim, so you tend to adapt more easily to different cultures."

While Dutta used the magical language of the pageant to describe her experience at Miss Universe, she was also quick to credit the Miss India training program with her success. This is part of the rhetoric of the pageant fairy tale, as it demonstrates how a relatively normal young woman is metamorphosed into a beauty queen. "I came from Bangalore, a small town," she said, "that's my background, and there you don't get the opportunity to actually know your Beethoven from your Bach, so every little bit of confidence helps."

Going from Bangalore to Miss Universe, in Dutta's estimation, constituted a sea change, and yet despite the rhetoric of the fairy tale, implicit in the process of competing in Miss India or any other pageant is the knowledge that not everyone can win. Not winning can be absolutely devastating to young women, who may place all of their hopes and dreams in the vehicle of Miss India, and being deemed not good enough to fit the Miss India mold after dedicating so much of one's time to it can be a fundamentally destabilizing experience.

**Miss India as a Platform**

A success as the lead actress in the 2002 Hindi film *Sur* (Melody), Gauri Karnik did not win Miss India 2000. Karnik came from a family of academics, had no family or friends who worked in the field of media, and was a graduate of the prestigious St. Xavier's College in Mumbai. Her story grants insight into how Miss India provides a platform from which young women without any connections can enter media-related fields. Karnik described her progression from college student to Miss India contestant as a result of the "huge amount of hype" that followed the 1994 victory of Miss India Sushmita Sen and Aishwarya Rai at Miss Universe and Miss World, and like many other young women, she credited the month-long training program with helping her to become who she is today:

> Miss India is a grooming school for a girl to become a lady, because in
> India there are no grooming schools. I've been a tomboy my whole life,

so I thought it could help me. I was unique in my looks. I'm not a conventional beauty—I'm not full-figured and fair with straight hair and I didn't have the grace and poise and streaked hair that the other girls did, so I had to cultivate that. It's a school where you can learn to present yourself as a lady, to think of yourself as a beautiful lady who can represent the country.

Karnik speaks to multiple issues in this passage, the most notable of which is the way she felt out of place at the pageant as a young woman who was beautiful with curly hair and a brown complexion, but did not fit the stereotype of what a Miss India looks like. The calculated description of how she did not meet the standards of the pageant is almost disturbing in both its conviction and its details.

Karnik was crushed when she did not win the pageant, but felt that the experience had taught her a great deal:

For two to three months after I didn't make it, I went into total depression. You lie low and then bounce back after you meet with failure. My path was to fulfill the requirements of the pageant as well as I could. Now, because I read so much, I know so much about the world and how to speak, which has stayed with me. It taught me how to cope with failure. Now I know that no one can be a landmark in history, because there's always someone better than you.

Karnik's description of entering into "total depression" before coming to terms with the fact that she did gain a great deal from the pageant speaks to issues of not measuring up. Implicit in entering a pageant like Miss India is the fact that some girls will win while others will not, a reality that is perhaps not emphasized enough at the training program.

Sadly, Karnik framed her failure to become Miss India as her fault, rather than the result of a flawed system that only considers one kind of beauty. When I asked her if she would compete again in Miss India, she said that she would not:

I gave it my best, there was no room for improvement. I lacked in grace. I can't flaunt my body. I am not conscious of how I walk. I am not a proper feminine person, even now. Maybe I lacked in height, because I'm five [feet] six [inches tall] and all the others were five [feet] eight [inches tall] and five [feet] nine [inches tall].

As I listened to Karnik say this, we were seated at a table at a café on Mumbai's Marine Drive, overlooking the Arabian Sea. I remember noticing how ethereal she looked with her hair blowing in the breeze and her eyes lighting up every time she heard something that interested her. Listening to her describe herself as less-than revealed that whenever individuals allow themselves to be made to believe that there are criteria for judging female beauty, they can also fall victim to the kind of inferiority complex that Karnik clearly displayed in the passage above.

Karnik also felt that certain aspects of the pageant, including allowing professional models to enter, were unfair. "How can a girl like me compete with a professional?" she asked, again positioning herself as inferior. This statement echoes former Miss World Yukta Mookhey's description of how intimidated she felt by some of the other contestants she encountered at Miss India. Karnik had much in common with Mookhey in her openness about certain elements of Miss India she found to be unpleasant, such as the idea of "sisterhood" at the pageant:

No one is nice at the pageant. They say everyone is a winner, but it's a lie. We're not sisters, we're competitors. There wasn't too much deliberate bitchiness, but there was a lot of competition. I made one friend there, because I was true to myself. I thought, "Why bother to bond with anyone just to abuse that trust?"

Karnik was quick to point out that had it not been for Miss India, she would not be on her current career path, as none of her family or friends were in the media. After Miss India, she acted on a soap opera for a period of time until Hindi film director Tanuja Chandra cast her in the lead role in *Sur*. The role on television was a result of a photographer she met during a Miss India training session who later contacted her for an audition.

"Miss India is a way for women to do something with their lives," Karnik observed in a way that espoused the rhetoric of the platform. A suburban girl like herself with no contacts in media never would have been able to become a film star without the pageant, yet Karnik was also quick to note that women who participate in Miss India often already have a set of characteristics that would allow them to succeed in any number of fields:

> Women who have won have been highly successful. They have power, fame, they are in demand. They're always treated like queens. We're talking about eighteen to twenty-three-year-olds, and to be successful with that fickle of mind takes a lot. The winners are not ordinary people. They are not ordinary at all.

As these examples of young women's lives illustrate, being a beauty queen means a variety of things: having a voice, being deemed the most beautiful woman in the country, a chance to further one's career, or being, as Karnik put it, "a lady." The most common theme that runs across such narratives is the hard work that young women put into winning, and the extraordinary amount of power they attach to the sense of responsibility it grants them.

## The Discourse of Responsibility at the Training Program

It is evident that being Miss India (or Miss World or Miss Universe, for that matter) does not really involve a great deal of real work for the winner and yet these responsibilities amount to much more than most women are given the opportunity to tackle in life. Not much is really expected of a Miss India winner beyond her appearance at various *Femina* events on behalf of the pageant and her representation of India at an international pageant. Similarly, all that Miss World or Miss Universe has to do is to serve as a spokesperson for charity groups while traveling on behalf of the pageant. It is as much the public nature of the title as it is the perceived hard work it involves that makes being Miss India a challenging prospect, and 2003 contestant Kaveri asserted "being Miss India means a big responsibility, because you have to carry the name. In India, people look up to celebrities, so indirectly you are responsible for thousands of others."

The notion of always being onstage implicit in Kaveri's example is rather daunting and parallels former Miss World Yukta Mookhey's description of the sense of immense relief she felt when she returned her crown after her year as Miss World came to a close. Although the more tangible responsibilities that a beauty queen has may be relatively few, the emotional weight of constantly managing a public identity can be quite overwhelming for a young woman in her late teens or early twenties. Forced to maintain a version of femininity and beauty that never happens naturally because it must be cultivated in some way or another, Miss India is never truly offstage.

Former Miss India Nafisa Joseph described the stress that being a contestant at Miss Universe caused her as almost unbearable and was adamant that the age of Miss India contestants should be raised to over twenty-five. Gender is always performed (and gendered beauty doubly so) and so it can be extraordinarily difficult to reconcile one's first real experience of adult independence with simultaneously embodying the standard of beauty for a nation. Joseph noted that she felt constant pressure to be more mature than she really was at the time:

> When I was Miss India I was traveling all the time, sometimes for social causes, sometimes for promotions. I didn't start really being a normal nineteen year old until I started working for MTV after Miss India, because Miss India was so much responsibility I had to be really grown up. Since I went to Miss Universe when I was only eighteen, I was really homesick and wasn't focused on winning.

Joseph's definition of a "normal nineteen year old" is somewhat skewed by the fact that her first job was with MTV India, but her statement reveals how the pressures involved in being Miss India make young women alter themselves in ways that may not be entirely age-appropriate. Stating that she "had to be really grown up," Joseph's description of being Miss India sounds more like a sentence she had to serve than a pleasant or empowering experience. If being Miss India is difficult, competing to be Miss Universe is even more so, and as Neha Dhupia prepared to leave for the 2003 Miss Universe pageant, she was emphatic that the competition would be much more difficult than it had been at Miss India:

There's the number of girls, for starters. The competition gets you down to $\frac{1}{80}$ of a possibility of winning as opposed to $\frac{1}{26}$. You've got to hold yourself and be aware of everything, starting from your body and your mind, everything, your face, your physical appearance, because you have to know that people are judging you. The standards are so much higher for everything. There are going to be women from all over the world. Just the level of things that happen, the entire event—it's just so much larger than a domestic level—it's a universal level, Miss Universe!

Dhupia described the feeling of constantly being onstage at Miss Universe "because you have to know that people are judging you," but with standards that surpass those at Miss India. Her repetition of the word "everything" in conjunction with descriptions of all the diverse elements of her body and self that were scheduled to be evaluated at Miss Universe reveals a great deal about the pressure she felt to perform.

These standards are kept in mind when the judges decide which contestants will go on to each international pageant, and the kinds of parameters that each pageant uses are carefully taken into account. In the 2003 Miss India pageant, for example, the winner of the Miss Ten title, which evaluated body type in the preliminaries, was not given to the contestant with most toned and fit body but rather to a young woman who had, as one organizer put it, "that very tall, lean, Miss Universe kind of a body."

The kind of beauty that is chosen to represent India is also crucial, and so former Miss World Yukta Mookhey noted in the course of a meeting with Ernst and Young consultants that it was important to acknowledge and effectively represent national difference at international pageants. In Mookhey's view, Miss India needs to "look Indian" in order to truly represent the country in an authentic fashion. "She can't be too Western looking with light eyes, like Miss Venezuela," Mookhey said, keeping the ever-present specter of the competition in mind, "because then she can't carry off a sari and look good." If a Miss India with light eyes cannot adequately represent the country, then a contestant who is deemed insufficiently "Indian" in her responses to questions at the pageant is equally unable to do so. Officials consistently used the example of former Miss India Madhu Sapre, who lost the Miss Universe pageant after answering a question about what she would do to help India in what was seen by the judges as an inappropriate manner. Sapre told the judges that because she had felt marginalized all her life as a sports aficionado in a country ill-equipped for athletes, she would help India by building a sports stadium. Miss India pageant officials and popular culture at large insisted that the reason she lost was simply because her answer "lacked juice," but this also had a great deal to do with Sapre's positionality as the representative of a poor country, which demanded that she answer such a question by referring to poverty and what she would do to eradicate it. Indeed, Miss India as an iconic figure must profess her passionate interest in helping the disadvantaged as part of her effort at maternal benevolence.

As I watched twenty-six young women be physically and psychologically altered throughout the course of the training program, I was consistently struck by how they carefully molded themselves into an image of an imaginary woman called Miss India. I spent a great deal of time conducting personal interviews with each of the contestants in addition to acting as a participant observer throughout the selection and training processes in order to present a clearer picture of what becoming this woman means to individual young women.

My interaction with the contestants led me to the conclusion that while being Miss India may have meant the world to all of them at some point during the pageant process, the degree to which this is the case varied based upon a number of factors including class, ethnicity, place of origin, and the amount of previous experience each had with media. Although the contestants were all unique in terms of their goals and motivations for entering, they shared certain things in common with other young women at the pageant and can be grouped into three broad categories: small-town girls, those who were raised outside of India and are often called nonresident Indians (NRIs), and professional models or actresses. Thirteen of the twenty-six young women at the training program were already working as full-time models or actresses, eight were enrolled in some kind of academic course, four were doing volunteer work or nothing at all, and one was working. Not all contestants' stories are included in the narratives that follow, but most are representative enough to spark discussion about the meanings individual women ascribed to being Miss India.

*Small-Town Contestants*

Of the twenty-six young women, there were only four contestants who were not from the major metropolitan areas of Mumbai and Delhi: two from Pune, one from Chennai, and one from Nasik. These young women were the first to be eliminated in the initial rounds of the final pageant; they were simply not able to compete with the professional models from Mumbai and Delhi who were possessed of a kind of symbolic capital that the contestants from small towns simply did not have. Always easily distinguished by their less fashionable clothing and accents, young women from outside Mumbai or Delhi were not in as good a position to compete as the others.

As is the case in most of India (and perhaps the world), it was relatively easy to visually gauge which of the contestants were from small towns. They were conspicuous in their clothing, which was not as expensive or trendy as that of the urbanites, and in their use of English. Contestants from urban areas had either been to expensive English-language schools that cultivated the British-accented English seen as prestigious in India or understood the importance of learning it, whereas the young women from small towns had done neither. Their pronunciations of English words with a dental "t" sound, one of the preeminent linguistic markers of class in India, distinguished them from their urban and more exclusively educated counterparts.

They also seemed much less mature and sophisticated, were prone to giggling fits, and did not, quite simply, have the tools with which to best take advantage of Miss India as a social network. This was painfully evident to the urban contestants, who often avoided or, at best, tolerated the presence of the small-town young women. Anjali, a professional model from Mumbai, was clear that the main difference between her and the contestants from small towns was that "they're naïve, whereas I live in Mumbai and see all kinds of things and people. They just don't have what it takes, because they're too different."

Indeed, the contestants from small towns were different. Sharayu from Pune was a graduate student in economics at the time of the pageant and described the intense process of preparing to come to the training program as one that involved her entire family. Sharayu's mother shopped for eight days as her daughter prepared to come to Mumbai, which the family considered a fantastic opportunity for Sharayu to establish herself in life. Like many other contestants from small towns, Sharayu described her rationale for entering Miss India as part of a greater project of creating a whole new self, noting that "this is a very good platform for me to evolve into a woman of substance and be an ambassador of my country, which has always excited me. To me, this is about being confident and endorsing my confidence in myself."

In envisioning herself as evolving into a newer and more confident person, Sharayu employed *Femina* magazine's former slogan of "woman of substance." This usage is not accidental and in fact underscores how the Miss India pageant, the *Femina* project of creating a vision of idealized femininity, and the goals of individual women are all intimately connected. Perhaps because they were not as practiced in vocalizing their opinions as their urban counterparts, small-town contestants often provided me with the best examples of just how much of a work-in-progress femininity can be.

Sharayu was emphatic that the training program allowed her to discover new sides of herself. In this newly uncovered self, which Miss India helped her to cultivate, she experienced a major life change that she described as "mainly related to my femininity, which has been subdued for so long." Insisting that the training program "brings out the best in a woman," Sharayu subscribed to the rhetoric of transformation that is so prevalent in the discourse surrounding Miss India. She also insisted that "every woman has Miss India in her, it's just a matter of getting it to come out."

Kaveri, from the semirural town of Nasik, best known for its rich temple culture and place in Hindu epics, was a journalism student who worked part-time for a cell phone company and wanted to be a model. Kaveri described the process of entering as one that made her feel extremely conscious of her small-town roots yet simultaneously very empowered:

> Nasik is very small, and before that my family was posted in Patna, in Bihar. I had no exposure to the world, and I thought I wouldn't stand a

chance. I didn't have a portfolio to send, I just clicked a picture and sent it, and when my father called me at work to tell me I got selected, I was jumping up and down, it was the happiest day of my life. But when I got here, I faltered because they were all professional models. In my swimming costume, I thought I would faint on the ramp at the tryouts.

Kaveri cited her lack of experience as a major hindrance to being selected and described the day she learned that she had been chosen to attend the selection as "the happiest day of my life." To move from provincial Nasik to the very glamorous world of the Miss India pageant based on a snapshot is itself an achievement, as the vast majority of entry forms for the pageant included expensive portfolio-style photographs that are simply not available outside of Delhi or Mumbai.

This sense of accomplishment was short-lived, because once Kaveri came to Mumbai, she felt distinctly out of place without the same sort of polish that the professional models had. She remained convinced of the fairness of the pageant, and when I asked her if she felt that anyone could be Miss India, she nodded emphatically and used herself as an example. "Look at me," she began, "I had no idea about makeup, I'd never been on-stage, but I still made it because Miss India looks for the raw material to be molded, not the finished product." With the use of a rather interesting reference to her pre- versus post–Miss India self as "raw material" and "finished product," Kaveri employed a telling metaphor of construction.

It was perhaps because they put in the most effort in terms of this project of self-construction that the young women from small towns were the most devastated when they did not win. Through a process that taught them to expect to win if they successfully mimicked an urban form of classed femininity, the small-town contestants grew especially invested in winning toward the end of the pageant. They had the most to lose if they did not become Miss India on the final day, as they were the farthest removed both geographically and culturally from the urban social networks of Mumbai and Delhi.

Some young women from small towns were also the victims of unrealistic expectations as a result of their limited exposure to urban beauty culture. When Harsimrat was eleven years old in the South Indian city of Chennai, she watched Aishwarya Rai and Sushmita Sen win the Miss World and Miss Universe titles with her father. Her father turned to her and said, "You have to win the crown." Since that day, she grew up fully expecting to someday win and was not surprised when she was selected for Miss India, but once she got to the training program she was overwhelmed by the number of beautiful women. "Back home," she said, "I'm always made to feel I'm the best, but here I get to see that there is so much more out there in the world than me." Because becoming Miss India is a process that combines internal monitoring and emulation of a certain stereotype of Indian beauty, many small-town contestants simply could not compete with their more professionally experienced urban counterparts.

### Miss (Nonresident) India

When choreographer Hemant Trevedi asked Ami, a contestant raised in the United States, how long she had been in India, she responded in a self-conscious and clipped American tone by asking, "Why, is it my accent?" He ignored her question and announced to the room, "Everyone cares about how she looks, and how you carry yourself is a very important thing." Trevedi drew attention to the way in which contestants raised outside of India were different from the others with his implication that Ami was not as graceful or feminine in her mannerisms as the Indian contestants.

Despite Trevedi's comment, NRIs are the subject of a great deal of privilege and respect, as well as numerous matrimonial advertisements and government investment plans. They are often seen as India's best exports, and so NRIs who return to India are accorded a kind of admiration ordinarily reserved for things that are altogether foreign. It seemed that young women who were raised outside of India had an unfair advantage that surpassed that of even the contestants who already had well-established media careers behind them, largely because of their firsthand knowledge of American and Western European popular cultures.

I was especially fascinated by how the NRIs made sense of media culture in urban India, and when I asked Payal, who was born and raised in Zambia, why she wanted to be Miss India, she couched her answer in a description of celebrity and voice:

In India, people are just fascinated by famous people and people listen to you when you're famous. People will listen to me more if I am Miss India, while in Zambia people will listen to anyone because there are not so many people and there is less poverty.

Payal underscored the amount of public sway celebrity provides in India by drawing a distinction between Zambia, where "people will listen to anyone" and India, where fame is necessary in order to have a voice. Payal was representative of some members of the Indian diaspora in her knowledge of Indian popular culture and cites the year that Aishwarya Rai won the Miss World pageant in nearby South Africa that she decided to someday enter an event that many contestants mentioned as a major formative influence on their lives. Describing the Miss Zambia pageant as "not such a big deal over there," Payal offered a bit of insight into why returning to India might offer her expanded career options in media.

Payal had never been to India until 2003 when she decided to explore her career options in Indian media before starting university in Zambia. She knew far less about India than anyone else, could not read or write Hindi, and yet because the contestants are expected to voice sentiments about "tradition" and "Indian culture" while simultaneously embodying modernity, someone like Payal underscores the way in which Miss India is an extraordinarily complex site for the construction and negotiation of national identity. As Payal sat studying a map of South Asia one day, I jokingly asked her the name of the capital of the Eastern Indian state of Orissa. She bit her lip nervously and exclaimed, "You mean the states also have capitals? There's so much to learn!" Payal did not win the pageant, but she did place fairly highly toward the end, a fact that illustrates just how foreign it is acceptable for Miss India to be.

The NRI contestants have additional issues to face at Miss India, most notably where to situate the diaspora understanding of India they grew up with in the cosmopolitan world of the pageant. Having grown up in an affluent Indian family in Zambia, Payal observed that her ideas about India were largely shaped by popular culture in Southern Africa: "When I was in Zambia, every time I saw a video on India it was all about shanty towns, and people would ask me, 'Payal, are there buildings in India, or is it all just shanties?'" Her description of a childhood understanding of an impoverished India that was made up of shanty towns stands in diametric opposition to the five-star hotels and media elites of Miss India. Payal was firm that if she won Miss India, she would use her voice in order to "tell the world that Indians are not cheaters like everyone thinks." Drawing on an African stereotype of South Asians, Payal asserted that her opportunity to be in the spotlight would be used to build a positive image of the Indian diaspora.

The NRI contestants were also more focused on the inequalities that exist in India, perhaps because they were accustomed to addressing them at a personal level. Ami, a financial analyst from Los Angeles who worked for a Mumbai nongovernmental organization, was adamant that she wanted to revamp India's class-based education system by insisting, "I would use my voice as Miss India to address education, because the education system here needs to be improved. We lose a lot of our good people, because the system discriminates based on social class and gender. Ideally, we'd have total reform, but I'd help by starting a school that bases admission on merit." Echoing Payal's statement about celebrity and voice in India, Ami was very clear about how being Miss India would allow her to improve a discriminatory system of education.

Ami insisted that she was qualified to represent India as Miss India because she made the choice to come back to India after growing up and working in the United States. Citing the yoga class she taught in college as well as her summers spent in India studying classical dance, she positioned herself as a culture bearer. Her grandmother, who sent in Ami's application to the pageant, was especially encouraging and envisioned Ami as a part of the family that emphasized their Indian heritage.

Swetha grew up in Dubai, moved to Mumbai a year before the 2003 pageant, and as Miss India United Arab Emirates, was already entrenched in the culture of the Indian diaspora. Possessed of the same sort of foreign authority as the other NRI contestants, Swetha was not very impressed with the urban Indian popular cultural obsession with beauty pageants, which she regarded as rather silly:

When I tried out for Miss India this year, it was funny to see women there who were five [feet] two [inches tall] trying. It's a craze to enter, so they do it. One girl was screaming, "I'm five [feet] six [inches tall]!" and I was thinking, "Yeah, maybe in your three inch heels." Even the girl who cleans my house wants to be a model, and says, "I know how speak English" in her funny accent, because those are the only words she knows, and she thinks she's pretty. I don't want to say anything to hurt her, but she can always come back and clean my house after she gives modeling a try!

Swetha pinpointed the Miss India phenomenon in a way that none of the contestants who had grown up in India did in her description of the "craze to enter." Because they had not seen or experienced life in a country other than India for an extended period of time, the other young women firmly believed that every country in the world had an equally important culture of national identity and femininity expressed in the form of a highly regarded beauty pageant. I was asked repeatedly by non-NRI contestants why I had never entered Miss America, and when I responded as politely as I could that I had never been interested in doing so, many assumed that there was really another reason, such as what they perceived as my lack of self-confidence. Swetha had modeled in both Dubai and Mumbai and was extremely critical of what she described as the lack of professionalism in Mumbai, a situation that she insisted was in dire need of reform. She felt she was at a distinct disadvantage because of her darker skin and her lack of professional experience in Mumbai:

There is so much favoritism in the modeling industry here. In advertising, they want the fair girl next door, and on ramp, there are the same fourteen models, and they're scared to take newcomers because maybe they'll trip and fall. It makes me so mad, because new girls get half the price for double the amount of work. The established models make comments like "fatso" behind your back at shows when they see you're a newcomer.

Swetha hoped that Miss India would allow her to transcend her newcomer status in order to succeed in Mumbai as a model with the help of connections to important media figures made at the training program.

Nupur, another NRI contestant, was raised in Delhi but had spent the two and a half years prior to Miss India 2003 working as a model in Milan, and returned to India exclusively to participate in the pageant. She was certainly the most well-established professional model in the eyes of the other contestants, because she held a contract with a European agency. Indeed, the kind of cultural currency that Nupur's international career held served to supersede her East Asian features that were unfortunately considered by many to be insufficiently "Indian." Several young Indian women of East Asian descent who were much more beautiful than Nupur had tried out for the pageant and were rejected by judges who positioned them as Other, or as not quite Indian enough. However, the judges were so impressed by the concept of a model from Milan participating in the pageant that Nupur was selected to add an international element to the training program.

Like the other NRI contestants, Nupur was rather specific about what she would like to change about India. Rather than social work, she wanted to professionalize the modeling industry in India once her career was over at the age of thirty-five. Nupur used her foreign authority to position India as an absolute opposite to the professional world of Milan:

> Modeling in India is unprofessional, so I want to introduce my agency here so I can use what I've learnt to train women here. There, in Milan, before you even start working you go through a whole training process. I don't see it getting any more professional here, because people just don't understand simple concepts like punctuality. In Milan, everything is so organized.

This sort of attitude prompted one of the judges to informally ask Nupur why she was in India at all if she was doing so well in Milan, as Europe has a much more well-established and respected modeling industry. Although Nupur was adamant that it was the prestige of Miss India that led her to participate, there was a great deal of gossip on the part of the organizers about how a young woman who would leave a career in Milan to participate in Miss India was possessed of what one pageant official called "a questionable set of priorities." Although it was clear that Nupur's presence at the pageant was really the result of a career in Europe that was probably not as stellar and lucrative as she claimed it was, the mystique of her independent life in Milan prompted quite a flurry of speculation about her.

In what I grew to somewhat humorously identify as "the cult of Nupur," she became the focus of almost constant gossip, and some chaperones eagerly insisted that she was the mistress of a much older Italian man who dealt in exports from India. Some even claimed to have seen him violating pageant rules by visiting her at the hotel during the training program and named him as the source of Nupur's extremely expensive wardrobe of Italian designer clothes. Organizers often expressed their concerns about what they termed her "lack of morals," vowing to have her thrown out of the pageant at the first sign of her "bad behavior." Though some of this speculation was perhaps a bit warranted given the pageant's focus on maintaining a good reputation and Nupur's haughty behavior, I wondered how much of the speculation surrounding Nupur's life was really the result of her ethnic minority status at Miss India.

Nupur's story and the corresponding level of attention it received sheds light on how young women brought differing degrees of knowledge about media and the larger world outside of India to the pageant. More than half of the contestants were already professionally established in the sense that they had either modeled extensively or appeared in Hindi films, and so the next section discusses what the training program meant to young women who hoped to use Miss India to cross over from the cusp of stardom.

*The Professionals*

When Parmita entered Miss India 2003, she had just finished acting in her third Hindi film after winning two major beauty pageants. A model since she was in college in Bangalore, she was very clear on her career goals and how participation in Miss India would help her to achieve them: "I entered Miss India because I strongly believe that it guarantees you success in any field. Being Miss Universe lasts only one year, but this training gives you confidence for life." Parmita exhibited a kind of motivation and determination that was striking even in contrast to the other contestants, as unlike the others she positioned even the Miss Universe title as transitory. The 2003 pageant was Parmita's second attempt, and her mother had cautioned her against competing in Miss India again after seeing the trauma that not winning had put her daughter through the year before. When I asked her why her mother did not compete in the pageant, she mentioned the equalizing force that she felt the pageant had become in terms of class, observing that "in her time there was no organizational support, so middle class people would feel intimidated by those who were better off. Nowadays, it's not that way because they give you everything—clothes, portfolio, hair, makeup—so there's no need to feel less than anyone else now." Parmita positioned herself as a middle-class contestant who could benefit from the pageant in a way that would otherwise be impossible. Citing the very real difference between the more class-stratified Miss India of her mother's day and the greater infrastructural support that she experienced at the pageant, Parmita pointed to the way Miss India is perceived as a step on the ladder to stardom by some contestants.

Shonal, a professional model from Calcutta, cited the much broader world that Mumbai would offer her in terms of a modeling career. In her opinion, the pageant provided much more than a beauty queen title through the opportunity to come to the center of the media world and interact with those in power:

> This is a gateway to other opportunities, and I wanted to come to Bombay [Mumbai] for modeling because everyone will notice me because of my height. A lot of women from Calcutta have come here and been transformed—Celina Jaitley, Reshmi Ghosh, Dipti Gujral. I've modeled for two years in Calcutta and did two shows in Delhi, but this is a better way to get in.

Positioning herself as part of a social network of young women from Calcutta that perhaps made her chances of doing well seem even more real to her, Shonal described the pageant as "a better way to get in," using a very physical metaphor to describe the social mobility that Miss India offers. Mareesha was from Mumbai and had also been modeling for several years, during which she had done everything from ramp shows to hosting events for corporations. A management student, she tried not to plan for the future in favor of putting her full focus on Miss India. "This line is very competitive," she noted, "and planning probably isn't such a good idea." Despite this, she was emphatic that the pageant would shape whatever career she chose.

Nikita, a fashion design student from Delhi, participated in her first beauty pageant when she was just thirteen. A winner at all four pageants she entered, she eventually won the 2003 Miss India–Universe title. Nikita's extremely early entry into the pageants points to the way in which a certain kind of family background is necessary in order to compete successfully, because the kind of preparation Nikita received via so much experience in pageants over a period of years made her more likely to do well at Miss India. Nikita hoped to use the contacts she made at the training program to establish herself as a designer.

Anurithi, a model who aspired to get a degree in journalism from Berkeley, loved traveling and had already modeled in shows in Asia, New Zealand, and the United States. She entered in hopes of becoming better known internationally as a model, as did Sunaina, a model and former flight attendant from Delhi, who also entered Miss India at least in part because her grandmother wanted her to. "She wants to live her life through me," Sunaina explained. Citing the enormous range of media opportunities that she will be able to "tackle head on" as a result of the training experience, she noted that the pageant was definitely a platform for her.

It is clear that the pageant means different things to individual women depending on their background and goals for the future. From the prospect of getting in touch with one's Indian heritage to the opportunity to become a film star, Miss India can serve as a variety of vehicles depending on how contestants choose to make use of it. Some women are clearer than others about what they hope to achieve from participating in Miss India and understand just how many life-altering changes they will have to make in order to spend at least a period of their lives as women under the gaze of the media.

# 3

# Watching Miss World

As part of the training program, the contestants watched approximately two dozen DVDs of past Miss Universe and Miss World pageants. The young women sat in the audience as choreographer Hemant Trevedi provided a running commentary on his opinion of each contestant's behavior at the international pageant being viewed as part of a fascinating process that helped contestants to visualize themselves onstage as the embodiment of national identity. Trevedi sighed dreamily as Miss India Diana Hayden appeared onscreen at Miss World 1997, lip synching to a pop song on the beach with ninety-four other contestants. "You have no idea how it makes me feel when a Miss India I've designed for gets somewhere," he said. Watching Miss World, or any other international pageant in which Miss India participates, is part of a dialogical process of becoming "on par" with the rest of the world for many urban Indians, as it provides an opportunity to gauge India's presentation of beauty vis-à-vis the rest of the world. Trevedi was adamant that India should be proud of its achievements at international pageants:

On globalbeauties.com, Lara Dutta has been nominated the best Miss Universe ever, which is a huge compliment. Lara, coming out of a Third World nation, was not only beautiful, but could hold her own no matter who she was talking to, even the South American journalists who have a big chip on their shoulders because other than us, they have a cakewalk, and so they hate us.

Each contestant was introduced onscreen, and the commoditization of national identity began with footage of each smiling contestant accompanied by a voiceover that introduced each young woman by using the features associated with her country, such as "and, from the land of the Taj Mahal, Miss India!" while Miss Thailand was "from the land of a thousand smiles" and Miss Brazil hailed "from the land of the Amazon." Each contestant was introduced by regional grouping at Miss Universe, with Europe first, then the Americas, then Asia and the Pacific, followed by Africa, which in and of itself speaks to a ranking of nations and, by default, beauties. As each contestant walked onstage in a bikini, a split screen showed her posing in her national costume, underscoring the dual role of each as both a representative of her nation and an embodiment of an "international" standard of beauty that has roots in North America and Western Europe.

Trevedi skipped over the introductions of women from regions that had not produced Miss Universe winners, and so Miss India contestants did not see a single contestant from Africa. This is also part of an entrenched "colorism" in India that preferences lighter skin and became an issue several times throughout the training program with both contestants and pageant officials. When the contestants noticed that Miss USA and Miss France were of African descent, Sharayu from the smaller town of Pune asked, "Why do the U.S. and France keep sending such dark girls who could never win?" Trevedi answered, "It just goes to show that there it doesn't matter what color you are, and here we're too hung up on that." Sharayu and Kaveri from small-town Nasik were both unsatisfied with his answer and continued to murmur that "dark girls" could never win at an international pageant. This was not so much a condemnation of this fact as an acknowledgment of the reality that they lived with in India, especially in nonurban areas where fairness is unequivocally equated with beauty and remains uncontested by the broader cultural dialogues on the subject.

The conversation about skin color continued with Nupur wielding her knowledge of the modeling industry in Europe as a tool to both educate and humble the other contestants as she said, "In Italy, agents seek out dark-skinned models. This just goes to show how backward India is." Deepica, whose brown complexion was a point of professional concern for her as an actress, agreed by citing the example of the successful black supermodel Naomi Campbell. The rest of the young women remained silent after interjections by Nupur and Deepica as if their claims to knowledge about Western Europe and diversity did indeed make Indian standards of beauty as well as their own life experiences seem inappropriate and outmoded.

Each contestant at Miss World and Miss Universe was viewed by the Miss India contestants and Trevedi as representative of all the stereotypes that surround their respective countries. Trevedi described Miss USA as "an aspiring Barbie doll from a small town in the middle of nowhere," and South American contestants were all "pageant queens with no substance." Watching Miss World and Miss Universe became a process of observing strikingly different forms of femininity, and yet Miss India was always described as the warmest and best-behaved contestant. Former Miss World Yukta Mookhey recalled that

> when I got to Miss World, Diana and Aishwarya had won already, so everyone was waiting for me. Indians are known to be warm and loving, so if Miss Brazil gives you an attitude, don't give it back, because then that's the end of our reputation.

The behavior of some contestants was held up as an example of how not to act, especially that of a Miss Thailand who was visibly angry when she did not win Miss World. "Be good Indian girls," Trevedi told the contestants, "you have gotten so far in life and this is only one small stepping stone." Miss USA was admired for her candid admission of the family problems she had faced growing up in response to the final question that determined that she was the winner of Miss Universe 1995. Trevedi used her as an example of the importance of self-confidence to the contestants:

> For a woman who has had a pretty bad personal life, despite divorce and acrimony, she has been able to achieve all of this because she believed in herself. So whether you're worried about your height or your figure or some domestic crisis, remember to believe in yourself because

*4. Miss India is said to embody all of the historical and cultural symbols associated with her country, yet the majority of these are drawn from the more powerful north, such as the cutout of the Taj Mahal in the background of this photograph of Aishwarya Rai.*

no Hemant Trevedi or Anu Ahuja or Mickey Mehta can do that. The first time the audience sees you, you'll be in your swimsuit baring your soul and your body to some extent.

When Miss USA continued her response to mention that if she could change one thing for her country, she would make men treat women as equals in the workplace, Trevedi paused the DVD and asked the contestants rather thoughtfully, "Isn't that interesting to hear that from someone who comes from a country with so many opportunities?" Trevedi was rather incredulous that Miss USA should feel that gender inequality was a problem in a country where, in his view, women are relatively privileged.

Language was also a factor in the way that the Miss India contestants watched international pageants. Former Miss World Yukta Mookhey advised contestants that "half of the girls there can't speak English, so they're not competition to you." The young women were taught that more than half of the contestants at international pageants have translators, which makes them less likely to communicate effectively, and that because Miss India always speaks perfect English and is relatively articulate, she has a better chance of winning. However, when I asked pageant organizers why Miss Venezuela, who is often not able to speak English at all, wins so consistently, they were firm that it was because she is "always six feet tall, blonde and perfect." This raised an interesting point about how Indian contestants at Miss Universe and Miss World are seen to be at a distinct disadvantage because of the association of beauty with fair skin and light hair color.

Venezuela is described by Miss India officials as a land of beauty queens, and one pageant organizer explained to me as we drove to a dress rehearsal that beauty pageant culture is far more advanced and entrenched there than it is in India. "You know, in Venezuela, the girls train for a year before Miss Universe, and they get plastic surgery, whatever," she began, before adding, "They're obsessed with beauty over there, even the men." She continued to note that although beauty culture in general has penetrated Venezuela to a greater extent that it has India, India's enormous population should make it a greater target for international beauty products. She then grew more reflective as she pointed to a pot-bellied man dressed in polyester trousers and a stained shirt standing on the street outside the car window in order to illustrate her point:

> It's funny, because despite all the focus on beauty here, the average person just isn't bothered. Like on the train, the women are just a mess. I don't know whether they just don't care enough to go buy a five rupee [eleven cents] bottle of nail polish at the market or they are just too

busy trying to survive. So, it's funny, because although the international beauty companies are just catering to the elite 10 percent here, it's still a huge market. But still, just look at the average person here—I bet no one in Venezuela looks like that guy!

The positioning of Venezuela as a country of stunningly beautiful people points to a fascinating hierarchy of "development" at work at Miss India. Venezuela and India share numerous historical similarities: both were colonies exploited for their raw materials, both continue to face a number of socioeconomic crises as a result of their colonial legacy, and both highly prize femininity in its extremely idealized form. However, the similarities end there. Miss Venezuela is part of an extremely professionalized industry of creating beauty, at the head of which is the Miss Venezuela Academy. Similar to the Miss India pageant training program in theory, the Miss Venezuela Academy trains young women physically and mentally for competition at the international level, and it is so successful that it also attracts aspiring beauty queens from Bolivia, Brazil, Colombia, and the Dominican Republic. The scale of the Miss Venezuela Academy is enormous in comparison to Miss India, with the average cost of training a beauty queen at $60,000 per year, and the Miss Venezuela pageant is a vastly more entrenched cultural phenomenon that 90 percent of Venezuela's twenty-one million people watch on television each year.

Miss India's chief weapon against this formidably constructed Miss Venezuela, then, is fluency in English. A. P. Parigi, head of the 2003 pageant, advised contestants that language was crucial to winning a title at Miss India:

> In British English, the mouth doesn't move too much. Try to keep your mouth still. It's a foreign language, there's nothing to be embarrassed about, but by listening to your accents, the experts can tell what your background is and what kind of school you went to. But you can hide it, if you talk to yourself all the time. Diction counts at Miss World, so you have a responsibility to yourself to practice.

The insistence that "diction counts" speaks to the fact that not all types of fluent English are equally highly regarded in India and that slower forms

*importance of English* (handwritten marginal note)

of speech that lack the harsher consonant sounds found in Hindi and several other Indian languages are considered more prestigious. Language is a powerful index of class background in India, which made the question and answer sessions particularly uncomfortable for young women who had not been educated at expensive English language schools. "See," worldly wise Anjali quietly pointed out to me during the course of a question and answer session in which a contestant from a small town was speaking English using the kind of hard, dental "t" consonant found in Hindi, "you can make out their backgrounds by the way they talk."

Anjali's assertion was more delicately put than some others, as both Hemangi and Kaveri faced a great deal of harsh criticism for their regional accents that had not been altered by expensive schools that privilege anglicized accents. Hemangi was a native speaker of Marathi, the language indigenous to Maharashtra state, and often spoke in the same brusque, low-pitched tone of voice when speaking English that she would use with her first language. Ami was raised in the United States and was not accustomed to the lilt that women in particular have in their speaking voices in India, and her American accent sounded nasal and unpleasant to some pageant officials. "When those two speak," a chaperone pointed out to me, "I get a complete headache." Parigi's insistence that contestants such as Hemangi and Ami have a responsibility to practice a form of English that does not come naturally to them was remarkably similar to sentiments echoed by the contestants as part of the pageant's consistent theme of the responsibilities that Miss India has to shoulder.

Seeing and being seen are accorded a great deal of importance in South Asia and beholding, known in Hindi as doing *darśan*, is essential to Hindu forms of worship. As part of a dialogical process with the divine that individuals engage in when they stand in front of representations of gods and goddesses, lines between the viewer and the viewed begin to blur, so that the distinction between what is subject and object, ideal and real, becomes only a matter of a degree. Images are very important throughout South Asia, as they are absolutely essential for Hindus and Buddhists to pray, and doing *darśan* is critical to Hindu ritual because the eye is the vehicle through which an individual is able to communicate with the divine (Eck 1998).

The concept of *darśan,* and of seeing and being seen, are both granted central importance in Hindu textual and cultural traditions. The notion of *burī nazar,* which can be loosely (albeit inadequately) translated as "the evil eye," is especially powerful because it illustrates how the gaze can be a source of greater authority than the object of the gaze. Gods and goddesses are often depicted as being possessed of a third eye that signifies superhuman powers of perception or, in the case of Shiva, the ability to destroy with one unfavorable glance. The concept of the gaze as the repository of both power and wisdom underscores the extremely visual nature of India at large, and pictorial representations of the eye are common throughout the subcontinent. Whether hand-painted on the backs of especially beautifully decorated transport trucks to ward off bad luck, staring out from the forehead of an image of a goddess at a temple, or in the form of the famously beautiful eyes of actress and former Miss World Aishwarya Rai glancing at the viewer from the front page of a fan magazine, the eye, and its ability to behold, are accorded exceptional powers.

Hinduism in particular has always placed an extremely high, and even divine, value on representation. It is never entirely clear in Hindu temples, for example, where the image of the idol stops and the divine entity that it represents begins. This sort of adoration of images extends to all facets of social life and is at work in Indian media culture in which certain individuals are accorded a degree of respect and adoration that sometimes borders on the religious. Beyond the extreme importance accorded to seeing in Hindu textual traditions, India has a long tradition of venerating some groups of people as embodiments of knowledge and power. Whether in the guru system, the feudal system of Rajasthan, or in the culture of celebrity in sites such as Miss India, situating some individuals at the center of complex webs of power is by no means a new phenomenon in India.

What is new, however, is the extent to which this is now done in urban India. As Walker (2003) notes in his discussion of art and celebrity, the increased role of media in daily life has necessitated the creation of cults of personality surrounding increased numbers of individuals, in essence, new celebrities to fill spaces in the pages of magazines and on the screens of theaters and televisions. So while this phenomenon is not uniquely Indian, it is compounded at Miss India by the preexisting class and ethnic inequalities that are endemic throughout the subcontinent and the newness of diverse forms of media in India.

Power is necessarily both about seeing and being seen, and the two interact in complex ways in order to produce even more intricate hierarchies. When young women enter the Miss India pageant, they do so with the hope that they will become visible enough to reach stardom and to place themselves even nearer the center of what is almost a closed system of celebrity. It is for this reason that learning how to behave as a public figure, and how to be scrutinized under the public eye, is an integral part of the Miss India training program in which contestants are evaluated and observed twenty-four hours a day.

## Foucault and the Politics of Miss India Training

> Remember, the moment you're out of this hotel, you're onstage twenty-four hours a day. (Choreographer Hemant Trevedi to contestants at rehearsal)

Resembling Foucault's (1995) concept of the panopticon in which individuals are so closely monitored that they begin to monitor themselves, pageant choreographer Hemant Trevedi's comment exhorts contestants to regard themselves as constantly under observation following the completion of the training program. As emblematic of the Foucauldian total institution, the Miss India training program completely takes over the lives of the contestants for a month by placing them under the gaze of experts who are seen as uniquely able to transform the young women into glamorous icons who meet what are known in India as "international standards."

Miss India as a concept represents gender inequality writ unabashedly large, as the contestants are watched every minute by chaperones, some of whom are their age or younger, who make sure that they eat, sleep, and do exactly as the experts advise them to. Although I never witnessed a confrontation between a contestant and a chaperone, I was constantly aware of the pressure of always being watched that contestants felt. One chaperone mentioned the responsibility of making sure the contestants followed the diet regimen assigned to them:

Every week they get a new diet assigned in a private consultation with Anjali Mukherjee, nutritionist. I have to make sure they stick with it. Poonam is seven kilos underweight, so she's on a weight gain diet, and she can eat pastries and cake in front of everyone, which bothers them.

Put in the odd position of supervising grown women's caloric intake, the chaperone's quasi-complaint illustrates how contestants are always under observation. Yet the contestants also observe themselves and each other, thereby internalizing the process of monitoring. The very fact that all meals were eaten as a group, where consumption could be watched and commented on by all, was in itself part of this. I was the target of the observation, "You're quite hungry today, Susan," by contestants and chaperones alike on at least six separate occasions over meals at the training program.

I sat with the young women over breakfast one morning as they entered into a complex discussion of the diets assigned to them by the nutritionist. Harsimrat complained, "I've lost two hundred grams, that's it. I'm 61 and one half kilos right now, and I want to be 60. She says I can't have fruit today, because it's fattening." Payal commiserated that she had been assigned bread and eggs for breakfast, followed by two days of cucumber and chutney. As part of the odd speculations that are inherent in playing the diet game, the young women at the table decided that fruit does not actually fall into the category of "fattening" because "it's more of a maintenance food."

The disturbing intensity with which the young women discussed their consumption patterns shows how the total institution of the training program enforces a kind of self-monitoring. However, the observation of contestants' consumption of food also extended to outright policing at times. When the young women were taken to a resort complex to meet the press, their first full day outside of the hotel in a month, a pageant organizer warned them as a group that "there will be normal food there, but control yourselves. I don't want to have to come up to you and ask you to stop eating."

The politics of eating were the subject of much discussion throughout the training program. Contestants filled their plates for every meal from a buffet table on which three large tureens of food were arranged for them. For breakfast they had cereal or fruit as an option, while for lunch they had two vegetables and soup, and for dinner they had rice and a protein-based dish. From these selections, contestants were expected to pick out what they had been assigned to eat by Mukherjee. Mealtimes were rarely occasions for the enjoyment of food, because contestants were usually between training sessions and would eat in the same seats they planned to use in the session held after lunch. The food was all very healthy and well-prepared but contestants still constantly complained about its quality to one another as part of a form of protest that not only allowed for some form of individual agency in an extremely controlled setting but also for group commiseration about the imperative to monitor food intake as a matter of course.

Some of the contestants who were not involved in media had clearly never dieted before and were unfamiliar and uncomfortable with either the sensation of deprivation it caused or the emotional risks that a sudden obsession with food consumption could spark. I asked all of the contestants about their perceptions of eating disorders and feelings about the focus on becoming thinner at the pageant. Young women who had greater exposure to Western European and American popular cultures and so were more familiar with eating disorders were perhaps more sensitive to my intentions in asking such questions and thus more detailed in their responses. Ami from Los Angeles was quick to note that she did not see anorexia as a problem in India because "here people always eat together and so it wouldn't be possible to hide something like anorexia." Payal, who had spent her formative years in a girl's boarding school in Zambia, mentioned that "it's hard not to think about eating all the time, and I think it affects some of the girls mentally."

The fear of overconsumption and the pressures of being constantly watched by the competition served to make it painfully clear to the contestants that their ability to win was dependent on both their self-control and their attention to expert advice. Although some young women worked harder than others at doing this, the message of having to struggle to be beautiful was constant at the training program. Being beautiful was defined as having extraordinary height, fair skin, and very little body fat, and

5. *Contestants engage in a rigorous diet and exercise routine as part of the thirty-day training program that transforms them into slender beauty queens, some of whom are so thin that they would be considered unmarriageable in certain areas of rural India.*

since no one could have any of these three qualities in excess at Miss India contestants constantly compared themselves to one another in a silent process of self-monitoring. This closely corresponds to Foucault's concept of how the panopticon works to force prisoners to begin monitoring themselves, which is extremely relevant and important given the power Miss India has not only to reinforce standards of beauty for the contestants, but also for the urban population who eagerly follow details of it.

Even the allotted one hour visits from family members between nine and ten P.M. nightly in the hotel's coffee shop were supervised by chaperones. The coffee shop was rather conspicuously placed in the center of the lobby, which all the open-sided hallways of the hotel's twenty-four floors looked down upon. This made it impossible for the contestants to show any emotions with family members that they may have felt uncomfortable expressing in front of others. One chaperone explained the rationale behind this policy by saying, "It's because the reputation of the pageant is at stake, and we can't have ugly rumors cropping up." As a result, she argued, it was necessary for the contestants to be in full view of the chaperones at all times.

When I questioned pageant organizers about why the contestants were not allowed outside of the hotel during their limited amount of free time, a chaperone explained that the outside world was a very different place from the Miss India training program:

> The other day when we took them shopping we had to push them onto the bus because all the *janta* [common people, in a negative sense] was gathering to stare at them. In India, women can't wear short things and those things all the girls wear make all the *kacrā log* [literally, "garbage people"] stare at them. That's why we have to keep them in the hotel all the time.

The chaperone utilized the language of protection to underscore the sharp division between the closed world of Miss India and the outside reality of India. Although the contestants were free to roam around the hotel in varying degrees of undress without attracting much attention, the average man on the street would not be able to take his eyes off a glamorous woman in a short skirt, simply because it is something that he would usually see only on television, because he is unable to frequent the kind of spaces in which this sort of dress is acceptable.

Contestants who had a considerable amount of freedom in their personal lives found this kind of surveillance more difficult to deal with than young women who were familiar with family supervision as a normal part of everyday life. Those who were already working as professional models or actresses and thus accustomed to traveling alone at night and dealing with a wide variety of men in the process were especially candid in their assertions that such tight regulation of their behavior was unnecessary. Swetha from Dubai joked privately that she felt she was "back in school" when she was asked to hold hands with her fellow contestants in order to stay together as a group as they crossed the street on a rare outing from the hotel. These feelings of frustration and embarrassment were echoed in a more explicit fashion by model Anjali from Mumbai, who asked another contestant rhetorically, "Do they think we're a bunch of prostitutes who are going to get out of line if they leave us alone?" Anjali's statement directly targets the unspoken sexual threat posed by the contestants' few journeys outside the hotel, although small-town Kaveri was quick to note in response that the contestants "look like a bunch of *būdīyā* [old ladies] in saris anyway" as if to highlight how unnecessary she perceived supervision to be if contestants were dressed in the conventional attire worn by most Hindu women over thirty.

The discourse of protection was employed throughout the duration of the pageant; if the contestants need to be watched by the experts, whose gaze was designed to help them improve their chances of winning, then the chaperones were required to make sure that their behavior did not cross over into the realm of the immoral. Noting that "the reputation of the pageant is at stake," many chaperones were quick to mention that it is necessary to maintain vigilance over the contestants that occasionally borders on the extreme. Mediating, or even controlling, the behavior of women is by no means a new phenomenon in South Asia. *Parda*, the seclusion of women from men not related to them, is a mark of prestige for many village families throughout South Asia and also serves as an ideology in urban India, where women are not as numerous in public space as men are. Female seclusion is intimately connected to the culture of male honor that positions women as barometers of family integrity, and numerous scholars (e.g., Abu-Lughod 1986; Hejaiej 1996; Mernissi 1985) have noted the way in which female seclusion is directly related to male authority and exists as part of a system in which such authority is paramount in women's social worlds.

Seclusion at the hotel during the course of the training program is very important precisely because it is perceived to maintain the integrity of the pageant. If men, however innocuous their relationship to the contestants, were allowed to visit the young women at the hotel, the gossip surrounding the pageant would serve to fundamentally destabilize its carefully constructed rhetoric of women's empowerment. Women throughout India must be very careful to monitor their behavior vis-à-vis men, as the segregation of the sexes is extreme enough that, following Hejaiej (1996, 69), "Sexuality is seen as the only realm of interaction between the sexes."

If women at Miss India are isolated under the gaze of chaperones and experts, it is a small price to pay for what they get in return in that being watched is also tied to the power of being looked at. One contestant laughed as she described how her servants "just love" watching her in her thong underwear, which she named as her garment of choice when she is at home. Although the stares may be out of sheer disbelief about the practicality of such a garment from a servant's perspective, the opportunity to be gazed at is a coveted one in Mumbai and Delhi. Page Three of the *Bombay Times* (or, in Delhi, the *Delhi Times*), a supplement of the *Times of India,* visually chronicles the social lives of celebrities and is avidly consumed by a middle-class readership.

Shonal, a successful model in her native Calcutta before she was selected for the training program, noted that doing well in Calcutta and at Miss India were two completely different things.

> I'll lose my privacy if I win. In Calcutta, people know me and there I have to be cautious about what I say and do. But as Miss India, I'll never be able to relax. Here, they turn you into a complete lady, but when people watch you more and more, your concept of individuality just goes.

Shonal's assertion that she will "never be able to relax" points to the kind of constant public scrutiny that the contestants are subjected to and how it increases tenfold if they win. When she insisted that "people watch you more and more," the metaphor of the panopticon and the double-edged compliment of the gaze become especially clear given her matter-of-factness: being observed is simply a part of life as a beauty queen.

Indeed, numerous sessions at the training program were designed to prepare the contestants to be the focus of public scrutiny. Diction expert Sabira Merchant led the contestants for several hours one afternoon through an exercise designed to prepare them to be on television, that ultimate instrument of the gaze. One by one, each contestant came to the podium, where Merchant advised:

> Everyone is watching you. Hold the mike level to your chest; make sure it's an extension of yourself. You'll sound sexy that way, well-modulated.

> You've got to sex up the audience, let's be honest. Everyone will be watching you, so be breezy, happy and in control, cool.

In a few brief sentences, Merchant summed up the need for contestants to be sexual yet nonthreatening and calm, and still in control. The more I learned about how difficult it is to present oneself as a beauty queen, the more I realized that it is unfortunate that, like most things feminine, women's work in the space of the pageant is so profoundly devalued. However, given the chance to be looked at via the opportunities made possible by the training program, the strain of being observed may very well be seen as worth the effort by many young women.

Foucault (1980, 98) is clear that humans are possessed of agency in the complex schema of power: rather than simple targets for the imposition of power, individual social actors "are also the elements of its articulation." The Miss India training program would not function if young women did not ascribe a great deal of importance to changing themselves under the gaze of the experts, as many contestants see their own self-modification as their duty in order to fulfill the role of Miss India, a reality that directly relates to the amount of importance attached to forming networks within Indian media industries.

## Qualified to Judge: The Culture of Celebrity in Urban India

India is probably unique in the world in terms of the sheer amount of deference and attention that celebrities receive, as to be famous in India is almost to be revered: newspapers chronicle your attendance at parties (sometimes on the front page), magazines speculate about your life choices, and sometimes, as one man did in Chennai for film star Amitabh Bachchan, people build temples in your honor. Reading the *Times of India,* the newspaper with the largest circulation in the country, I often learned more about the lives of Hollywood celebrities in the span of a month than I would have in a year of newspaper reading in the United States. It may be that there is such a limited scope for social mobility in India that those who are fortunate enough to be at the top of a highly stratified social structure provide an opportunity for millions of middle-class consumers of popular culture to live their fabulous lives vicariously.

I spent almost two years living such a life in Mumbai, during which I was a part of numerous relationships, albeit with varying degrees of intensity, with individuals whose lives and careers were largely dependent upon the kind of celebrity I have described above. These social networks function as a complex matrix in which media visibility is the ultimate barometer with which to gauge one's place. Miss India officials were careful to choose members of social networks who were close to the center of the matrix of power and visibility in the culture of celebrity, and so the judges at the Bangalore preliminaries were composed of the same panel of names that are omnipresent in urban Indian culture. Beauty queens and models Namrata Shirodkar, Aditi Govitrikar, and Sushma Reddy sat next to Hindi film director Pooja Bhatt, actor Mahesh Manjrekar, advertising guru Piyush Pandey and television actress Neena Gupta, and the only nonmedia celebrity on the panel was Indira Hinduja, who facilitated the first test-tube conception in India.

Chosen because of her status as what Parigi described as "a woman achiever," Hinduja stopped the PowerPoint presentation being made by the Ernst and Young consultants to the judges by interjecting, a bit embarrassed, "I'm sorry, because I believe that everyone else here is in the media field and knows each other already." Hinduja's brief interruption pointed to the strikingly insular nature of the culture of celebrity. Indeed, the other judges had been talking among themselves prior to the entry of the Ernst and Young consultants, as they were all part of the same social network, but because Hinduja was not involved in the media she was an anomaly at the pageant.

The judges were asked to select the winners for the titles of Miss Ten, Miss Beautiful Skin, Miss Beautiful Hair, Miss Beautiful Smile, and Miss Photogenic, the purpose of which was to allow contestants to go on to certain fields in media. Miss Photogenic, for example, usually becomes a well-known model. As Ernst and Young briefed them on the judging process and criteria, the judges expressed curiosity about why the guidelines were so strict, underscoring how beauty pageants as a concept are firmly

6. *The judges and "the experts" at the Miss India training program work in media-related professions, especially the Hindi film industry, making the pageant a conduit to stardom for many young women.*

subjective things, which in turn raises the question of who is qualified to judge.

The judges found Ernst and Young's detailed explanation of procedures a bit boring and showed their lack of interest by asking no questions at the end of an extremely complicated presentation, although this may have been partly due to the extremely clear-cut definitions of beauty presented. For example, "beautiful skin" was defined as "the absence of blemishes and presence of radiance," and the winner of the Miss Ten title would display "physical fitness, tonal quality of body, shape/length of legs and symmetry of body." Given these criteria, it is fairly bizarre that a pretense of objectivity was given. During the judging round, the contestants walked out onto a ramp in their swimsuits. The sight of all twenty-six young women in identical swimsuits and numbered sashes standing silent for a full three minutes in front of the judges in contestant order was remarkable. As the song "Absolutely Flawless" played in the background, the judges took notes on each young woman's appearance to refer to when making their final evaluations. The judges at the final pageant were better

known than those at the preliminaries and included Infosys chairperson
Sunil Mittal, Kinetic Honda chairperson Sulajja Firodia Motwani, tennis
player Mahesh Bhupathi, actress and sex symbol Shilpa Shetty, diplo-
mat Nirupama Rao, Hindi film directors Yash Chopra and Sanjay Leela
Bhansali, and Hindi film action hero Jackie Shroff.

The contestants who were aspiring actresses or models were especially eager to meet directors Chopra and Bhansali, who were doubtlessly
evaluating the potential of the contestants as Hindi film actresses. In fact,
the potential of judges to make stars out of the contestants is consistently
(and breathlessly) described by *Femina* editor Sathya Saran in her annual
report on the pageant in *Femina,* the title of which often reads something
to the effect of "the connoisseurs will select," thereby validating the perceived expertise of the judges in evaluating beauty. Yet not all judges are
comfortable with this role; Hindi film actor Jackie Shroff, whose wife was
Miss India 1980, spent almost an hour with me expressing his reservations
about beauty pageants in general. He taught me how to roll a cigarette
with the tobacco and rolling papers he kept in his cowboy-style bandana
as he explained that he found the culture of beauty pageants inherently
unfair. "I know how girls are," he said. "They'll all be so sad if they don't
win. I hate to do this. I could never do what these girls do." Shroff's rather
candid admission that he "could never do what these girls do" reveals just
how difficult it is to be judged, especially by those who all of urban India
holds up as icons.

### The Dark Mystique of Indian Media

There is a very dark side to the film and media industry in India, and so
if media is actually reality writ large, then the rumors of the sexual compromises that young women have to make in order to succeed can be seen
as representative of the difficulties that women face in a male-dominated
country. I was consistently struck by this when I was conducting research
on the Hindi film industry prior to beginning work on the Miss India pageant, as everywhere I looked there were signs that emphasized just how
easy it is perceived to be for women to slip into a dark world of sexuality
exchanged for power and glamour. From the pictures of beautiful young

7. *Significant differences in age, class, and social status between contestants and the men who have control over their success in the media provide much fodder for salacious gossip in the Indian press. Pictured are Lara Dutta and Pradeep Guha.*

actresses with aging, pot-bellied film producers in the pages of the tabloids *Filmfare* and *Cineblitz* to the advice columns of women's magazines like *Femina*, the message seemed consistent and clear: women need to be careful how they negotiate their presence in a male world.

Indian popular culture accepts and even dwells on the fact that young women do not have it easy in media. Stories abound about naïve young women who come to Mumbai to make their mark in the film world only to be exploited by an assortment of nefarious male characters. Their naïveté and vanity are usually the reasons given for their predicament, as well as the fact that, as one film producer succinctly stated, "The amount of trouble you get into is directly proportional to how desperate you are." Urban legends abound throughout urban India about the secret lives of celebrities, especially women. Popular public sentiment holds that women who work in media have made some kind of dark pact, some compromise, which has transgressed the boundaries of the moral universe at a fundamental level to allow them be so wealthy, powerful, and, above all, visible. Individuals in high profile media-related fields thus inhabit a strange nether-realm as people who are both known and unknown and exist in a liminal landscape in which identities are often constructed for them by audiences, fan magazines, and even the film roles they are assigned by production houses.

The celebrated Hindi film actress Rekha has a cult of personality surrounding her that is unparalleled among other actresses and is often the subject of particularly fascinating urban legends. Rekha began her career by acting in South Indian Tamil-language films, which most Indians place lower than Hindi films on a hierarchy of quality and substance, until she received her first starring role in the spectacularly successful Hindi film *Umrao Jaan* (The Good Life) as a Mughal courtesan and subsequently became the subject of male fantasies throughout the subcontinent for decades to come. Throughout the course of her career, Rekha's skin color and youthful appearance have been the object of consuming interest to her fans and to popular culture at large. Her complexion was initially much darker than what is ordinarily acceptable for Hindi film actresses, and now in her fifties Rekha's skin is as pale as her counterparts in the film industry, a fact that does not go unnoticed in the highly public world of cinema. Women often discuss Rekha's transformation in terms of what she must have done in order to enact this miraculous change. Most insist that it was simply staying off sun-drenched film sets that changed Rekha's skin tone, but by far the most interesting account of her transformation is the urban legend that was circulating throughout Mumbai in early 2002.

Supposedly told to a friend of a friend whose security guard knows the security guard who stands outside Rekha's house, the story takes the form of most urban legends in that the teller of the story has a link, however nebulous, to someone who has access to some special knowledge about the subject of the story, in this case, Rekha's security guard. It is common knowledge among film fans in India that Rekha does not leave her house, a fact that no doubt adds to the mystique that already surrounds her. This popular cultural knowledge forms the backdrop for what comes next: the information that Rekha's security guard has seen a string of young men entering her home at odd hours of the night and that he is under strict orders to let them in.

At this point, the story is explicitly questioning Rekha's moral character, as Hindi film actresses and other women who are active in media are often stereotyped as sexually promiscuous. In her study of film fans in South India, Dickey found that actresses in Tamil cinema are often the subject of vicious gossip, so much so that directors in the Tamil film industry were shocked when Dickey asked if they would allow their daughters to become actresses, because "actors and actresses have no privacy, and actresses develop bad reputations because even when 'they're extremely good, the public talk nonsense'" (1993, 47). This mirrors the public ambivalence that surrounds actresses in Hindi cinema, because thinly underlying the public's fascination with them is the assumption that fame for women always comes at a terrible moral and psychic price.

In the case of Rekha and the urban legend, the price of fame is the endless stream of male night visitors who arrive under the eyes of the security guard. The young men, the teller of the story carefully narrates in a low tone, are never seen again, even though their numbers sometimes reach into the dozens each week. The story reaches a crescendo when the teller reveals that the security guard fears that Rekha's fair, youthful complexion is the direct result of her bathing in the blood of adolescent males, who are obviously lured to her gate by her beauty and legendary sex appeal.

That such bizarre stories can circulate about an established actress serves to illustrate just how difficult it is for young women to negotiate the culture of celebrity and how it can be nearly impossible for young women with no connections in media to overcome the kind of institutionalized sleaze that pervades it. Because Miss India provides a direct route to media stardom, it serves as a means by which young women can negotiate the gender inequality that is omnipresent in the film industry. Participating in Miss India guarantees young women an enormous amount of media exposure in the country's largest women's magazine for the duration of the pageant, and as one of the few opportunities for young women to be noticed without the patronage of a lecherous older man, Miss India provides social mobility to young women in a way that no other group or institution in the country can. An aura of decency surrounds the pageant, not only because it has *Femina*'s trusted stamp of approval, but also because of the allure of "international fame."

Every contestant who makes it to the semifinals wins a title that is linked to a sponsor: Miss Beautiful Skin and Miss Beautiful Hair are sponsored by soap and shampoo companies, and Miss Photogenic is predictably sponsored by a camera or film company. These titles provide young women with increased exposure that helps them to build media careers after the pageant is over because the network of what is called "the glamour world" in Mumbai is extremely small. From the circumscribed film world to the repetitive cast of characters in the Miss India training team to the faces on the society page of the *Times of India*, media comprises a tight, tiny circle that is extremely difficult to break into. By allowing young women at least a chance to access that world, Miss India acts as a powerful agent of social mobility.

Former pageant director Neeta Asnani noted, "There are plenty of pageants on a national level, but they don't have a brand like *Femina* behind them. We've been doing this for over forty years. We know what we're doing." Miss India does create an unparalleled opportunity for applicants, but the process of selection is so biased in terms of class and ethnicity that many would question whether moving into a media industry in which women are largely decorative constitutes any kind of progress at all. Former Miss World Yukta Mookhey was adamant that Miss India contestants should avoid Hindi films as a career choice:

> Winners do Bollywood because they have nothing better to do, but that means a lot of degrading yourself and male ego to deal with, and you'll realize that isn't what you want to do with your life. It won't last long, because there's always someone to replace you. It's an okay place for two or three years, but after an international pageant, which I believe is really uplifting for a girl, to waste it away where you're getting paid for your looks, it's stupid. Miss India is about what's inside, and in Bollywood all girls do is change their clothes. There is no message. Unfortunately, in India the only larger than life stars are cricketers and film stars. In Bollywood, there is total disregard and disrespect for you, and if you can deal with that, do it. There is no quality or substance at all.

Mookhey listed every commonly voiced opinion about the Hindi film industry in her characteristically forthright style while positioning the Miss

India pageant as the direct opposite of Bollywood. If Bollywood is superficial, Mookhey argued, Miss India is substantial; a line of reasoning that utilized the language of the pageant that organizers were careful to tailor in a way that illustrated the positive aspects of femininity rather than the display of women's bodies in order to fit into cultural norms surrounding womanhood and modesty.

Despite this, however, the Miss India pageant does not escape the kinds of criticism that the rest of media receives. Miss India organizers received a request to use the sets for the 2003 pageant to shoot a film called "Miss India: The Mystery." The synopsis of the plot sent by the producer read strangely like a comment on the presumed immorality of contestants:

> Our film "Miss India" is based on the backdrop of this contest. Being a thriller in its genre it unfolds into a murder mystery, which takes us into the behind the scenes activity and the politics involved in it, showing how some that are willing to get exploited do get exploited.

I was struck as I read through the screenplay by the writer's assumption that the pageant is characterized by the same patterns of degradation and sexual exploitation Yukta alluded to in her argument against Hindi film careers for women. The screenplay was not at all subtle in its implications or its execution: in one particularly bizarre scene, a contestant's dead body is found lying naked, "the victim of a judge's lust."

Family connections prove invaluable for those who want to establish themselves in an industry that is clearly seen by both outsiders and insiders as an abusive and dangerous place for women. Coming from what is known as a "film family" helps immensely, and those who have relatives who are well established in the industry are thought to have fewer problems with the constant (usually sexual) compromises that many others are believed to make in order to succeed. As a result of this, the industry as a whole has a sordid reputation and is not seen as a very reputable career choice for women. Some individuals in media, however, noted that this was changing as budgets improved; director Pankaj Parashar observed that "this kind of money changes a lot of people's minds about sending their daughters into films, because once they see that their daughter can make crores [tens of millions of rupees], they'll call up directors and send her to Bombay [Mumbai]."

Modeling is not unlike the film industry in that it is rather consistently described as both dangerous and sordid. The media industry is almost completely dominated by older men and so the potential for the exploitation of unsuspecting women is often explained rather matter-of-factly by people both in and outside of the industry. Of course, this potential is also extremely sexist in its implicit assumption that women are unable to take care of themselves and manipulate networks of power to their own advantage. This negotiation of the media industry was a common subject of discussion among women when they described their work to me in the course of interviews, and many women stressed the difficulty of living alone in Mumbai. It was often taken for granted by both men and women that women are forced to navigate power and gender in ways that men do not need to because of their gender.

Model Diya Abraham, who came to Mumbai from Bangalore in her late teens, expressed deep concerns about teenage girls entering the media industry in Mumbai. She observed that they are often unequipped for the kinds of dangers that they must face; what was most interesting was that these dangers described by women are always sexual. This system is so entrenched that implausible rumors also abound that Sushmita Sen won the Miss Universe title via sexual favors she supposedly performed as part of the infamous "godfather system" in the Hindi film industry, in which young women attach themselves to powerful older men in order to further their film careers. Abraham described the process of navigating what she called "the sleazy people in the field" as a process of diplomacy in which older men "learn not to mess with you, but also don't get angry with you." This elaborate, gendered, and highly sexualized dance is difficult to perform and yet its performance largely, if not completely, stems from the view of women as showpieces with little talent who are near-accessories to male actors who are the real performers. This negotiation of gender and power even affects women from established families, and a third-generation actress described two instances in which even she was subjected to the sort of sexual manipulation that the media industry is so notorious for:

Mom always warned me about this, but I was shocked when it actually happened. This woman came to my house and she was sitting and my maid had gone, and she was this big, huge woman, and she was asking me if I would meet the financer and stuff like that, and I was really shocked! And I was so scared that I didn't even know what had hit me. So I said, "Um, I'll call you back!" I didn't know what to say to her. And she left. And then it happened again! There was another woman who came over saying she wanted to meet me about a film and she said, "I want you to have a personal meeting with the director," and "this is how it goes nowadays." And I understood what she was saying, and what she was trying to get at, and I was scared again. There are a lot of bad people in this industry.

The actress's description of the fear that she felt when she was forced to navigate the film industry's complex networks of gender and power illustrates the near-showpiece position that women are sometimes placed in. The most unfortunate thought that occurred to me in the taxi home from the actress's house that day was that someone like her has the power to say no, whereas other women who are faced with fierce competition for ad campaigns and films do not.

The question remains as to why women choose to be a part of a network that is known to be so exploitative to women in general. Both women and men who are not part of the network except as viewers of films and magazines often describe Bollywood and media in general as "dirty," a strong choice of adjective to characterize an industry that is so much a part of popular culture. When I asked individuals in the industry why women choose to be a part of this network, the answer was often the fame and the adulation that they receive if they are successful. A female documentary producer in India who had worked on a documentary on Hindi cinema for the BBC observed that "there's nowhere else on earth that people get the kind of adulation that film stars and models get here."

Although beauty is enacted as a competitive sport between women in many other geographical regions, it is particularly strong in Mumbai and perhaps even in India as a whole. This adds to the incentive for women to join the industry, because, as entertainer Ruby Bhatia observed, being successful in the industry proves that one is beautiful. Bhatia further commented that women enter the industry because "every woman wants another person to think she's beautiful, to pay her money because she's so beautiful." Actress Riya Sen echoed Bhatia's comments in noting that it is the seductive power of glamour that encourages women to participate in the project of beauty as a professionally competitive sport:

> Everyone wants glamour; every girl wants to have it. Someone might say, "Please, I don't want to model," but given the opportunity, anyone would want to be sitting there in front of the camera, in front of the light, being recognized as beautiful by the public, and at the same time being paid a lot of money.

Sen went beyond the simple insistence that glamour is an alluring force to contend that glamour is so powerful that "every girl" wants to have it. A *Femina* cover story in 1997 by model coordinator Imam Siddiqui capitalized on this seductive power when it asked readers, "So You Want to Be a Model?" and laid out the steps from getting a portfolio to walking the ramp. Siddiqui (1997) very clearly outlined the requirements: women, for example, need to be at least five feet six inches tall and weigh between 110 and 130 pounds, and they were advised to invest approximately 38,000 rupees (about $800) on a portfolio, clothing, cosmetics, and shoes in order to begin their careers. That amount seems like a prohibitively high cost when college graduates are lucky to earn such a sum after several months of work.

Beauty culture exploded in Mumbai with *Femina* at the helm following the opening of the economy in 1991, and between 1993 and 2000, *Femina* ran a pageant called "Look of the Year" that promised international fame and modeling contracts to the winners. The advertisement for the pageant read:

> The connoisseurs will select. The specialists will groom. *Femina will create.* Yet another star. *Femina* is on the lookout for the perfect model. The perfect face. The perfect figure. Perfect poise. Confidence. Charisma. Presence. That extra something that distinguishes a potential supermodel from

other mortal models. If that's you and you are under 21 and over 5 [feet] 6, go right ahead and apply. And what's in it for you? If you are the winner, you will be India's representative to the contest for the international title, "Elite Model Look 97." There you will compete with the best potential models from all over the world. The victorious top 15 will get international ad contracts ranging from US $50,000 to $150,000 each. And fame. And stardom and power. (Saran 1997)

Utilizing the seductive and almost magical language of the pageant, *Femina* literally promised the world to entrants. This language is important, as it points to the reason why modeling and what in India is often called "the glamour world" is seen as a viable career option by many young women.

Mumbai offers few prospects for young women who have grown up privy to media images of life in the United States and Europe, and modeling is perceived to grant young women a chance at independence similar to what they have seen in films and on television. As such, *Femina* may not be exaggerating in describing the Look of the Year pageant in an editorial as "a night of magic and promise." Look of the Year winner and Parisian model Ujjwala Raut's article in *Femina Girl*, a version for teenage readers, breathlessly recounted fascinating details of her life, such as the time that she fainted at an Ungaro fitting because she had not eaten breakfast. "Luckily, girls fainting is quite commonplace," she wrote, "so before I knew it they had me back on my feet with some sugar and water" (Raut 2002). Despite such pitfalls of the profession, modeling is often seen in urban India as something of a fantasy world that involves glamour, international travel, and fame.

Postliberalization India's enormously expanded media industry combined with the perceived international status that modeling and beauty pageants give to young women means that these fields are becoming more acceptable to urban Indians. As Saloni, a Miss India 2003 contestant noted,

Ten or twenty years ago, parents were hesitant to let their daughters enter this field, but lots and lots of TV and media have changed this perception, so that what used to be not so good is now very good.

While Saloni credited the media with changing negative prevailing social sentiments on pageants and media, I contend that the deeper structural view of women expressed in the vehicle of the beauty pageant is actually very Indian.

## Beauty as a Competitive Sport: Pageant Cultures

> *Merē khūbsūratī merē sabse baṛai duśman hain* / My beauty is my greatest enemy. (Miss World 1994 Aishwarya Rai, quoted in *Merī Saheli* [My Girlfriend] magazine)

Rai's statement resonated with readers throughout India who sympathized with the double-edged sword that being beautiful presents to women. Beauty is often described as dangerous in India because the beautiful female body is always an object of display whether by choice or not. Women feel extremely free to comment on the appearance of other women in their presence, noting changes in weight, appearance, or even overall beauty. I ended one screening of an Aishwarya Rai film with a friend noting that the twenty-five-year-old actress was "looking really old and haggard."

Yet what may appear malicious is actually a product of a cultural system that is extremely accustomed to the standardized evaluation of beauty. What is considered beautiful is often very clear: beauty is fair, tall, and slim, as the matrimonial ads placed by families in search of brides for their sons consistently mention. The practice of judging women is deeply ingrained in India from the practice of "seeing girls," in which young women are brought for the evaluation of a young man's family as part of a prospective marriage proposal, to the reduction of female bodies to "item numbers" who do nothing but perform undulating dance sequences as plot interludes in Hindi films. I often found it extremely odd that critics of beauty pageants in India would criticize them as Western, because the concept of objectively judging female beauty has been institutionalized for quite some time in India. As one young woman succinctly mentioned, "If you are relatively young and maintain yourself, you will be evaluated and judged."

This stems from a misogynist element of a cultural system that separates women and makes them competitors for potential mates via practices ranging from "seeing girls" as part of arranging marriages to evaluating male prestige and wealth by the beauty of the woman he is able to marry. Beauty in India is nonnegotiable, something that is a fact that needs no further explanation. Women often describe each other as "my beautiful friend," using the adjective as freely in the course of conversation as they would any other identifying marker. It is not uncommon to hear women say "it is because I am so beautiful" as a way of explaining why an event transpired in a particular way. There are some cultural systems that lend themselves particularly well to the commoditization and packaging of female beauty, so although beauty pageants are a profoundly capitalist phenomenon in the sense that they use women's bodies in order to market products, they are also cultural performances in which ideas about femininity and gender norms are reinforced.

At the Miss India 2003 semifinals, presenter and former model Malaika Arora Khan casually announced that "contrary to popular belief that women are women's own worst enemies, this group has been supportive of one another." It was the casual, offhand tone of this remark that provided the most disturbing statement about a system that pits women against each other. The concept of beauty as a competitive sport is perhaps nowhere more evident than in the Hindi film and media industries, which are a part of everyday life for many women in the forms of soap operas and films that they watch at home. It is perfectly normal, even expected, that women will comment on the appearance of women they see on films, on television, and in everyday life, because women are always presumed to be onstage when in public. Female friends who belong to the social milieu to which Miss India contestants aspire routinely greet each other after an absence of just a few days with observations on weight loss or gain, on clothing, or on other aspects of their self-presentation. I have always been rather conscious of my appearance, and yet it took several months in the field before I was able to become fully accustomed to having my weight evaluated as a matter of course by women I considered my friends.

Public space in both urban and rural India is almost exclusively male, and it is fairly normal (albeit socially unacceptable) for men on the street to irritate the majority of women to no end via sexual comments or singing of particularly racy songs from Hindi films. This powerful distinction between inside/outside and female/male provides an important means by which women judge what domains and forms of dress are appropriate. Women negotiate public space by staying in cars en route to places where more revealing clothes are appropriate, such as nightclubs, or by wearing loose shirts or shawls over tight or revealing clothing.

Nightclubs are often thought to be especially fraught with danger for women, especially since the type of behavior that seems very normal in such spaces, including conversations about sexuality that more often than not have an androcentric tone, are anything but normal elsewhere. The one occasion that the Miss India contestants were allowed out after dark (to celebrate New Year's Eve), they were taken to a nightclub that was closed to the public to ensure that they would not receive undue amounts of unpleasant male attention.

This construction of the nightclub as a space laden with dangerous sexuality is underscored by my own experience, as I was often advised by well-intentioned men not to go out at night throughout the course of my fieldwork. The following example, in the form of just such a piece of advice, this time from a film producer, illustrated the sort of dangers that women face when out at night when he noted, "You're a nice girl, Susan. You're not like these Bombay [Mumbai] women. See, once a man sees you smoke, he automatically assumes that you drink and do all sorts of other bad things." "All sorts of other bad things" in South Asian parlance generally refers to sexualized forms of behavior, because the danger that results from going out is primarily sexual. Because certain "sets" of stereotypically male behavior, such as smoking, alcohol consumption, and overt sexuality are often lumped together in India, women who find themselves in the spaces in which these behaviors are normal risk having all three ascribed to them should they choose to engage in one of them.

The concept of "normal" is fraught with complexity for media professionals in Mumbai, who have little in common with the rest of the city because of their wealth, power, and class privileges, a disconnect that results in standards of behavior that are fluid and often relative to the amount of money one has. Going out at night involves a dialogical process by which women negotiate their desire to participate in the kinds of activities urban popular culture associates with modernity and pleasure with their need to preserve a public face of morality. Although the sexualized attention of attractive young men might be viewed by young women as an exciting and inevitable part of participating in social networks in which moral standards are relatively more relaxed than in the rest of India, it is also crucial that these women maintain an image of respectability in order to eventually find a marriage partner not only for themselves but also for their female family members.

Mumbai is constituted of a moral terrain that offers extremely limited behavioral choices to women, and the sharp division between those who are conservative and those who participate in the kinds of activities Miss India contestants do leaves many individuals with conflicting desires surrounding identity. This contradiction is particularly striking in terms of the reality of life in Mumbai, or in India at large, as opposed to life in the space of media and popular culture. Mumbai, after all, is not a cosmopolitan city; it is however, home to participants in a cosmopolitan media world whose presence in turn informs the character of the city.

Nonetheless, the characterization of Mumbai as a cosmopolitan city is quite a common one in India that serves to veil the more embedded discourse of sexuality and danger. Women are present in large numbers in the space of the night out, and individuals often contend that women have access to a lifestyle in Mumbai that is simply not possible in the rest of India. Nightclub owner Devesh Sharma noted, "People have become more civilized. That's why Mumbai is so great, because a woman can come into the club and rest assured that she can have a great night, and a safe time, without a second thought." Sharma's reference to people becoming "more civilized" is a common statement about poststructural adjustment behavioral shifts, and yet the fact that he needs to point out that women in Mumbai can have a "safe time" highlights that other spaces have the potential to be unsafe and that defending oneself against both the perceived and real dangers of male public space is a legitimate concern for women.

Whatever way women choose to negotiate the cultural norm of the female body as an object of beauty and display, the fact remains that women are positioned as embodied subjects for male consumption. This new urban cultural norm of the beauty queen on display is, like most other things Indian, writ large on the Hindi film screen, especially in the form of the postliberalization actress. The resulting influx of European and American images of beauty since the economy opened to foreign investment has deeply impacted the notion of what a beautiful actress looks like, and many avid consumers of popular culture in India have commented on how today all actresses look the same. The postliberalization actress is easily identifiable with long, straight hair, extraordinary height, tiny waist, and tight-fitting clothes. A made-to-order film star, she represents a great deal, stands for very little, and although she cannot truly be called an actress, because she often has little to do in a film except sigh and pout, she is on every film screen as a beautiful accessory to an actor.

There are hundreds of others who look exactly like her, which makes competition for work extremely stiff, and in an era in which beauty is perhaps more rigidly defined than it ever has been before, the image of what an actress or model should be is becoming circumscribed into a specific physical type. Although young women have been largely defined and measured by their beauty for centuries, the decade-old media explosion in India has meant that more and more young women are interested in media as a viable career option. This interest combined with the lucrative rewards such a career promises and changing norms for female behavior has made for incredibly tough competition among women. This is precisely the reason why the Miss India pageant serves as such an important vehicle, because it places contestants into direct contact with prominent individuals who can help them in their careers, thus serving as a springboard into what is known in India as "the glamour world."

The fact remains that media is everyday life writ large, and in the beauty pageant of everyday life things are no different. As a writer for a prestigious fashion magazine in Mumbai noted, "Now, the glamorization of life makes it so women are always judging each other," highlighting the pressure women feel to cultivate themselves. Economic liberalization

with its onslaught of beauty products and images of beauty has seriously compounded issues that women may have faced before in regard
to beauty. As such, while acknowledging that the Miss India pageant
provides wonderful career opportunities to young women, it is important to also raise the question as to which women it does so for; namely,
those women who fit into a mold of being female that is idealized at best
and harmful at worst.

PART TWO | *Gender*

# 4

## Strī Śakti and the Rhetoric
## of Women's Empowerment

Standing in front of the contestants, 2003 pageant director A. P. Parigi sought to emphasize the tone that the young women should take in their introductory speeches to the audience. The theme of that year's pageant was "strī śakti," a rather formal Hindi translation of "woman power." "Stand there and speak slowly," he said, "because if you talk about woman power too fast, then the guy in the audience will throw up his hands." The contestants began to nod their heads in approval as he added, "That guy in the audience will say, 'Hey, I came here and sat in the audience, I never said I didn't believe in strī śakti!' so be gentle."

Although positioning "that guy in the audience" as an advocate of strī śakti as a result of his presence at the pageant is rather dubious, this statement shows how contestants must adhere to stereotypes about femininity at all times. By being "gentle," no one in the audience will be offended, and the concept of female beauty as submissive will not be disturbed. Beauty pageants are profoundly about reaffirming patriarchal values, and as Perlmutter (2000) notes in her analysis of Miss America, although contestants may articulate statements about women's empowerment, they only do so at a very superficial level. Contestants at Miss India perform femininity in much the same way, all the while espousing the rhetoric of social mobility, which serves to legitimize the pageant in countless ways.

## The Rhetoric of the Platform and the "Fair" Pageant

> Miss India is a platform for a girl to do whatever she wants. All the
> winner needs is beauty and a mind, destiny, and her parents' blessing.
> (Deepica, Miss India 2003 contestant)

Miss India 2003 contestant Deepica observed that Miss India is perceived as a platform from which young women can do anything that they
want. Although this "anything" usually means careers in media-related
fields, Miss India is seen as sort of a fairy godmother who grants contestants an opportunity to enter social arenas that they would not have access
to were it not for their participation in the pageant. During the two-day
period that comprised the selection of candidates in Mumbai, public relations consultant Malati Puranik made sure to have photographers capture
images of young women from the predominantly middle-class suburbs
of Mulund and Vashi, which ran in the *Times of India* the next day. This
was part of a concerted effort by pageant officials to send the message
that anyone can be Miss India, even a young woman from a middle-class
suburb in Mumbai.

The 2003 pageant's focus on fairness and transparency provoked numerous discussions about who has access to the pageant and who can
become Miss India. From contestants who insisted that only the elite be
allowed to represent India because, as one contestant put it, they are "the
best of the country" to experts who argued that they would have far too
much work to do with young women from nonmetropolitan areas, class
and geography were highly contentious subjects throughout the pageant.
Yamini Gupta, the head of public relations for the pageant, was insistent
that although not everyone can win, everyone has potential.

> I agree that the *gajrāvālī* [street vendor who sells flowers] doesn't stand a
> chance and that the girls who come to do the contestants' hair and nails,
> they may not do it because they don't feel they have it in them. But I'll tell
> you that everyone has potential. When Sunsilk goes to the villages, the
> women feel the difference in themselves once they use shampoo instead
> of *śikākāī* [homemade herbal cleanser], they feel more beautiful.

Gupta's choice of the *gajrāvālī*, a female street vendor who sells strands of jasmine to adorn women's hair, is rather ironic, because such a woman also deals in beauty and simultaneously earns an income with which to support herself and her family. Since the *gajrāvālī* has no access to the kind of cultural knowledge that would allow her to participate in Miss India, Gupta's reference to her classed beauty clearly associates "potential" with the ability to invest money in beauty products. The recognition that a self-employed woman like her "doesn't stand a chance" is a sad illustration of the hollow rhetoric of women's empowerment at the pageant.

Geography was also a subject of discussion in regard to the politics of becoming Miss India. Akuno was a contestant from the troubled state of Assam in Northeast India, best known for its Marxist insurgencies and tea plantations, who unsuccessfully attempted to use her membership in a marginalized group to improve her chances of being selected by the judges. When asked why she wanted to be Miss India, she answered, "Because I come from the East, and being Miss India will let me help people there overcome superstition and poverty and uplift their life."

With the East Asian features that characterize people from the Northeast, Akuno stood out from the rest of the applicants at the selection round in which individual contestants were privately interviewed by a panel of judges at an opulent hotel. The judges unfortunately seemed to focus more on her identity as a northeasterner rather than her chances of being Miss India, and the questions that they asked her reflected this. The first question was, "Why does the Northeast understand Shakespeare more than other parts of India?" to which she answered, "Maybe because they have more visual beauty." In a mode strikingly similar to racist stereotypes of African Americans in the United States, another judge asked her why "people like singing and dancing so much" in the Northeast. Akuno was then asked why the Northeast does not have much representation in the rest of India, to which she replied, "Everyone is poor in the Northeast, so we don't have people who are powerful enough to speak up." The way in which Akuno was made to feel keenly aware of her membership in an ethnic minority group at the selection round was extremely disappointing.

Nazani, a Muslim applicant who had come from Saudi Arabia in order to compete in the selection round, was first asked by the judges whether she would marry a man who already had another wife. All of the judges were Hindu with the exception of one Christian, and they made Nazani keenly aware of her status as a Muslim by beginning the interview with a confrontational inquiry about her practice of Islam. She answered, "I would marry an already married man as long as he gave me what I wanted." Following a curious line of questioning, the next judge asked her if she would have sex with a man in exchange for money. In implicitly positioning the Qur'anically sanctioned practice of polygyny alongside prostitution, the panel of judges made it fairly clear to Nazani that her religion made her a minority at the pageant. I am fairly certain that the judges were not aware of the uncomfortable situation they created for contestants who came from minority groups, and yet it is clear that the effect of their bias reduced the chances for selection of such young women.

Certain regions were also the subject of unfair questioning by the judges. The sole contestant from Goa, a state best known for its idyllic beaches and rave parties where expatriates primarily from Western Europe and Israel often use psychotropic substances, was asked if she had ever tried drugs. She answered, "There is a big drug scene in Goa, but I've never tried drugs." None of the other contestants were asked a similar question. Although last names were blocked at all levels of the pageant in order to ensure that there would be no bias on the part of the judges, these examples reveal that bias clearly did take place. I do not believe that this was a conscious effort on the judges' part, but rather that the stereotypes outlined above are so deeply ingrained in India that the judges subconsciously reiterated them in their line of questioning.

The first time that I was given access to the last names of the contestants was after they were brought to Mumbai, when it became obvious that there had been a clear preference for women of North Indian ethnic ancestry. I had suspected this due to the number of young women with the lighter skin color that generally characterizes people from the North and the unfortunate reality that it is extremely rare that women from the South are regarded as beautiful in the rest of India. Only three of the twenty-six contestants were ethnic southerners, two of whom had roots in the state of Karnataka and one in Kerala. The rest of the contestants were ethnically northern, including nine Punjabis, one Sindhi, five Gujaratis,

*stereotypes & judging*

seven from Rajasthan and Uttar Pradesh, and one Maharashtrian. Some South Asian scholars would situate Maharashtra in the South because of its cultural norms that grant greater freedom to women, but linguistically it bears more resemblance to the North, and most Maharashtrians prefer not to be grouped as a part of South India.

Locating the precise division between northern and southern in India is extremely problematic for scholars, as there are numerous regions, including Maharashtra state, which have cultural allegiances to both the North and the South. As such, I have defined "northern" Indians as native speakers of languages that are Indo-European, whereas "southern" Indians speak languages that are Dravidian in origin. Prejudice against the South is deeply ingrained in the more politically powerful North, the language, culture, and architecture of which are more frequently represented as "Indian" both internationally and within India itself. It is not incidental that India's national language of Hindi is itself a northern product, or that the nation's capital is located in the northern city of Delhi.

The domination of the South by the North in India is centuries old, yet political power remains centralized in the North, and northern features such as lighter skin color and greater height continue to be marked as desirable in both North and South India. If ethnicity was a contentious (albeit unspoken) issue, the young women who tried out for the Miss India pageant in 2003 were very vocal about what they perceived as other unfair aspects of the pageant. The most common complaint about bias involved the height requirement of five feet six inches in order to participate; most Indian women are petite, which ruled out many possible contestants.

One contestant was particularly adamant that the height requirement was unjust when she was told she was unable to participate because she was only five feet four inches tall. When she complained, the judges told her that they were simply following the rules that had been written to maximize India's chances at Miss Universe or Miss World. She responded by arguing that "this international pageant argument is stupid, because I'm quite sure Miss China isn't going to be five [feet] eight [inches tall]!" and thus positioned herself as a distinct member of an Asian female community that does conform to the supposed "international" standard of beauty as tall. The height requirement was the one aspect of the pageant

8. *The Miss India pageant has been heavily criticized because of its reinforcement of the South Asian cultural association of fair skin with beauty. In this photo, Miss World Diana Hayden looks strikingly different from the children who surround her.*

that was never considered negotiable by judges or pageant organizers, and although contestants at the selection rounds complained bitterly that it was not fair, pageant officials continued to insist that they were only following "international standards."

Other contestants resented the idea that they had to feign concern for social causes as part of their participation in the pageant, and their complaints were most often couched within broader discussions of class. One contestant noted, "We come here for fame and recognition, so we'll do whatever they tell us. No one cares a damn about charity. This is the only chance a lot of us have to get out and do something for ourselves." Although she understood that part of being a beauty queen means evincing concern for social causes, particularly those surrounding children and general social well-being, this contestant was clear that her goals were very different, and she described Miss India as "the only chance" that many contestants had to improve their lives. This is a heavily classed remark that draws attention to how social mobility is not a reality for most young women in India, because many, if not most, aspects of life are dictated by one's social network, and it is extremely difficult to move from one class group to another. The Miss India pageant is by no means an exception to this, as when I asked a group of contestants waiting to try out for the pageant at the Delhi selection round if they felt that class made a difference in one's chances of winning, many girls insisted that it did:

> Money does make a difference, because a glamorous dress makes you look glamorous. People who have a lot of money have a better chance, so the whole process isn't fair. If a girl just comes with a snap and a borrowed dress, she'll get rejected.

Indeed, the young women who were selected for the pageant all came from upper-middle-class or wealthy families. This is partly because of the large amount of time that the pageant requires, as the contestants must devote approximately two months of unpaid time to the training program and the period before the pageant. Sixteen of the twenty-six contestants had mothers who were employed outside the home in such fields as teaching, politics, banking, boutique ownership, medicine, spiritual healing, and directing the Federation for Indian Industry and the Sports Authority of India. The nonworking mothers had trained in Ayurvedic medicine, teaching, English literature (doctorate), and law. The contestants' fathers all worked in prestigious professions: eleven held positions of high rank in the military or the government, and there were six heads of corporations, three bankers, two doctors, one jewelry designer, one architect, and two commercial pilots.

There was also a clear bias toward young women from urban areas, and if the women who spent their lives outside of India were counted as residents of the Indian city they lived in when they entered the pageant, thirteen were from Mumbai, eight from Delhi, two from Pune, one from Bangalore, one from Nasik, and one from Calcutta. This urban bias results from the fact that young women from rural areas do not have the English language skills, knowledge of global popular culture, or family support necessary to participate in Miss India. The negative associations that the Indian film industry has with female promiscuity make careers in media unthinkable for most women, because their families would not allow them to be a part of it. Although much of this speaks to class, the broader reality is that there exists an enormous disconnect between images of beauty in the majority of India and at Miss India.

### The *Bekarī* Body and the Beauty Queen Body

On my way to a Miss India training session one day, an extremely thin young woman approached the rickshaw I was seated in. She was begging for food. As he placed a coin on her bony palm, the rickshaw driver said to me, "*Bahinjī, road par bahut bekarī hain—dekhō, itnī patlī bekarī laṛkī!*" [Sister, there's a lot of poverty on this road—look, such an impoverished, emaciated girl]. When I reached the training program's opulent ballroom, where the contestants were in the middle of a ramp walk session, I could not help but notice that several of them had the exact same body type that the rickshaw driver had taken pity on.

The only thing that separates the beauty queen body from the *bekarī* (emaciated) body is context, and so oddly enough, a *bekarī* body surrounded by wealth becomes an object of beauty worthy of representing a nation. I had noticed this trend before during the course of fieldwork I conducted at an expensive Mumbai gym and spa where because everyone knew that I was working on research that related to beauty and body image, individuals often pointed out to me what and whom they found particularly attractive. Interestingly, the body type that was most consistently described as perfect by men was that of the *mazdūr*, manual laborers who are extremely lean and muscular as a result of the heavy physical work that they do everyday.

Recruited from the North Indian state of Rajasthan for work in Mumbai, *mazdūr* carry cement and other similarly heavy materials for ten to twelve hours a day, seven days a week, in exchange for very little money and no benefits if they are injured on the job. As a result, they cannot afford to indulge in the same kinds of high calorie and fat-rich foods that the patrons of the gym and spa were able to on a daily basis. *Mazdūr* are not viewed as fitness role models because of their lack of formal knowledge and training (glossed as "awareness" in Indian English) about exercise; their bodies are fundamentally different from those of gym and spa clients because they have acquired their lean, muscular physiques from sheer physical labor rather than workouts with weights in a gym. As such, although the *mazdūr* embody the ideal male form, it is fashion and media that dictate whose form is the result of more prestigious specialized knowledge.

The cultivation of what are effectively *mazdūr* and *bekarī* bodies by privileged men and women reveals much about the classed nature of beauty and sexuality, as neither affluent English-speaking women described *mazdūr* as attractive nor did men of the same background call the *bekarī* bodies of poor women desirable. This sharp disjuncture in terms of gender indicates the importance of class in defining beauty in the opposite sex, as it would be wholly inappropriate for a relatively privileged Indian woman to evince admiration and tacit sexual attraction for a man of a lower class status. Men of the same background would be similarly unlikely to express desire for a woman who is thin due to poverty, which points to how the thin female body can be seen as a cultural performance. To be thin and female in most of India generally suggests sickness or poverty rather than the cultivation of a regimen of fitness and dieting, and yet as part of Miss India's cultural performance the body was the focus of both spoken and silent scrutiny throughout the training program.

During one fitting session for designer Ritu Kumar, I glanced through an elaborate sizing chart that listed every possible measurement of each contestant's body, including knees and ankles. The reduction of women's bodies to such an extent is part of the comically antifeminist quality of the pageant as a concept. It is clear that tailors need measurements in order to structure garments accordingly, but there is something profoundly dehumanizing about being clinically measured and having those measurements publicly announced as a mark of shame or pride. It was very disturbing to watch two contestants in particular clearly struggle with eating disorders throughout the course of the training program in a desperate attempt to achieve a beauty queen body that did not come easily to them.

By the end of the training program, I was struck by how the majority of the twenty-six contestants looked almost identical from behind: the same straight black hair with red or gold highlights, the same height and identical thin bodies. Twenty-six young women who had been similar only in height at the beginning had metamorphosed in four weeks into twenty-six separate versions of a woman called "Miss India." The enormous amount of deprivation and exercise that this body required was often the subject of humor and even derision on the part of those who were not directly involved in the training program. During the semifinals in Bangalore, one contestant told the judges that her hobby was eating cookies, to which Hindi film director Pooja Bhatt responded, "You look like you haven't had a cookie in a while" as the other judges laughed. Another judge said to a particularly thin contestant, "You must be looking forward to eating tonight," referring to a postjudging party that was being held in the contestants' honor.

The cultivation of the beauty queen body and the deprivation that it requires is often seen as a ridiculously female pursuit. This sort of language is deeply misogynist, because it underplays the kind of work that women have put into their bodies as superficial and frivolous, even silly. While men who cultivate their bodies as part of competitive sports are taken seriously and admired for their hard work and dedication to their bodies, women who do the same in beauty pageants are regarded as the subject of humor, even by those who are supposed to be evaluating them.

A techno-remix song entitled "Absolutely Flawless" played from a small speaker as each contestant stood individually in her swimsuit in front of the judges, and a pageant official read her chest, waist, and hip measurements aloud. All of the contestants were almost identical in height: eight were five feet six inches, eight were five feet seven inches, seven were five feet eight inches, and three were five feet nine inches, five feet ten inches, and five feet eleven inches, respectively. Their physical measurements were also similar, and although the outliers in terms of size were a tiny 28-23-26 and a more statistically average 34-27-39, the rest of the contestants had a chest size that ranged from thirty-one to thirty-four, a waist measurement between twenty-four and twenty-six, and a hip measurement between thirty-five and thirty-six.

If the purpose of the training program was to produce a homogenized form of beauty in all twenty-six contestants, it also sought to create a simultaneous social transformation in them. This process was even more complex than the physical changes the contestants underwent, as it involved an amalgamation of cultural norms that were quite unfamiliar to the vast majority of contestants.

## Cultivating Class

Every session grooming expert Rukhshana Eisa led on etiquette dealt with the twin themes of social class and femininity, both of which she described as central organizing principles in the life of every woman. Interestingly, she always began her lessons by noting how important it was for the contestants to be cosmopolitan individuals, repeating over and again that "you must remember that you are a representative of your country, all of you will be at some point in your life." Eisa also consistently stressed the obligation that she perceived individuals such as herself have to educate those who lack a firm grasp of what she defined as "proper behavior." This is firmly in keeping with the concept of the culture of experts, which positions those possessed of symbolic capital in a paternalistic relationship to those who do not have it. In the course of a lecture she gave to contestants, she described this responsibility to educate:

> Indians have a herd mentality. You must tell people, even at the bus stop, to stay in queue. In our Indian culture, men are used to pushing their way through, and they need to be educated. I'm talking about educated people in ties and shirts and trousers who ask my daughter and I to get up while we're eating at McDonald's, imagine. But never have a public argument with anyone. No fisherwoman behavior, please.

Eisa prepared the young women to take on this mantle of responsibility to educate others as experts in their own right by referencing a complex set of class-based behavioral norms. When she positioned Indian men, for example, as badly behaved in public, she employed the experts' shared assumption that although they are Western European–oriented in manner, the majority of Indians are not. Further, she used the stereotype of the fisherwoman as a means to index bad behavior. Common sights throughout Mumbai, these women are the brokers who sell fish that their husbands catch. Negotiating a predominantly male world as businesswomen in their own right, they have to be tough and strong in their behavior in order to survive and compete for customers. Yet the fisherwoman, it seems, is not fit to be Miss India material and is an example of what not to emulate in terms of behavior.

However, the fact remains that like the fisherwoman, the contestants also have to negotiate a male-dominated world. Eisa also went into detail about how to do this in a socially acceptable way:

> At parties, there are always men that you cannot offend who will keep asking for your phone number. Your body language should communicate what you mean in this case. If he leans forward, lean back, and he'll understand that you're not an easy type.

Although the fisherwoman may be able to tell the persistent men described above exactly what she thinks of their behavior, the Miss India contestant cannot. This reveals what a difficult path the contestants have to tread in negotiating between being single women in the media industry and potential male playthings in order to further their careers. This kind of difficulty extends to public space as well, where the presence of lower-class men, whose gaze is perceived as insulting to middle- and upper-class women, complicates what women should wear.

Eisa advised the contestants to "carry a shawl to pass the *caukīdār* [security guard] in your building" while going out, hinting that while it is acceptable to wear revealing clothing at a party under the gaze of men from the same social class, it is inappropriate to allow men such as the *caukīdār* visual access to one's body. The *caukīdār* who stood at the entrance to the Mumbai apartment building I lived in with a man who worked at night could have featured in one of Eisa's examples of how important it is to dress appropriately in public space. One night I left the building alone and, in a hurry to meet a friend for a late dinner, I forgot to wear a shawl over my sleeveless dress. Before I could reach the heavy iron gate that led to the street outside, the voice of the *caukīdār* boomed in abrupt Hindi, "*Sāhab kahān gāya?*" [Where is sir?], three simple words that overtly inquired not so much as to the whereabouts of my flatmate as it did the reason I was out at night alone with bare shoulders. The cultural framework of the *caukīdār* was such that he probably believed that I could not possibly be going to any respectable location in such revealing clothing and that had my friend been home he would not have allowed me to go out dressed that way. It is notable that the *caukīdār* never spoke to me on nights when I remembered my shawl and thus showed appreciation for an unspoken code of social norms that allow the exposure of women's bodies only in certain classed spaces.

One very interesting trend that was present throughout Eisa's lectures was the similarity between cultivating a privileged lifestyle and flouting cultural norms in India. She repeatedly insisted that spouses must "socialize independently at parties, and meet only at the end of the evening to go home together," which is rather contrary to cultural norms even in urban India, where men still have manifold freedoms in public space that women simply do not. The idea that women are actors independent of their husbands or immediate family is still fairly new in urban India, and Eisa's adherence to strict rules that seemed to be directly imported from a Victorian book of etiquette seemed almost bizarre at times:

> If a man asks you to dance, you must never refuse if you are sitting alone. If you are with a partner, you must ask his permission, and he should give it. Even if he's a sleazy gentleman, you should still accept. You must never leave your partner on the dance floor, just suffer through it if he misbehaves, and try to lean away from him if you can.

In an urban Indian context, the idea that a young woman should dance with any man who asks her is extremely foreign, and could even be dangerous to her reputation. I asked Rukhshana Eisa about the basis of these rules, and she insisted that it is important for contestants to understand how to behave in Western Europe and the United States as a way to expand their way of thinking of the world, and thus better prepare them for participation in an international pageant.

Although perhaps inseparable from the cultivation of social class, the performance of femininity was another topic that Eisa frequently addressed. This was highlighted in one especially fascinating session in which ballroom dancers were brought in to teach the contestants how to waltz, tango, and foxtrot. The sort of language that was used throughout the session evinced a focus on an extremely dichotomous system of gender, and as the young women watched the dancing couple gliding across the floor, Eisa kept up a running commentary about their movements that spoke volumes about gender and power:

> All of these are male-dominated dances, but that doesn't mean that you have no role to play. The man is the stem, the woman is the flower. No one ever looks at the stem, they look at the flower. The job of the stem is to tell the flower where to go, and it is the responsibility of the flower to go there.

Eisa concisely reaffirmed old gender stereotypes in utilizing a less-than-subtle metaphor that regarded women as passive and decorative accessories to the active bodies of men.

This sort of reaffirmation was not uncommon throughout the training program and the need to be more feminine was often voiced as a criticism to the contestants as they struggled to answer questions. The twin themes of cultivated class and femininity converged when the contestants needed to speak, and as I sat with a pageant official as she asked the contestants questions, I was struck by the number of times that she exhorted the contestants to be "ladylike":

> Remember that there is a fine dividing line between confidence and aggression. Say, "good evening, ladies and gentlemen," because it sounds more ladylike than "everybody." You have to maintain the dividing line between being diplomatic and nice all the time and having a mind of your own.

The question of what "ladylike" meant was never entirely answered for me, but seemed to comprise a constellation of behaviors and beliefs that center around a respect for traditional gender norms, a complete absence of radical or controversial views, and a willingness to voice platitudes about the positive qualities of women. These positive qualities that were most often stated by contestants to the satisfaction of judges and experts were the ability to give birth, the strength of character to sacrifice one's own goals for the sake of her family, and the creativity to be beautiful.

These positive qualities are hardly revolutionary and yet must be described and listed by beauty queens in such a way as to make them seem noble and not entirely antifeminist, which is no easy task. The ideal answer to a question at Miss India as we practiced it at the training program starts with a greeting, reaffirms a cliché without sounding clichéd, and is a bit witty without sounding condescending or too thought-provoking. When asked, for example, what she would like to change about herself, Shruti from Delhi answered that she would like to become more tolerant, with which a pageant organizer disagreed by noting that it made Shruti seem intolerant. Shruti was instead advised to say, "I would like to embrace the uniqueness of others," to the satisfaction of the other experts.

Beauty pageants as a concept reinforce the idea that women do not have radical ideas, and so when Diana from Mumbai honestly answered that she felt that the worst leader in world history was Bal Thackeray, the head of a right-wing Hindu political party called the Shiv Sena, a pageant organizer dramatically threw her head in her hands. She then asked Diana, "Do you know how many Shiv Sainiks [followers of the Shiv Sena] will be in the audience in Bombay [Mumbai], Diana? Do you want the pageant ruined?" Contestants are taught how to answer questions that can only have political answers in a way in which takes away from the real meaning of their answer. For example, choreographer Hemant Trevedi was unhappy with the responses volunteered to his question, "In a country of starving millions, are beauty pageants frivolous?" Parmita from Mumbai answered the question using P. T. Barnum's famous line, "The show must go on," and another young woman made an attempt at talking about role models. Trevedi disagreed with both approaches:

How are you helping the underprivileged? You must specify this. Why not have entertainment as well as starving millions? Show me one other area where a young woman can come forward and speak her mind to millions, even if it's only for thirty seconds?

Trevedi's argument for "entertainment as well as starving millions" is problematic on countless levels and yet also points to the way in which the contestants have to negotiate the reality of India as a country with a large impoverished population. Although his answer was perhaps no different in substance than Parmita's, it reveals the points of unspoken tension that exist between the extravagance of Miss India and the kind of consuming poverty for which India is so internationally well known.

It is the short amount of time granted to contestants to speak, as well as the lack of time that they have to prepare their thoughts, that is part of the underlying sexism of the beauty pageant as a concept. By limiting women's speech and tailoring it to suit gender norms, the rules at the pageant are such that it is virtually assured that none of the contestants are able to, as Trevedi put it, "speak her mind." As Trevedi points out, when a young woman gets an opportunity to speak to millions it is for only thirty seconds, and in that brief span of time she draws upon what she has learned in the training program rather than upon her own internal voice. These processes are embedded in larger Indian sociocultural trends that are tied to economic liberalization but have deeper roots in South Asian ways of thinking about women and their bodies.

## Femininity as Cultural Performance

In the morning, the woman feeds her husband and her kids, dresses the husband, the kids, sends them to office, to school, and gets back into bed, desperately fighting off inexplicable tears and feelings of low self esteem by immersing herself in the lives of *Page Three* people. Every one of them is thinner than her. That makes her feel even worse. After this, she showers, dresses and eats an egg white only omelet, drinks a cup of tea (no sugar, no milk), potters around the house attending to this, fixing that, dusting this, stocking up on that, all the while pretending to work on her novel-in-progress or prêt *salwar kameez* [a North Indian garment] collection. The rest of her day is spent screeching at the maid, re-re-organizing the linen cabinet and waiting for the evening when she can be of service again. In the meantime, she eats half a box of chocolate-coated caramels and does three personality tests in a women's magazine, left convinced that she is indeed a worthwhile human being. (*Femina Girl*, February 2003)

This passage is taken from a *Femina* article titled "The Fear of Freedom" (2003) that illustrates how different the lives of even most economically privileged Indian women are from the lives of what are commonly called "Page Three people." Such individuals (who include Miss India contestants) have their attendance at parties and other social events chronicled daily on the third page of the regional section of the *Times of India*. Particularly interesting is the way in which the passage positions the wealthy stay-at-home urban wife as a consumer of the images of Page Three people's lives: in finding that she simply does not measure up to them, she seeks (and fails) to emulate their thin bodies.

The sheer act of altering one's habits in order to reshape the body is a powerful statement because it entails both the consumption of an image and the attempt at the replication of that image onto the consuming party's own body. As part of a cultural performance of femininity, dieting becomes a means by which women can attempt to become more like their role models as they appear on Page Three. Much has been written about the way in which women are thought to contribute less to society in comparison to their husbands and partners, and in a world in which it is considered very normal for women to stay at home with their families even before they have children, women understandably deal with weighty issues surrounding self-esteem. Two solutions to this have presented themselves in Indian popular culture: the self-help book and degrees in what are viewed as "impractical" disciplines.

The notion that women need to cultivate themselves in order to compliment men's "practical" knowledge is widespread. As one woman noted about the male aversion to self-help books:

> Men don't read self-help books, just like men don't read books, because they like action better. They'd rather go out and do it than just read about it. All women read self-help books because they help you grow, and women really need to grow.

This positions men and women as opposites on a familiar continuum of gender in which women are passive and men are active. The assumption that women "need to grow," while men do not, directly implies that women are lesser than their male counterparts who do not require the assistance of a self-help book in order to improve themselves. As the bearers of cultural knowledge, women who are in a position to do so often pursue higher education in subjects that are thought to be impractical because they are not economically lucrative, such as English literature or sociology. "That's just like a hobby, reading books," sniffed one man at a dinner party I attended in honor of a woman's immense pride at receiving her master's in English literature. This sort of profound devaluation of female achievement is striking in the sense that it is so casual.

Yet femininity as cultural performance also takes on another fascinating form in Mumbai in the wearing of so-called skimpy clothes. Being scantily clad in the United States is often understood by feminists as a form of male domination, but being so in Mumbai is a symbol of independence and being "fashionable" for many young women. As a way of wearing modernity, clothing that exposes the body allows certain women to communicate their emancipation, however cursory, from cultural mores that insist women be covered. Modernity, it seems, does not wear many clothes, and wearing revealing garments is also a way of referencing a Western European and American way of life that many women believe to be liberating. This lifestyle is often seen as highly desirable and results in the condition of many women being in a state of permanently planning to move to either Western Europe or the United States. As one woman explained in the bathroom of a nightclub, "My uncle has this fabulous chateau in Switzerland, with a beautiful fireplace and all. Everyone keeps saying, 'Go, you'll be happy!', but I don't know. I just want to have some freedom, that's all." The desire to have "some freedom, that's all" is commonly voiced in Mumbai, and throughout the course of my research, it seemed that every semisuccessful woman I met was planning to permanently leave for a place that she described using the words "equality" and "independence."

This kind of language underscores how life for many women is conditional upon approval from male family members and, more broadly, a male-dominated society, as even the unemployed men who spend their spare time standing on the street dictate female movement with their lewd comments, lecherous stares, and singing of racy Hindi film songs.

My own comparative freedom in Mumbai made it a bit difficult to find female friends during the first few months of my research, because some women resented my ability to make decisions independent of my family. This kind of marginalization not only crosses the lines of class and ethnicity but continues throughout women's lives to shape their entire identities. As one Miss India organizer's spouse commented:

> The wealthiest people in Bombay [Mumbai] live in my building and every week I have a *mālisvālī* [masseuse] who comes to give me a massage, and she tells me stories about the other women. She says *"madam pūrā din palang meṅ baiṭhī hūī hain, tv dekh rāhē hain"* [Madame spends all day sitting in bed watching television]." That's all they do, once the children have left home and their husbands have lost interest in them because they're fat, then they fall apart. They do socialize, but in a very empty way, and their friends are just as depressed as they are.

This extremely vivid image of middle-aged women wasting away for lack of stimulation and love in their lives is sadly a common theme voiced by urban women. Many young women insisted to me that their mid-twenties was the only time that they had to enjoy themselves, because "once you get married, you have to have a baby, then you get fat, and no one wants you anymore," which positions women as useful and valuable only when they are young. This misogynist notion is part of a cultural system that clearly views women as objects of display rather than valuable contributors to society, a necessary condition for the existence of a pageant culture. Yet some young women contend that it is women themselves who allow such conditions to persist, and at least one female Miss India organizer who asked not to be identified by name insisted that Miss India contestants were simply perpetuating a flawed system of gender via their participation in the pageant.

The organizer closely questioned my views on beauty pageants and, upon discovering that I was extremely ambivalent toward them, told me she felt that the contestants were, in her words, "all whores." She observed:

> You must have noticed that most of them aren't really doing anything in life. They're lazy, they just want to get married to a rich man and be

pampered, but they don't want to work. They use these old men and the old men use them, that's how they live, and that's all they want.

In an extremely striking parallel between prostitution and partnering with an older man from a higher social class, the organizer underscored how social pressures often force young women to choose between compromising their values in order to possess the material things they want or alternatively remaining middle class their entire lives. Miss India offers an opportunity for women to achieve a certain degree of independence via social mobility in a space in which women are profoundly devalued both in popular culture and via the social structures that shape their lives. Although this is an extremely cursory and short-term freedom, the opportunity to develop one's own career based upon (perceived) merit rather than the social network of a family is not only absolutely unique in South Asia, but also a chance to profoundly transform individual lives.

**Miss India as a Life Transition**

Although participating in Miss India serves as a life transition in some way or another for all young women who participate, some experience the pageant as more of a testing ground for possible selves than others. Miss India can be seen as part of a cultural system involving class and gender that allows women to take extended periods of time away from remunerative activities, as it necessitates that contestants devote a substantial amount of time to the training program. It is still perfectly acceptable for all urban Indian women who have the means with which to do so to stay at home before they get married to help out with the family business or take classes in cooking or various other domestic art forms.

Miss India can provide social mobility even for young women who do not seriously want to pursue a career as an actress or model because it grants them access to a wider social network in which they are able to consider relationships, including marriage, with men from a higher social class. Beauty still acts as the ultimate form of female currency in the South Asian marriage market, and as the primary source for the validation of beauty, participating in Miss India situates young women as the most desirable partners for men.

*Femina* editor Sathya Saran underscored this point particularly well during the course of a conversation we had about how the pageant has changed over time. As she described how Miss India was transformed when *Femina* magazine underwent a radical change to a color glossy format in 1994, she was adamant that the pageant is a vehicle of unparalleled transformative powers, observing, "We discovered that we had a very powerful tool in the pageant to build an image of the magazine, and to launch young women into life. Earlier it was only to launch them into the glamour world or into good marriages." Saran's casual linkage of "the glamour world" with "good marriages" illustrates how both are seen as the best that life can offer to young women.

It is perfectly acceptable in India for women to stay at home with their families both before and after marriage rather than cultivating a career, and so Miss India is a means for young women who only want to get married to improve their chances of meeting a partner from a more affluent background. Perhaps nothing illustrates the sheer degree of social mobility that Miss India confers upon contestants than the stamp of approval they receive from participating in the pageant. This raises serious issues surrounding class, which came to the fore again and again during the course of interviews I conducted with contestants who saw the pageant as a life transition. Although I had to question some of them more than once before they admitted that not everyone can participate equally in the pageant, contestants were usually rather forthcoming about the social inequalities that are endemic both in India and, by extension, Miss India.

Contestant Nalini Dutta noted that, "you do need a little financial backing to enter, because if you are worried about eating, then you can't spend time doing this." Although Miss India does offer social mobility, it does so only to the middle and upper-middle-class young women who, as Nalini succinctly put it, are not "worried about eating." Indeed, most of the contestants were fairly privileged in terms of English language education and the ability to devote at least a month of time to the pageant. Of all the contestants who participated in 2003, Diana was the most representative of young women who enter Miss India as part of a life transition. Not particularly interested in a career of her own, Diana worked with her mother at the travel agency they own together, and her father was a chartered accountant. She had never modeled or participated in a pageant before, and she entered Miss India on a whim. Diana described Miss India as her opportunity to experience a world she does not normally have access to. "I wanted an element of change and excitement in my life," she said, "I saw the ad and said, 'this is my chance to do something different before marriage.'"

This opportunity to do "something different" can mean the world to a young woman in her early twenties in a culture that does not do a great deal to encourage beautiful young women to cultivate themselves intellectually, as they often receive cultural and familial messages that their beauty is currency enough for the world. A less-mentioned form of marginalization, beauty often works against women throughout the world in much the same fashion, as beautiful women, after all, are not supposed to be intelligent. In true Indian beauty queen style, Diana said that her only goal in life was to make positive changes through "education and the upliftment of slums," a superficially noble cause that was shared by a number of contestants. Beauty queens are expected to choose topics that are curiously perceived as apolitical in India, such as poverty or education, as part of a larger culture of female charity that is pervasive among women who do not work for an income outside the home.

The charity group is largely the realm of economically privileged women in urban India, if only for the reason that they have the largest amount of time and money to devote to charity causes. Such women learn to present a public image of caring for those who are less fortunate than themselves, as doing charity work displays one's class status due to the fact that devoting a significant amount of time to a social cause is a luxury that women who have extensive child care or employment responsibilities simply cannot afford. Although gendered charity work is not unique to South Asia, in India it functions both to create a social network for privileged women to pass their time and to demonstrate their class status. Miss India's focus on charity work highlights the way in which femininity at the pageant is a cultural performance that incorporates broader cultural discourses about class and the perceived responsibility of privileged women to serve as role models to the poor.

This sort of cultural performance is definitely learned long before most young women get to the pageant phase of their lives. I led a conversation about social class with fifteen-year-old female students at the private Alexandra School for Girls in Mumbai and was a bit surprised by the way in which the young women made sense of their relationship to poor people. One young woman described the sense of emotional fortitude necessary to live with the ubiquity of inequality in India in a rather disturbing way:

> In the train, you know, you identify with them sometimes. My mother was talking to this one girl, telling her to go away and stop begging, and she was just my age and a prostitute and she had a baby. It just upset me so much that I started crying and my Mom slapped me and said, "Don't cry, because if you start crying in this country, you'll never stop."

Charity work helps privileged women to negotiate the divide between the comfort in their own lives and the deprivation that exists among people who live on the streets outside their homes; how well they actually do this in practice, however, is a different story. As I sat in on a session of the charity group Akanksha (Sunrise), a group that voluntarily educates disadvantaged children by utilizing the classrooms of private schools after the school day has finished, I was struck by the classist nature of the dialogue led by women who were not able to successfully transcend the divide between themselves and those they work for via the charity group.

One session was led by a young woman who had just finished her master's at an American university, who began by telling the seven-year-old children in her group how important boiled water is for health. As she explained to them that they must drink ten glasses of boiled water a day, she revealed her lack of knowledge about how expensive the gas necessary to boil so much water for a child's consumption would be for an impoverished family in an informal housing settlement. Despite the ineffectiveness of many charity groups, most women who belonged to them insisted that membership was a necessary part of being a good human

9. *Miss World reinforces gendered associations of women with children and family through her occasional social service activities. In this image, Aishwarya Rai appears with her mother (center), who smiles approvingly.*

being. A stay-at-home mother who became involved in a group that educates underprivileged young women was quick to note that the inequality that is so pervasive in urban India makes charity work a necessity by saying, "You're growing up with the haves and the have-nots, and you should know what you have, and what the others are lacking. It should be part of your life." That charity work is personally enriching for women is self-evident, yet it is also crucial to note the way in which charity groups serve as a social network for many women.

Most economically privileged women do not work for an income, and so they are put in the position of either socializing with their friends from school or college or making new ones in order to fill their time. The charity group serves as an excellent means by which to make new friends, as well as to announce one's social status, and in addition to this charity groups can also be a great deal of fun, although they may not actually benefit anyone except the women who participate. Ever alert to the intricacies of social class in urban India, socialite and newspaper columnist Shobhaa De observed that

> starting December, all the heavy-duty *cause-wallahs* [leaders of "social causes"] get into overdrive. The weather is conducive to staging outdoor events. Socialites want to show off their latest Shahtoosh shawls. . . . However, I'm pretty sure power ladies flocked to the venue to gorge on gourmet nibbles and feel better about themselves after leaving a generous "tip" for the orphans/flood victims/girl-child/lepers/mentally disadvantaged. Designer charity is here to stay. (De, 1999, 6)

Charity groups thus serve a dual purpose in functioning first as social events for the wealthy and secondarily as actual assistance to the disadvantaged. Similar to the way in which charity work grounds women in the reality of India by situating them in a custodial relationship to it, Miss India contestants are quick to stress how they have a responsibility to be role models. Diana was quick to stress how normal she is, and how this makes young women who would not be able to compete in Miss India admire her:

> Girls draw inspiration from us once they learn we are from the same background as they are. We were chatting on the Internet the other day with some girls, and they all said that we inspire them. We're all very simple girls from the same typical Indian families with similar social values.

Diana's statement works to subvert the concept that beauty is inherently a mark of female superiority, a notion itself representative of the pageant culture that is so pervasive in India.

However, the fact remains that the contestants are anything but normal Indian young women. Shruti, an aspiring model and final year psychology student from Delhi, was nervous that other students at her college would be "in awe" of her after the pageant. Her use of the word "awe" shows just how iconic the contestants are to their peers. It is perhaps because of this high regard for contestants that Parvati skipped the beginning of her MBA program to take part in the pageant. When I asked her why she had chosen to participate in Miss India, she laughed a little and said, "I just wanted to prove to myself that I could be the best." In Parvati's case, the pageant served as something of a validating mechanism, and she was emphatic that she did not expect to be selected for the pageant: "Being called to preliminaries was a huge thing for me. I didn't know if my pictures would be good enough, because they were next to pictures from professional models. I'm really surprised they called me for this." Parvati's worry over whether her ordinary pictures would be "good enough" points to how the pageant is an enormous self-esteem boost to young women who are not professionally established models or actresses.

Miss India still serves as a powerful tool with which to navigate the social world even for the young women who do not explicitly seek to use the pageant as a means to enter the world of media. Family life in India requires that women serve as the social barometers of family honor, and the carefully cultivated veneer of "women's empowerment" and concepts such as charity work serve to make the pageant wholesome enough that its display of physical beauty does not take on undesirable sexual overtones. The seclusion of the training program makes the pageant acceptable to more conservative families because although female seclusion is certainly not socially mandated among the upper-middle-class families that contestants typically come from, it is still a reality of life for them in practice. Young women are rarely accorded the same freedoms of movement and choice that their brothers and male peers are, and so while such women may not be in formal seclusion, numerous social monitoring mechanisms still serve to restrict them. As Ring (2003) points out in her discussion of women in *pardā* in Karachi, seclusion serves as a social shield between the self and the larger world that functions to reduce the possibility for behaviors that are not socially sanctioned. Such seclusion at the training program serves as incontrovertible proof of the moral integrity of the contestants whose behavior is so carefully monitored.

*Pardā* as it is practiced in the rural Indian context "demands that married women, both Hindu and Muslim, of families that seek high status or good reputations remain secluded" (Gold 1994, 53). Such a practice affects all aspects of life, as it effectively removes all of the middle- and upper-class females from public space, and scholars (e.g., Mernissi 1985; Paul

1992) have noted how architecture, employment, and basic infrastructural services must develop around the reality that an entire segment of the population does not frequent public space. Women's potential contributions to public life in such a system are sacrificed in order to increase family prestige and honor, known as *izzat*, as part of a moral economy in which one's actions are never free of gendered implications (Wadley 1994).

Such a moral economy is clearly at work at Miss India, where young women's seclusion at the training program also takes place under the watchful eyes of the experts and chaperones. The contestants emerge from the pageant's training program not only as potential actresses and models, but also as socialites who can increase male prestige in ways in which ordinary upper-middle-class women cannot. If Miss India contestants make desirable marriage partners, it is in no small part due to the way in which the training program so carefully cultivates them as paragons of Indian femininity.

PART THREE | *Globalization*

# Structural Adjustment and "International Standards"

## Structural Adjustment and the Culture of Experts

> For a long time in this country, because the women had not evolved, I don't remember honestly whether past Miss Indias met with any success. In 1991, the then-government decided to deregulate the economy and then Star TV and a slew of other channels came in. Previously, exposure was restricted to those who traveled abroad, but through TV it was broad based, so people started developing faster and aspiring for more.

$\mathcal{Q}\mathcal{G}$ ampark communications consultant Malati Puranik, who worked in public relations for the Miss India 2003 pageant, positioned the postliberalization entertainment revolution as part of a linear path toward a sort of national development. This fascinating rhetoric of evolution was consistently espoused by pageant officials, contestants, and popular culture as well as individuals I spoke to who were unconnected to the pageant. In Puranik's estimation, economic deregulation and the influx of satellite television allowed for increased economic aspirations on the part of the urban middle class:

> After the economy opened up, people started shopping all the time rather than just at festival times, because they desired to look better. Earlier Miss Indias had made it near the top, but in those days no one

cared about beauty, but when Madhu Sapre missed the crown by a whisker in 1992 that was the turning point. So, the *Times of India* decided to try harder.

Puranik's insistence that "no one cared about beauty" before economic liberalization is particularly interesting, mostly because it is patently untrue. South Asian women have always been inordinately concerned with beauty and even in the most remote villages women know dozens of recipes for herbal skin and hair care products that can be made in the home. The difference lies in the kind of beauty that Puranik is referring to, namely, the expensive kind that results from using chemical preparations made by foreign companies. This underscores the kind of real, as well as symbolic, capital required to win an international pageant, as Puranik's underlying message is that exposure to white European standards of beauty is necessary for this "evolution" to take place.

It is in response to this perceived need to cultivate what pageant officials called "international standards" that the *Times of India* began the training program that is described in detail in chapter 3. Puranik extended the discussion of the training program to include the complete reconstruction of young women's bodies:

> The *Times of India* decided to institutionalize the training process with a regime of diet, because in India we have a different bone structure. So, if you want to compete on an international level, you need to change yourself. People are very different every fifty kilometers here, so you need to regularize beauty. If we want to get people to conform to international standards, we need to work toward a healthier body and spirit, which is where the trainers took over. It's education, a mind shift.

The concept of regularizing beauty is both frightening and fascinating, as it speaks to deep-seated concerns voiced by critics of globalization. Although it is one thing to talk about standardizing business practices along international lines, it is another entirely to casually mention that female beauty needs to, in Puranik's words, "conform to international standards."

The Miss India pageant was consistently positioned throughout the 2003 process as a part of India's evolution in a trajectory toward development. A contestant from the Western Indian state of Goa who left the training program early due to illness insisted that "this is a stage countries go through" in response to my question about why pageants are such a sensation in urban India, but not in the countries that India regards as "developed." Indeed, the discourse of progress informed nearly everyone's discussion of the pageant and what it means to live in urban India. Samantha Kocchar, a hair and beauty expert at the pageant, noted that because long hair was back in fashion in the United States, "Now we're on parallel lines with the west."

This rhetoric of evolution closely mirrored Gupta's (1998) assertion that "underdevelopment" has become a form of identity in India. Although his work focused on a village in Uttar Pradesh and my own on one of the most privileged and exclusive spaces in urban India, I found striking similarities between the two, as the entire pageant was geared toward winning an international title that would serve as a form of validation for the nation at large. As former Miss World Yukta Mookhey mentioned in the course of a discussion we had over lunch, "India has an advantage at international pageants because everyone looks for Miss India. She goes there to say, 'look, I come from a slummy country and here I am! I'm going to wear my saris and win!'" Yukta's use of "a slummy country" to describe India highlights the sense of inferiority that many Indians feel vis-à-vis Western Europe and the United States. This results from an extremely complex process that involves, in brief, British colonialism, the regime of "development" that followed on the part of industrialized nations, and the postliberalization influx of images into popular culture of an urban lifestyle that the average urban Indian cannot afford.

Yet perhaps this is the reason why winning Miss Universe or Miss World is so important in India. As a space of national validation that is glamorous in the same way as the images on satellite television, winning Miss Universe seems to position India on a pathway to "development" in the eyes of many urban Indians. The Miss India pageant has sent contestants to participate in Miss Universe and Miss World since 1964, and although Indian Reita Faria became Miss World in 1966, the rest of India's winners emerged only after liberalization. "International standards" can also be oppressive, and although contestants were clear that it probably was not fair that the vast majority of Indian women cannot meet the five feet six inch height requirement and are barred from competing as a result of this rule, they were also adamant that the choice of taller women was necessary if India was to win. One contestant was especially vehement in her insistence, noting that "a normal Indian girl can't compete with someone who is six [feet] two [inches tall] and towering over her, so at Miss Universe, we need to be global."

If being Miss Universe means being "global," one wonders just whose "global" standards are being employed. It seems that in India the mutual exclusivity that height and beauty share has everything to do with the way in which ramp models are always over five feet six inches tall. As part of a frighteningly overzealous desire to embody what are essentially white European standards of beauty, the vast majority of Indian women are unable to measure up to what are fairly unrealistic standards. The rhetoric of evolution espoused by Puranik and others places even beauty on a path toward "development," positioning it as something that can be created with assistance from those who are sufficiently equipped with appropriate cultural knowledge. The following "recipe" for a successful Miss World contestant featured in the *Times of India* ascribes nearly all of the credit to the experts at the training program:

**"Making Miss World: Ingredients" (1996)**

A suburban Bombay-ite [Mumbai-ite]
The *Femina* Miss India pageant for marination
The essence of a diet, á la Anjali Mukherjee
A powder blue concoction from Hemant Trevedi
Large helpings of Mickey Mehta workouts
Dermatologist Jamuna Pai's skincare, peeled to perfection
Finely grated talk by the high priestess of politesse Sabira Merchant
A dash of timely marketing
Swarovsky to sprinkle
Sundry advice (optional)

The contestant herself contributes rather little to the process of becoming Miss World in this "recipe"; rather, it is "the experts" who do the majority of the work by sculpting her into the ideal of what Miss World should be. The initial ingredient of an anonymous "suburban Bombay-ite" is followed by a list of the names of the experts in a rather snide reference to the enormous class divide that exists between a young woman from the suburbs and the South Mumbai-dwelling experts.

It is precisely this class difference that allows for social mobility on the part of the Miss India contestants at the pageant, and as Mareesha mentioned, "Even if you don't win, you gain something, so it's not a wasted effort. You make so many contacts, by the end of it you have fifteen different options—serials, ramp, whatever." Mareesha's statement points to how the training program gives contestants the opportunity to create a social network that allows them to enter numerous fields in media. India is so socially stratified that building such a network would ordinarily be impossible for a young woman from a middle-class background. Citing the benefits that simply participating in the training program provides to young women, Mareesha underscored how Miss India acts as a gateway to social mobility.

The culture of celebrity that positions those known as "the experts" as authorities on everything from their actual field to the future of India is largely the result of economic liberalization, which necessitated the development of a group of individuals who could incorporate international trends into an urban Indian context. The experts are treated with deference and positioned as sophisticated individuals of the highest caliber both at the pageant and in popular culture at large. The panel of experts who comprised the 2003 training staff was not significantly different from the list of celebrities and individuals well known in the field of media in Mumbai in years past. They are chosen to impart knowledge to the contestants through the culture of experts that pageant officials see as crucial to the training program and at the 2003 pageant the experts included a fashion designer, dermatologist, dietician, trichologist, two hair stylists, makeup artist, self-styled "grooming expert," personal trainer, cosmetic dental surgeon, spiritual guide, diction coach, head of an art foundation, and photographer.

The larger-than-life nature of the people designated as experts is overwhelming in urban India, and most of these individuals have been part of the training program for so many years that they are cited in the press for their opinion on everything from lifestyle to women's rights, and they form part of a new postliberalization elite who are role models for what the urban Indian is supposed to aspire to be like. When I worked for *Femina* and the editor would ask me to find out "how prominent people feel" about a certain issue, it would invariably be the experts whom I would contact to solicit their opinions.

Being an expert brings with it a variety of privileges and responsibilities, the most striking of which is the right to be exceedingly impolite without cause, and fashion designer Ritu Kumar, who designs some of the clothing the contestants wear at the pageant, is an excellent example of this. Because she is known for her temperament as well as her elaborately embroidered saris, choreographer and designer Hemant Trevedi had to warn the contestants to be polite to Kumar by saying, "Ritu Kumar may not be the warmest person in the world, but that does not mean you give her any bad vibes. Be gracious, as she is our most senior and respected designer." As an expert, all those who were not experts were expected to defer to her behavior, regardless of whether it was appropriate or not.

This is reminiscent of the guru system, which positions those with specialized knowledge in an exalted position to be unconditionally honored by those who seek to gain the same knowledge. In an extremely interesting case of cultural extension, then, Miss India contestants treat the experts in much the same way that religious scholars treat their teachers. The benefit in the end, of course, is the enormous social network each contestant will receive, as well as the skill set that will enable them to deal with each expert and possibly even to become one in the future.

The contestants are consistently reminded of how they should behave toward the experts, sometimes even by other experts themselves. As makeup artist Cory Walia explained to the contestants during a session that he conducted, one must never presuppose that one has knowledge that the expert does not, even if it concerns oneself. "Do not tell the makeup artist what suits you," he insisted, "that person is a professional, so you will end up in tears and may even get a slap."

Over and again, I watched one particular pageant organizer chastise the contestants for their behavior; during the auditions for the Miss Talent title to be performed at the final pageant, she snapped at a contestant who in her opinion was giggling too much, "You're a *Femina* Miss India contestant now, and you need to behave like one! Be more ladylike." The organizer's harsh tone made the contestant, who had been under an enormous amount of strain throughout the previous week of training, start to cry. For one month, the contestants' lives are controlled and dictated by the experts; from skin care to diction to diet to spirituality, the training is designed to provide what *Femina* consistently describes as "a comprehensive crash course in life." Of course, the kind of life that the training program prepares young women for is one that revolves around physical appearance, and although the body and diet were consistent points of attention, the most striking focus was on skin color.

I sat in on weekly individual sessions that dermatologist Jamuna Pai held with the contestants in order to examine their skin. Every single one of the young women at the 2003 pageant was taking some sort of medication to alter their skin, particularly in color. In a disturbingly casual manner, Pai emphasized the need for all the contestants to bleach their skin by prescribing the peeling agent Retin-A as well as glycolic acid and, in the case of isolated dark patches, a laser treatment. I asked Pai, who trained as a plastic surgeon in London, why fair skin was such a concern at the pageant and she offered the following explanation.

> Fair skin is really an obsession with us, it's a fixation. Even with the fairest of the fair, they feel they want to be fairer. I feel it's ingrained in us. When an Indian man looks for a bride, he wants one who is tall, fair and slim, and fairer people always get jobs first. We still lighten their skin here because it gives the girls extra confidence when they go abroad.

In the name of "extra confidence," the contestants undergo chemical peels and daily medications, some of which have rather unpleasant side effects. Harsimrat, for example, often complained to the doctor that she felt nauseous and weak as a result of the medication prescribed to lighten her darker South Indian skin.

The contestants also received vitamin supplements to make their skin appear healthier. These did not always work, and in one contestant's case Pai sighed and said, "I'm giving you ten multivitamins, but you're still not glowing. I'm afraid that the only solution is to eat more." The notion of being "afraid" to tell a contestant to eat more and that contestant actually looking concerned at the prospect of having to do so in order to make her skin appear healthier partially reveals the impact of a cultural system and an institution that combine to position women's bodies as never quite beautiful enough.

As part of the project of constructing the Miss India body, the contestants were given a diet designed by nutritionist Anjali Mukherjee, best known in Mumbai for her weight loss centers and line of packaged health foods. Mukherjee used a combination of allopathy and traditional Indian Ayurveda to advise each young woman on how to eat to suit one's constitution. Interestingly, her description of the diet plan to contestants sounded much like the concept of the body as a machine, as she noted that "the blood becomes purer and cleaner with the diet that we're giving, and your machinery is working better with it. The body is like a car that needs servicing, it's that simple." Mukherjee's use of a vehicular metaphor to describe the body is particularly apt in the case of the training program, as in her conception of diet each young woman needs to improve the "machinery" of her body. Like Mukherjee's concept of the car, each contestant's body is envisioned as a machine whose functioning can be improved under the guidance of the experts.

The question of how thin is thin enough remained with me throughout the pageant. Although many of the young women were already slightly underweight when they tried out for the pageant, this was not necessarily the result of disordered eating. I watched at least two young women clearly struggle throughout the training program with anorexia that no one attended to, despite the recognition by other contestants that these young women needed help with their eating patterns. Neither the pageant nor the experts encouraged the development of disordered eating in any way, but the atmosphere of competition and surveillance at the training program certainly did. Watching the anorexic contestants in particular silently evaluate who was the thinnest of all the young women made me constantly aware of the power of the gaze to mold the female body. Perhaps because of my consistent concern with what the contestants were eating, Mukherjee was quick to note that the contestants were being adequately nourished when I asked her how she defined ideal body weight. Although she noted that "ideal body weight has a range," she curiously described that range in terms of the four to twelve pounds each young woman needed to lose. It is important to note, however, that there was one contestant who was put on a weight gain diet after Mukherjee deemed her fourteen pounds underweight when she entered the training program.

Mukherjee's diet plan combined with exercise routines designed by personal trainer Mickey Mehta in the project of creating the Miss India body. Mehta led the contestants through a two-hour exercise routine that began at seven A.M. every morning and mainly involved aerobic exercise, which allows the body to maintain a lithe form without building up muscle. Unusually focused on the totality of being, Mehta took a spiritual approach to fitness that made use of an eclectic and syncretistic cocktail of different beliefs:

> I take what I like from different religions. Dao, Tao, Zen, yoga, my focus is on holism. I don't believe in branded spirituality. I believe in oneness, everything is just one. When a person looks into the mirror and sees herself and not an illusion, she is deluded. The lotus is the illusion, mud is the reality. This has nothing to do with weight loss—a beautiful body is a body that is in proportion, not a thin body.

Mehta's charismatic mélange of spiritual beliefs is fascinating, but the fact remains that Mehta's job is to cultivate thin bodies rather than spiritually pure beings. When I questioned him further about his views on the kind of body he was being asked to help engineer for the contestants, he confessed that this body was a prerequisite for the world of media. Mehta characterized thinness as something of a necessary evil, noting, "I think that some of them are too thin, but that's not me, that's the demands of the line of work that they're getting into after this. . . . Some girls were so huge around the hips that they needed to lose weight;

otherwise they would look out of place and probably spoil the show for the other girls." As an actively involved participant from the beginning of the pageant, I was conscious of the fact that there were never any young women who were, in Mehta's words, "huge around the hips." All of the young women who tried out for Miss India were of normal weight, and many of them had been underweight before they even came to the training program.

As we walked around the grounds of the hotel where the contestants were getting ready to begin their exercise routine for the morning, Mehta pointed to Swetha, who went on to win the Miss India–Earth title, as an example of someone who had worked very hard. Swetha was slumped against a pillar and clearly exhausted when Mehta congratulated her on the eight pounds she had lost in two weeks. She smiled and thanked him before dozing off again, trying to catch a bit more sleep before her morning run began.

Other young women also seemed perpetually exhausted because most were trying to lose weight in order to improve their chances of winning, and almost none of them were consuming enough calories to sustain a schedule that demanded sixteen hours of active participation each day. As a result, it was never much of a surprise to see physically exhausted young women propped against chairs near the end of the day. Yet this effort was highly rewarded, contextualized as it was within the rhetoric of achievement, and Mehta noted with pride that it was the young women who worked the hardest to lose weight who often went on to win:

> The ones who keep working hard despite everything are the ones who win. I've seen many such girls. I worked the hardest with [Miss World 1997] Diana Hayden, who lost almost fifteen kilos [thirty-three pounds], and then there was [Miss World 1999] Yukta Mookhey, who was so huge that people just wrote her off completely, but during the training she worked so hard she lost twelve kilos [twenty-six pounds] and then on her way to Miss World she lost more.

Mehta's association of weight loss with hard work is part of the interesting language of Miss India, where young woman "work hard" to become underweight and use their "confidence" to answer largely vapid questions while simultaneously aspiring to "represent India" at events that privilege white European standards of beauty.

Mehta softened the obvious imperative to lose weight with his use of spirituality and was insistent that "we are not looking at FTV here, because we are looking at women who will make changes and be positive." In his reference to the Hong Kong–based Star TV network's Fashion Television (FTV) channel, which broadcasts twenty-four-hour footage of fashion shows around the world, Mehta describes the training program as set apart from the purely superficial world of modeling. He situated the cultivation of spirituality as essential in order to do well at the pageant:

> People can go paranoid about winning the crown. The primary drive for them is to make it big, but after they meet me, they may think they should become nuns. Some of them don't like meditation, and they just mediate on winning the crown, but I tell them that spirituality with intent is not spirituality.

If Mickey Mehta used spirituality to distinguish himself from other fitness professionals, other experts used the language of science in order to explain their role in the pageant. Apoorva Shah billed himself as the only certified trichologist in India, a dubious distinction that qualified him as a member of the team of experts whose opinions are consistently cited in the press. Despite its rather scientific-sounding name, trichology simply refers to the ability to examine the condition of the hair and scalp under a machine that resembles a large microscope. Its recent popularity in urban India is related to a culture of foreign authority that continues to position American and Western European technology and commodities as superior to their Indian counterparts.

In a fascinating link between science and the construction of beauty, Shah described how the use of the sonographic trichometer, a small tube that contains a microscope that allowed him to view the condition of the patient's hair and scalp, was an absolute necessity. He explained, "If you have a heart problem, you go to a cardiologist and if you have a hair problem, you should go to a trichologist." In positioning a heart problem and a hair care problem in the same category, Shah posited that beauty is as important as health. Shah described how trichology is a science supposedly pioneered with funding from NASA and then provided a perplexed coterie of reporters with a demonstration of how the sonographic trichometer worked by grouping each contestant into one of three groups: maintenance, SOS, and red SOS, each with its own corresponding level of treatment. Nupur and her perfectly healthy hair were prescribed three months of multivitamins and a diet rich in hair foods such as spinach, dairy products, and almonds, after which she turned to the reporters' cameras and gushed, "I thought that I could never talk to anyone about my awful hair problem before, and now Dr. Shah has fixed it!" Nupur's enthusiastic assertion in front of the television cameras demonstrates how the experts enjoy an enormous amount of press coverage and free advertising from their participation in the pageant.

Every expert was very clear about the role he or she had to play in helping the contestants. Hair stylists Jawed Habib and Samantha Kocchar noted: "Our role is to prepare contestants for the future, because most of them are going into the glamour line, and this is essential for them, because sometimes they have to do their own hair and makeup." Kocchar started working in her mother Blossom's Delhi salon after she returned from a beauty school in Chicago in her early teens, and later was creative director for the Indo-American film *Monsoon Wedding,* and Habib was the most well-known hair stylist in India at the time of the pageant. Both Kocchar and Habib are proof that beauty is serious business; she as the spokesperson for Sunsilk shampoo, and he as the official endorser of L'Oreal hair color in India. "No one gets up in the morning and does *pūja* or *namāz*," Habib observed using the appropriate terms for Hindu and Muslim forms of prayer, "first you look in the mirror and try to worship you." Habib's equation of the cultivation of beauty with daily religious observations is particularly apt in this case.

Although I made sure to attend most of the training sessions, those conducted by former Delta Airlines flight attendant and etiquette expert Rukhshana Eisa were by far the most interesting, as well as entertaining in a way that almost mocked the urban Indian admiration of all things American and Western European. Eisa used the symbolic capital that being a flight attendant in India continues to command as a way to teach the contestants etiquette in addition to her responsibilities as head of her own grooming school, called Image Incorporated.

In a style characterized by a series of exhortations for proper behavior that often began with "you should" and "you must never," she advised the contestants on how to conduct themselves in a variety of social situations. Eisa was clear that the information she provided was absolutely essential for the contestants and that "this is important for the girls, because our own culture doesn't teach these things . . . after this they'll be able to sit with diplomats and heads of state and know what to do." Eisa's emphasis on teaching the contestants manners that are foreign to most urban Indians initially seemed simply a bit odd, but the reality that young women needed to learn an entirely new culture in order to effectively compete became increasingly clear as they struggled to remember the complexities of Western European table manners and waltzes.

The ability of the contestants to articulately answer questions was considered equally important, and so for nearly three hours each day the young women sat in chairs around a ramp that faced pageant choreographer Hemant Trevedi and his conspicuously placed microphone. Trevedi advised them on how to improve their responses as they answered questions I had written for them, and when contestants did not answer quickly enough, he commented, "When you hesitated, it showed you were unsure, which also makes me unsure about your sincerity." As contestants tried to answer questions about which person they most admired and what their views on subjects as diverse as abortion and reincarnation were in an apolitical, audience-pleasing manner, I saw how difficult it is to present views that seem to be the products of an independent thinking woman but are in fact platitudes that will not offend anyone. Kaveri often answered questions exceptionally well, and named Hillary Clinton as the woman she most admired "because she's a paragon of love, power and strength even though she's had a disastrous personal life." By naming Clinton, who so clearly reaffirmed patriarchal values by staying married to her philandering husband, as a role model, Kaveri answered the question perfectly in the context of the pageant: she named a woman in a nonthreatening position of power as a result of her marriage who had sacrificed in order to keep her family together. Trevedi was extremely happy with this answer, and said, "It's correct not to be specific about her problems."

The very formation of their sentences and the tone of voice in which they were spoken was also the subject of daily sessions for the contestants. Sabira Merchant was employed by the pageant as a diction coach to teach the contestants how to cultivate an accent that is a combination of British inflections and American usage that is generally marked as high status in urban India. These diction and pronunciation lessons were conducted separately from those led by Trevedi and Ahuja, but it was understood that each contestant would use knowledge gained from interaction with all of the experts in order to improve her overall performance in individual sessions. In addition to the other experts, several past Miss India winners were called in to speak to contestants about how to win. These young women were accorded the greatest amount of attention by the contestants, who often requested to pose for photographs with the past winners after sessions were finished. Positioned as the ultimate authorities on how to win, the contestants were absolutely absorbed by the advice of international pageant winners.

Miss World 1999 Yukta Mookhey worked as a consultant throughout the pageant and spent two hours advising the contestants on the amount of work they should put into both themselves and the pageant, noting that "there is never enough, so compare yourself to yourself and think 'I can do better than that.' Here you are just twenty-six, and there are ninety-four girls at an international pageant." Positioned as the ultimate role model for the contestants, Mookhey was clear that the competition would become even tougher at the international level. The rhetoric of achievement and hard work evinced by Mookhey ran through the entire pageant; young women were consistently and implicitly advised, whether in the form of medication to lighten their skin, exercise to make them thinner, or classes to change their accents, that they were simply not good enough.

The Miss India training program serves as a site in which young women are able to decide their futures, or at least expand their options in terms of media-related careers in exchange for participation in an extremely emotionally taxing training program that involves a rigorous sixteen-hour schedule each day and constant, unrelenting supervision of each young woman's behavior. During one of my first meetings with pageant officials to discuss the research for this book, I was asked to help determine what the judging process should be like in light of the 2003 pageant's focus on impartiality. One official was especially adamant about the need to define standards:

> We need to know what the pageant judging procedure should be like. If we are judging beauty, what is beauty? If we are judging poise, what is poise? What is a normal or abnormal breast size? What defines stage presence, or a good figure? What defines an evening gown?

Although I managed to avoid participating in the production of the 2003 pageant's definitions of beauty, these questions left me in the uncomfortable position of trying to determine answers for myself. Certain basic criteria for beauty in India such as fair skin and straight hair are so entrenched that they are virtual symbols of the preference for Northern features that pervade the subcontinent and as such, judging beauty at Miss India is a thousand times more problematic than, for example, evaluating performance at a sporting event. With its implicit connotations of subjectivity and transience, the concept of judging beauty is inherently problematic, as what is actually being judged is the ability of contestants to fit neatly into the preset mold of Miss India. The concept of how a Miss India should look is very clear and is not open to much negotiation, as pictures of winners since the pageant's inception in 1959 reveal women who are all light-skinned and slim. This disturbing continuity in appearance prompted a Mumbai-based friend of mine to remark, "What is Indian about any of them? They all look like European girls with a tan."

The 2003 pageant was no exception to these standards. Only one contestant had naturally curly hair, which made her stand out among the twenty-five others who, if their hair was not naturally straight, used a heated iron to flatten out their curls. Two of the contestants were what matrimonial advertisements in urban India would characterize as "wheatish" in complexion, a description that connotes a darker skin tone that resembles the color of whole wheat bread. Sadly, these women spent an inordinate amount of time concerned about their skin color and invariably mentioned it as a hindrance whenever we spoke about their chances of winning. These standards of beauty have combined with the precedent set by past winners to create something of a Miss India prototype in popular culture. The contestants who did not fit this mold were painfully aware of this fact throughout the training program and often felt that they received less attention than young women with lighter skin and longer hair. Purva observed, "You saw it yourself when we went to the Amby Valley. The photographers from the press only wanted to take pictures of the girls who look like Miss India, all fair and tall with long, straight hair." In summarizing what it feels like not to fit in with her concise description of "girls who look like Miss India," Purva from the small city of Pune perfectly described the Miss India prototype. Not a striking beauty by Indian standards with either long hair or very fair skin, she clearly was made to feel that she does not fit the model of what a Miss India should be.

The practice of evaluating female beauty is extremely widespread and commonplace throughout India, but it is the question of how and by whom beauty is evaluated that reveals key elements that construct the discourse surrounding appearance for women.

## Setting Standards: Ernst and Young

As a part of pageant organizer A. P. Parigi's plan to position and conduct the pageant along international lines, he appointed Mumbai branch of the New York accounting firm Ernst and Young to act as consultants throughout the entire pageant process and to tabulate the results. Ernst and Young has tabulated the results for Miss Universe for the past twenty-six years, and as a means of emulating standards, pageant officials could not have chosen a more appropriate firm. Parigi insisted that a three-year contract between Miss India and Ernst and Young would "enable the organizers of the pageant to institutionalize the selection process and make it more independent and prestigious."

Appointing Ernst and Young as consultants for the pageant served to add an international character to the rhetoric of "standards." The concept of using international standards to evaluate beauty was further complicated by the insistence of the two Ernst and Young employees who served as consultants throughout the 2003 pageant process that it is impossible to judge beauty objectively. After receiving a great deal of advice from the Ernst and Young office in New York that handles the Miss Universe pageant, both consultants were very clear that Miss India "is not an objective evaluation of beauty, it is a recording of a subjective evaluation of beauty."

I attended a meeting in the early stages of the pageant between former Miss World Yukta Mookhey and the two Ernst and Young accountants in which the subject of discussion was how to increase the international credibility of Miss India. Mookhey stressed the need to choose young women who are similar to international pageant winners from India's chief competitor, Venezuela:

> Get girls who are as tall as possible to increase our chances, five [feet] eight [inches tall] plus, because during the pageants, Venezuelans are six [feet] two [inches tall] without heels and Indian girls will just get lost. Make sure that the girls can walk in four to six inches of high heels, because there are one hundred girls at Miss World, and they need to be able to carry that off.

Mookhey's insistence that "Indian girls will just get lost" in the image she painted of Venezuelan women of Amazonian proportions points to the tendency at Miss India to choose only those examples of national beauty that simulate international images of beauty. This illustrates how Western European and American beauty culture has profoundly altered standards of beauty in urban India, as the prevailing logic at Miss India was that if beautiful women in other countries that won pageants were tall, then Indian women should also be tall.

Mookhey was very specific throughout the meeting about what types of women should be invited for the selection rounds in Bangalore, Delhi, and Mumbai and recommended that each of the five judges make what she called "a yes/no list" and "a doubt list" in order to narrow down the entries that they received into young women who could possibly win an international title. She stressed the importance of height and argued the judges should "first, separate them by height: these are my five [feet] nine [inches tall] girls, these are my five [feet] six [inches tall] girls." The focus on the criteria of height is a product of Pradeep Guha's tenure as head of the pageant beginning in 1991, as many petite former Miss India winners would not even be eligible to compete today. "International standards" loom like a specter for pageant officials, with frequent mentions of the ever-formidable description by organizers of the "six foot two in her bare feet Miss Venezuela."

Thus situated within an international framework, the 2003 Miss India pageant focused from the beginning not on creating a Miss India, but on creating a Miss World or a Miss Universe, and Ernst and Young maintained a concomitant focus on the standards that were perceived to be necessary to improve India's chance of winning at Miss World or Miss Universe. "We are following an Olympic scoring system," an Ernst and Young representative told the judges before the final pageant, meaning that each judge's votes would be independently tallied to reduce the effect that outliers have on the final score. The representative presented examples of past Miss Universe and Miss World winners from all over the world accompanied by brief descriptions of the kinds of career paths they followed as a way to encourage the judges to look for someone who could fulfill the responsibilities of a Miss World or a Miss Universe, which included the ability to "support charitable causes, be a goodwill ambassador, spokesperson, work with global media, help increase awareness and funding for a cause and be available for modeling assignments." The likelihood of a contestant to potentially fulfill this somewhat incongruous list of responsibilities was gauged as part of a four-part process that evaluated various parts of each contestant's body and self.

In a slide titled "Our Vision of Beauty," the Ernst and Young consultant listed the four facets of physical, spiritual, emotional, and mental beauty that the pageant was searching for. Physical beauty was defined as "an attractive, beautiful face, expressive eyes and symmetry of form," spiritual beauty as "honesty, integrity, what her eyes and aura tell you," emotional beauty as the ability "to express herself from the heart," and mental beauty as "good judgment, common sense and intelligence." In a somewhat amusing example of the last point the consultant added in all seriousness, "She shouldn't talk about *hindutvă* [Hindu fundamentalism] or anything." *Hindutva* refers to the Hindu nationalist philosophy that India is an exclusively Hindu nation and is a very real issue in the rest of the country, but not in the five-star hotels and corporate offices that make up Miss India. The judges listened eagerly as the consultant explained that he had spent over one hundred fifty hours of time on the phone with his Ernst and Young colleague in New York who was in charge of handling the Miss Universe pageant. He urged the judges to take the criteria he presented seriously, as it determined "which girl will represent your country." This kind of language was used repeatedly and often made the pageant sound more like a political training camp than a venue for the production of models and actresses. Several facets of the pageant had been changed for 2003, most notably the inclusion of a sari round that was designed to make the pageant "more Indian" as well as to replicate the national costume competition at international pageants. Prior to 2003, the contestants had worn the work of various designers that may or may not have been stereotypically "Indian" in appearance.

Yet Ernst and Young's sincere attempts at adherence to "international standards" sometimes irritated pageant officials who found the procedures far too cumbersome and unrealistic to actually implement. During a meeting to decide on judging criteria, several pageant officials confronted the two consultants from Ernst and Young about their continued emphasis on making the pageant "international." One pageant official literally erupted at a meeting about the procedures for determining the winner of the Miss Photogenic title and shouted, "Well, if you obsess about standards too much, then you can kiss your show goodbye, because you can't structure it so much in India!" Ernst and Young was eventually able to convince organizers that the Miss Photogenic round should "be judged solely on photographs, the way it is done internationally," rather than by meeting individually with contestants. Organizers remained somewhat frustrated with Ernst and Young's attention to detail, which they largely regarded as a waste of time. As one organizer said somewhat dramatically to the consultants at the same meeting, "I think you're fucking around with the show big time. Either the show or the judging goes into jeopardy because of your standards."

As these conflicts between consultants and organizers rather clearly illustrate, the fact remains that there are certain aspects of life in India that cannot be conducted along "international standards," no matter how much negotiation is done. Staging an event anywhere in urban India necessitates that there are bribes to be paid, officials to ingratiate oneself with, and political elements to be appeased, and although none figure into Ernst and Young's supposition of "international standards," these are ground realities that will result in the cancellation, police raid, or political boycott of an event if ignored.

For example, government regulations prohibit the use of loudspeakers after ten P.M., and any event that comes close to that deadline requires a special permit from the police. As one organizer complained in Bangalore, "I've spent two days fighting with the cops in this city and tomorrow I want to say to the police commissioner '*calō, sāhab, party ke līyē*' [come on, sir, let's go drink alcohol and enjoy life at my expense] and be done with this." The organizer's frustration at having to bribe the police in order to ensure the success of the event was evident despite it being a nonnegotiable reality. Budgets were also an issue, and although the Ernst and Young consultants wanted the winners to be known only to the judges and themselves until the names were pulled out of a sealed envelope, the pageant organizers insisted that this was not possible. Citing the Oscars as their point of reference, the consultants were adamant that these standards should be followed in order to make the pageant more professional. Miss India officials mentioned the reality of budget constraints at the pageant in response, asking, "If the winners aren't known to us, how will the camera know where to look to capture their reaction? We can only afford eight cameras. This isn't the Oscars in terms of budget."

Miss India is indeed not the Oscars, just as India is, by and large, not a country in which the elusive "international standards" can be easily implemented. The two Ernst and Young consultants deserve an enormous amount of credit for dealing with the sheer quantity of opposition they faced from officials throughout the pageant. However amusing they were at times in their insistence upon "standards," their presence at Miss India pointed to a very real disjuncture between the reality of urban India and the goals of the pageant.

## The Complex Mathematics of Beauty: Sites of Contention

Although the arguments I was privy to between organizers and Ernst and Young representatives were rather contentious, they were nothing compared to the severe internal conflicts that young women faced when they did not win. The pageant's training program had completely absorbed the lives of all twenty-six contestants for a month, and many of them had spent even more time preparing for the final night. As such, the pain of not being chosen was devastating for some of them. The concept of being judged onstage is in itself dehumanizing at a basic level, and although it may be stressful for the judges as well, this cannot compare to not being deemed good enough in front of the viewing nation. Inherent in the notion of participating in Miss India is that most young women will not win, yet the training program is administered in such a way that each contestant firmly believes that she has a chance of winning when she leaves for the pageant.

The training program involves a complete transformation, or at least the appearance of it, in the physical and emotional self. Young women learn how to present themselves as Miss India, an apolitical, pleasant being who largely reaffirms gender role stereotypes. The judging process determines how successfully the contestants have managed to mimic these standards for being female, and in a cultural framework in which being feminine is the ideal of what a woman should be, not being able to incorporate these characteristics into one's self-presentation is perceived as a great failure on the part of young women, whether they are Miss India contestants or not.

Being female in urban India involves a process of constantly evaluating oneself not only against the moral standards set by society, but also vis-à-vis icons of beauty, such as Miss India or actresses in the Hindi film industry. It is perhaps fitting, then, that the training program that prepared contestants for the eventual judging procedure focused so intently on teaching young women to answer questions in a way that made them appear to be of sufficiently good moral character. This primarily involved expressing the importance of family, motherhood, and sacrifice as feminine virtues. Interestingly, none of the contestants were from particularly conservative families, and yet it was deemed necessary that they voice convictions that echoed deeply conservative views about gender that they did not necessarily believe in. At every stage of the judging process, I was struck by how beauty pageants demand that women mask their real goals and selves in order to appear that they are self-sacrificing, visually pleasing, apolitical beings. When judges ask contestants, for example, what they would do with a million dollars, they need to couch their answer in a beauty pageant rhetoric that locates itself in a closely circumscribed view of femininity, and as such, an ideal answer is that the contestant would donate their million dollars to charity rather than spend it on themselves. Although the contestants, judges, and audience know that this is complete nonsense, it is in keeping with the role of women as sacrificing beings who put the concerns of others above their own. Contestants are acutely aware of this and tailor their answers in order to fit these gender norms.

However, because the judges obviously have their own views about life and gender that may not be informed by dominant social norms, contestants also have to modify their answers with the judges' lifestyles in mind. During the prejudging round in which contestants met individually with judges before the final day of the pageant, I followed ten young women through their meetings with the various judges to observe how each presented herself to the wide array of individuals to whom she spoke. I was stunned by the differences in self-presentation each contestant employed as she spoke individually to each judge, often altering key elements of her personality and life to suit each judge's view of gender-appropriate behavior.

Deepica, the Hindi-language soap opera actress, was particularly adept at this as she circulated among the six judges, who were all figures in the Indian corporate and media worlds. Deepica had often told me how much she missed her boyfriend at the training program, and yet when Hindi film producer Yash Chopra asked her if she had a boyfriend, she feigned shock by placing her hand on her heart as she widened her eyes for dramatic effect. "I'm sorry for my surprise, sir," she said breathlessly, "but I come from a very traditional family, and there is simply no question of boyfriends." The producer smiled at her and continued his line of questioning, secure in the knowledge that she was an example of conservative Indian femininity. Yet when Deepica sat with Hindi film star Shilpa Shetty, a sex symbol who was rumored to have an ongoing relationship with a married man, her answers were completely different. When Shetty asked her what she thought of extramarital affairs, Deepica nodded confidently and said that it was perfectly acceptable as long as both parties were consenting adults.

This is part of the complex terrain that young women have to negotiate in order to be judged sufficiently "modern," yet also adequately demure. Adjusting oneself under the evaluative gaze of the judges is a crucial part of becoming Miss India and as young women play at being paragons of feminine virtue, they engage in a reflective process in which the mirror of the self is never far away. To the young women who do not win, being deemed not beautiful and not feminine enough to be Miss India can be devastating. I have never seen so many young women as absolutely distraught as I did on the night of the final pageant, when I sat backstage as young women returned dejected from the stage.

Ethnic South Indian Parvati was among the most articulate and intelligent of the contestants at the training program and also one of the first to be eliminated by judges at the final pageant. Parvati returned backstage in tears and full of feelings of rejection, and while I tried my best to reassure her that much more exciting things would happen to her in her life, she was adamant that the judging procedure had not been fair to her:

> Some of the girls, like me, can speak such golden words, and who won?
> Just the same old Miss Indias, the ones who are fair and skinny and
> beautiful. Why do they even pretend they are looking for girls like me,
> who have a mind of their own?

I was not quite sure how to answer Parvati, because I knew she was right. As I looked at the contestants who had become finalists at the pageant, they all fit the Miss India mold she described. Parvati's darker skin and introspective nature had set her apart at the training program, and though she may have always had doubts about her ability to win, her final rejection gave a clear message to her: you are not Miss India material because you do not meet our standards. In the face of such rejection, all of the rhetoric she had listened to about "beauty with a purpose" and "*strī śakti*" suddenly rang embarrassingly hollow.

## Finding Miss India: The Urban/Rural Divide

Where does one look in order to find a woman who can be called Miss India? This question was foremost in my mind as I joined Miss India officials for the selection round of the pageant. Although statistically most women in India are illiterate agricultural workers in rural areas, these were not the women who were sought out by the pageant. Aspiring contestants for Miss India were instead made up entirely of urban, relatively privileged young women who were all well-educated and fluent in English and who hardly had anything in common with the majority of women in India. Former Miss India contestant and Hindi film actress Gauri Karnik was quick to point out that "it's not fair that a village girl who might be stunning, can't win." Interestingly, she was the only one who mentioned this fact as a point of inequality throughout the course of my research on the pageant. She further described other issues at stake regarding access:

> They need to come from non-conservative families. You can't tell a small town family, "I'm going to put your daughter in a swimsuit in front of 5,000 people." They'll beat you up and tell you you're crazy. You also need a certain amount of money and a certain diet in order to have glowing skin, and how many women in India have that?

Karnik was one of the most reflective individuals I spoke to throughout the pageant, and her statement concisely expresses the vast differences that exist between urban and rural cultural norms. It also points to the way in which women are always situated in a family context rather than as independent actors in India.

Family support is indeed crucial for a young woman to enter Miss India. Kismet from the North Indian town of Chandigarh was chosen to come to Mumbai for the training program but was unable to continue due to family objections she had anticipated at the selection rounds. Although she insisted that her family was supportive, she also added that,

"Chandigarh is a very small town, so not many girls participate. They'll say you're promiscuous." Dressed in a purple velvet gown she had borrowed from her aunt, Kismet discussed the politics of coming from Chandigarh to Delhi for the selection round with me backstage. Chandigarh is a large North Indian town in the state of Punjab, located in what is known as "the bread basket of India" and is culturally quite distant from the milieu of Miss India. Kismet had initially hoped that her immediate family's support for her participation in the pageant would allow her to complete the training program, but social pressures related to reputation later forced her to drop out.

Although the example of Kismet from Chandigarh can be extended to illustrate why more young women from rural or semiurban areas do not enter Miss India, it is crucial to mention that not all metropolitan areas are alike. Selection rounds were originally scheduled for Bangalore, Delhi, Mumbai, and Calcutta, the last of which was cancelled due to lack of entries; as one of the pageant officials' assistants explained prior to the cancellation, "We're not expecting too many girls, maybe ten for Calcutta, because it's conservative and they'll think 'Oh, I'll have to go all the way to Bombay [Mumbai] for the training,' so we're skipping it." Young women from the South, who are generally darker in skin tone, were largely ignored from the beginning of the selection process because of a deeply rooted bias in India that holds fair skin as an indicator of beauty and provides the skin bleaching cream Fair and Lovely with an estimated sixty million customers throughout the subcontinent.

Miss India 2003 received 532 entries, out of which 200 were deemed "invalid" because the applicant did not meet the height requirement of five feet six inches or above. The 332 valid entries had an overwhelming number of professional portfolio photographs, and there were only a few entries that were taken in small-town or inexpensive suburban photography studios with natural looking girls staring hopefully into the camera in front of an inexpensive synthetic red curtain. That so many young women had portfolio-style pictures from professional fashion photographers to send in is notable, as these are virtually unheard of outside of metropolitan areas. This is also heavily classed, as a set of professional photographs to be used in a portfolio costs anything from five thousand to twenty-five thousand rupees ($100 to $500), an enormous sum of money for most young women. As one contestant from Nasik, a small city in the western state of Maharashtra, put it, "In Nasik, people would hear ten thousand rupees [two hundred dollars] for a picture and think you were crazy!"

There was an enormous difference between the majority of the applications that came from urban areas and the few that were from smaller cities and towns: on one page, a professional photograph of a model posing seductively in a bikini by a pool listed measurements of five feet seven inches tall, one hundred ten pounds, 33-24-34, and next to it was a snapshot of a plain girl in a brown sari in front of a curtain, with measurements of five feet six inches, one hundred twenty-three pounds, 36-27-36. It simply was not fair to expect these two girls to compete against each other even in photographs, as the gulf in terms of class and symbolic capital was simply too vast.

However, the mere presence of such contrasts points to the permeation of global beauty culture into women's lives throughout India. Photographs of applicants with blue contact lenses, ironed hair with carefully placed highlights in gold or red, and professionally applied makeup consistently revealed a focus on the expensive accoutrements of beauty. These things are all costly and yet the applicants understand that they will impress the judges and help them advance their careers in media. From the applicant in the leopard print bustier to the bikini-clad model lounging by the pool, the message was clear: modernity does not wear many clothes.

### Finding Miss India: The Initial Selections

I sat in the Miss India office on Saturday afternoon with the 532 entries received for the pageant in front of me, feeling a bit overwhelmed by the way women's bodies could be evaluated in a way that could change their lives. The entries were housed in a clinical set of twenty white three-ring binders, with one page to each contestant. Each page had two full body shots and one close up of the face, along with a list of the applicant's entry number, age, height and weight, and bust-waist-hip measurements. Those who did not make the height requirement of five feet six inches tall had a white sheet over them with the word "invalid" typed across it in thick black letters.

Applicants were chosen for the selection rounds in Bangalore, Delhi, and Mumbai based on a set of criteria on a scale of one to ten. The sheet that each judge filled out contained a short description of their duties, which ended with the heavy-handed, "The final winner will go on to represent your country in international pageants." The deciding factors were divided into two categories: first was face/natural beauty, which was comprised of smile, expressiveness, complexion, radiance and attractiveness/magnetism, and the second was figure, which entailed proportion, poise, and confidence. The scale of one to ten was carefully graded, with one meaning "applicant has no chance of making it to the finals of the pageant," five signifying "applicant has a reasonable chance of making it to the finals of the pageant," and ten assuring that "applicant will definitely make it to the finals of the pageant."

Attempts were made to conceal all indicators of regional and ethnic identity in order to prevent judging bias, although it is difficult to determine the degree to which this was successful, as certain physical features often mark individuals as part of distinct ethnic groups. Individuals usually marry and socialize within their own ethnic and religious communities in most of India, and this attempt to mask ethnicity and religion was designed to encourage judges not to favor individuals from certain ethnic or religious backgrounds, which last names easily reveal. As a result, the twenty white folders contained 332 nameless and culturally unbound Indian women: the postindependence ideal of womanhood.

Some applicants submitted resumes that included descriptions of modeling assignments and photographs of them winning other beauty pageants, and these were covered in white paper to prevent them from being seen by the judges, as they constituted an unfair advantage. All of the entries were striking in terms of sheer physical homogeneity, and although all of the girls were thin, some were simply undernourished. One such girl's physical measurements read an extremely unhealthy five feet six inches, ninety-four pounds, 30-23-32. The final results were that ten young women were called to Bangalore, thirty-five to Delhi, and thirty three to Mumbai.

It was eminently clear throughout the selection round that the entrants were largely young women from cosmopolitan backgrounds, as a number of them were raised outside of India or had spent time abroad. Many contestants had traveled extensively; one had studied fashion design for a year in Australia ("because it was safer than New York") and another had traveled from Saudi Arabia specifically to enter Miss India. All the young women were from similar backgrounds but did vary a bit based upon the city in which they were called to the selection round in, which was usually the city they lived in or nearby. Although the majority of applicants came from Mumbai and Delhi, the Bangalore section of the selection rounds was conducted because it was the sponsor's choice of location for the semifinals. The selection rounds in different regions provided fascinating insights into regional understandings of what it means to be Miss India.

*Bangalore*

When I asked television producer Reshma Ghosh how it felt to judge the selection rounds, an Ernst and Young consultant who overheard insisted that I should "instead, ask her how it feels to play God." As we arrived at the venue for judging in Bangalore and I began to catch glimpses of nervous contestants, I wondered whether it would be so far fetched to actually ask her such a question. The Bangalore selection rounds were held at the Le Meridien hotel, and only ten young women were invited: three from Bangalore, two from Mumbai who were enrolled in college in Bangalore, and five from Chennai.

The five judges included Ghosh, former Miss India and MTV presenter Nafisa Joseph, former Miss India and Miss World Yukta Mookhey, photographer and actor Boman Irani, and Parigi, the organizer of the 2003 pageant. As celebrities in the field of media, the judges were deemed qualified to evaluate beauty and, more importantly, the potential of a young woman to become Miss Universe. The limited number of contestants in Bangalore made the judges' task easier, because they knew that there would be many more contestants in Delhi and Mumbai. After a six twenty A.M. flight from Mumbai, Miss India officials measured the young women in order to determine that they met the height requirement of five feet six inches tall. Parigi was adamant that no journalists were permitted into the hotel and that only the judges were allowed with the young women throughout the day. Because applying to participate in Miss India requires a certain degree of presumptuousness on the part of young women, namely the supposition that they are beautiful, rejection from the pageant can serve to unsettle that assumption. As a result, many of the young women who were brought to the selection rounds had not told anyone outside their circle of immediate family, fearing the embarrassment that not being selected would bring. As Parigi noted, "If my wife or daughter were participating, I wouldn't want them discussed in colleges across the city. This is very personal, so if a girl is selected then it's fine, but if she doesn't win then she doesn't want anyone to know she participated."

The judges were briefed for an extended period of time by the two Ernst and Young consultants who went through a PowerPoint presentation with the judges that featured the characteristics of former Miss Worlds, Miss Asia-Pacifics, and Miss Universes. This was to be the first of many times in which judges were reminded that they were not looking for a Miss India, but a Miss Universe. Beyond the need for those selected to meet "international standards," Parigi also mentioned the need to keep a buffer of five girls, as some were sure to drop out of the rigorous training program. Interestingly, he cited those with the class privileges to go elsewhere as the most likely to leave. He said, "They'll say, 'shove it up your ass, Parigi. My father's Merc is waiting outside.' They won't have the drive that a girl from a different kind of family would have." Parigi advised the judges to "pay attention to whether or not she will be able to lose weight, because there are certain body types which cannot lose weight because of their bone density." The judges were asked to clinically evaluate each young woman based on their perception of her body's ability to lose weight as part of a fascinating process that sought to gauge the potential of an individual woman's body to be molded into a Miss Universe. This physical type, combined with the ability to answer questions relatively articulately, was the primary criteria for selection at this level of the pageant.

In the first part of the Bangalore selection round, each young woman walked down a ramp in a sarong and bathing suit before removing the

sarong and introducing herself with her first name, age, and place of origin before sitting in a chair in front of the five judges. None of the girls
in Bangalore were extremely thin or toned, but they all had the kind of
figures that are the result of dieting and going for walks, a preferred form
of female exercise in India. Their bodies were in proportion, but the lack
of real pressure to achieve the kind of physical perfection that exists in
Mumbai or Delhi was evident. Yet, as judges noted down their scores on
a scale of one to ten, I wondered how any of this could possibly be objectively evaluated.

In the second round of the selections, the young women were supposed to show their poise and grace in an evening gown. Parading down
the catwalk in everything from a bustier with an attached purple micro
miniskirt to a full-length gold lamé ball gown, the contestants were striking in their interpretation of what an "evening gown" was. Former Miss
India Nafisa Joseph commented: "It's not fair, because half the girls bor-
row their gowns, like I borrowed mine from my aunt." Indeed, although
the judges were supposed to evaluate the contestants based on their poise,
not their gowns, I wondered how the contestant in the inexpensive stretch
cotton dress could possibly compete with the stunning Miss Universe
look-alike in the floor length, white sequined ball gown that she clearly
had tailor-made for the occasion. The young women then answered questions individually in front of the judges while wearing their evening
gowns. Parigi had asked me to compose a variety of questions that varied
from current events to personal preferences, and the answers contestants
gave in response varied from rather canned ("I admire Mother Teresa") to
extremely innovative ("I handled my anger problem by taking karate").

A consistent theme throughout their answers was their motivation to
enter careers in media; as Bipashana from Chennai said, "I applied because
I want to be a model and that's why I need to go to Bombay [Mumbai] and
meet the best, to have a platform. I want to know if I'm good enough to
grasp my dream and, if not, what I can do to improve myself." Situated
within the rhetoric of being "good enough," Bipashana, who did not make
it past the selection round, described her desire to change herself in order to
meet Miss India standards. This tendency on the part of contestants to display such willingness to alter their bodies and personalities was startling

at times and almost gave the impression that many young women viewed the pageant as an extremely serious chance at a once-in-a-lifetime opportunity for social mobility and access to a brighter future.

Judges listened to young women describe Miss India as "a childhood dream," as did Monisha from Bangalore who said that "to even have the chance to be even this much a part of *Femina,* it's a dream come true for me." The connections made by contestants between being considered beautiful enough for *Femina* and Miss India and the use of the word "dream" or "fantasy" were not mere linguistic coincidences, as the way in which both the pageant and the magazine can dramatically alter young women's lives is almost immeasurable.

The interview round of the selection process was designed to allow the judges to gauge the depth of each contestant's maturity and to get a sense of their convictions, and many of the contestant's responses were imbued with similar language involving dreams and fairy tales. The underlying task of each judge was to determine which young women would be able to fulfill commitments to Miss India without embarrassing anyone in the process, despite the reality that this is probably impossible to gauge in the four or five minutes each contestant spent with the panel of judges. Told to search for someone who was creative in her answers, the judges often cross-questioned young women in a way that made them very nervous; in one case, Parigi interrupted a contestant's reading of a poem she had written to ask her what constituted bad manners, hoping that she would have the wherewithal to tell him that his behavior was in fact inappropriate. Notably, the contestant did politely mention that "perhaps interrupting could be considered rude" and was selected for the training program in Mumbai.

The brief contestant interviews ended the Bangalore selection round and the judges gathered the young women together to thank them for coming. Photographs were taken by the pool to be distributed to the press, and the judges gave general career advice to the contestants on "competing with oneself, not with others." In the end, two out of the ten contestants, both of South Indian descent, were chosen to come to the training program in Mumbai. The judges expressed happiness that the pageant process had begun in Bangalore, where the limited number of eligible contestants made their task easier; already it had been decided that the most desirable candidates would be found in Delhi and Mumbai, the next cities on the itinerary.

*Delhi*

As a much larger city than Bangalore, Delhi had thirty-five young women chosen to compete in the selection round, and of these, twenty-two were from Delhi, six from Chandigarh, and one each from Assam, Calcutta, Dehradun, Ghaziabad, Indore, Nagaland, and Simla. There were a number of professional models and extremely thin young women, and as they paraded onto the catwalk in fitted and sophisticated bathing suits, their highlighted hair perfectly framing their faces, it was clear that they were different from the types of women we had seen in Bangalore. The selection round in Delhi seemed to showcase urban femininity in a way that Bangalore had not, and the majority of young women who competed in Delhi had expensive markers of beauty such as a diet- and gym-altered body with at least two inches of space between the thighs, straightened and highlighted hair, and a great deal of makeup. They also wore clothing that, although relatively difficult to find in India, sometimes oddly resembled the ensembles worn by women who worked at a topless bar I conducted research at during graduate school. This is simply in imitation of part of what Dwyer (2001) has called the "high street rather than high fashion" ethos present in fashion and film magazines in India, rather than an oversexualized pool of contestants. Most young women wore ill-fitting borrowed formal gowns and inexpensive summer dresses, and so the vinyl and PVC-clad contestants definitely stood out. As I watched an especially emaciated contestant who ended up as a Miss India finalist answer questions in a black PVC minidress that barely covered her underwear and outlined the prominent jutting of bones from her hips as she walked, it was impossible to forget that in most of India such a thin woman would be considered unmarriageable. In the space of Miss India, however, this kind of body was perceived as ideal.

Young women were rather forthright in their answers to the judges during the interview section, perhaps because of the greater number of contestants and Delhi's status as a larger city. When questioned about career goals, young women responded with a variety of answers. "I want to be a socialite," said Gitanjali in a short black dress, "so I can be there with my friends every morning in the pages of the newspaper." Shruti from Delhi, who placed very highly at the end of the pageant, noted that if a married man offered her money in exchange for sex, a question presumably designed to gauge her depth and breadth of understanding of how to handle unpleasant social situations, she said she would "first ask him why, and then ask him for more money."

These answers were part of a broader exercise designed to reveal the worldviews and moral stances of each contestant; in short, the judges were supposed to determine just how "broad-minded" the young women were. The term "broad-minded" as it is used in Indian English can have both good and bad connotations depending on the context, as it evidences an emphasis on individual choice while simultaneously implying a view of sexuality that does not highly prioritize female chastity and honor. Saying, for example, "She comes from a very broad-minded family," generally means that the woman in question is allowed a degree of freedom in terms of leaving the house and choosing her partner(s) that is simply not possible in the rest of India. Being characterized as "too broad-minded," however, can imply that one is possessed of a questionable set of moral standards.

"Broad-mindedness," then, was definitely a consistent theme throughout the Delhi selection round. A close second, however, was the more nebulous concept of "boldness." The term "bold" generally holds a more negative connotation in Indian English, and although it may be representative of the concept of a new, "modern" woman who speaks her mind and makes her own choices, "boldness" is more often than not an adjective used to chastise young women within a family environment. When I lived in Udaipur, an extremely conservative North Indian town, women would often use the English word "bold" in their Hindi language exhortations to their daughters of how not to behave and what not to be, namely, women who speak their mind without thinking of the social consequences of their words. However, broad-mindedness and boldness are both almost prerequisites for participation in Miss India, as both ensure a contestant's ability to withstand and enjoy a life of constant

10. *Miss India must maintain a careful balance between being sufficiently "Indian" and adequately "modern," the latter of which often takes the form of tight, revealing clothing such as this black dress.*

media attention. Yet boldness also has other connotations in the andro-centric space of India, and so while boldness may be necessary in order for women to venture into the extremely public sphere of media, it is not always discursively constructed as socially desirable.

Young women in Delhi also demonstrated determination and willing-ness to alter any part of their personalities and bodies in order to be Miss India. Using a metaphor that was extremely appropriate given the situa-tion, Gopika (who was selected for the training program) said, "I want to shape my future like 36-24-36, just like how I shape my body." The con-nection she made between her body and her future was striking in that it seemed so natural under the circumstances. At least ten other contestants in Delhi looked the judges straight in their eyes and simply said, "I will do anything to be Miss Universe, and I mean *anything.*"

Delhi also brought numerous class-related issues to the fore, espe-cially in the evening gown round in which one young woman posed in a fitted, floor length gown made of sheer white fabric with only a pair of thong underwear and push-up bra underneath, and another wore a designer evening gown made of red silk with an elaborate train made of gray and red silk roses. Still others wore tight black tube dresses, and some had on ill-fitting borrowed dresses that hung like potato sacks on them. It was obvious that some girls had been able to spend a great deal of money on their dresses, and others had borrowed theirs. This raises the question as to whether there can ever be such a thing as a fair beauty pageant, especially in a country like India that is so cross-cut by class and cultural preferences for lighter skin; not surprisingly, both of these issues were just as prevalent in Mumbai.

*Mumbai*

Mumbai had thirty-three young women called to compete, twenty-one of whom were from the city itself, five from a city one hundred miles south of Mumbai called Pune, and one each from Ahmedabad, Baroda, Delhi, Goa, Nagpur, Nasik, and Patna. As I watched the thirty-three young women milling around in swimsuits and sarongs at nine- thirty in the morning in the space of a luxury hotel, I realized that if any of them stepped outside, the men on the street would not know what to make of women in such a state of undress, as even street prostitutes in India wear saris. Mumbai was absolutely fascinating in the way that the contestants so closely mirrored the white European beauty culture that is depicted on FTV. The thirty-three women walked expertly down a narrow catwalk in very high heels, their lips forming a pout in carefully studied approximation of what they had seen on television.

The twin themes of broad-mindedness and boldness were as consistent in Mumbai as they had been in Delhi. One young woman explained to the judges that if the Miss Universe pageant had a problem with the large unicorn tattooed on her back, she could have it covered with makeup. Interestingly, nearly every girl who answered a question in a controversial manner was selected for the pageant. One of the more common questions designed to provoke an attention-getting response was whether a contestant would pose nude for *Playboy* magazine if offered a million dollars. I suspect that this question was designed not so much to test an applicant's moral character, but rather to gauge how "modern" she was in her outlook toward life. Most contestants chose to answer the question in some variation of Meghna from Mumbai's insistence that "if Playboy offered me a million dollars to pose nude, first I would fulfill my duties to Miss Universe, and then I'd do it." Such an answer positions the contestant as open-minded enough to not take issue with certain things that may be asked of her, but not so Machiavellian that she would embarrass the institution of Miss India.

Not all young women were equally able to express these kinds of sentiments, especially those who were not from Mumbai or Delhi, as the young women from small towns stood out both in terms of the way that they looked and their answers to questions. They almost always revealed the wrong things to the judges (such as one contestant's example of an abusive boyfriend who hit her mother), were too explicit in their attempts to demonstrate their flexibility and ambition (such as the applicant who volunteered that she would agree to exchange sex for an improved chance of winning), or did not appear open-minded enough to participate. Maushmi, a contestant from a small town in the foothills of the Himalayas, detailed the struggles she faced as an aspiring actress in Mumbai as her reason for entering the Miss India pageant:

> I was raised in Simla, the capital of Arunachal Pradesh. As a girl from a small town, my journey to get ahead in Bombay [Mumbai] was really bad, because people wanted to exploit me. With Miss India, I'll be able to have a platform which will keep me away from such people and out of danger.

Maushmi's candid assertion that her experiences with the Hindi film industry had been rather sordid did more to unnerve the judges than it did to convince them that she was Miss India material. In so easily confessing that she had been victimized, Maushmi did not appear to be the kind of young woman who could navigate the fame that Miss India confers.

Maushmi's case also illustrates how young women who are not fluent in English were marginalized in the Miss India selection process. As one of only two contestants who asked the judges to question her in India's

11. Each Miss India pageant produces three winners who then go on to represent their country at international pageants that are seen to be much more prestigious than Miss India. Featured are winners Sara Corner, Celina Jaitley, and Maheshwari Thyagrajan.

national language of Hindi, Maushmi did not have the cultural capital of fluency in English essential to be Miss India. Young women from small towns were further marginalized because although not every young woman in Mumbai or Delhi has equal access to the kind of symbolic capital necessary to be Miss India, they all have the potential to be exposed to it via television, print media, the Internet, and social norms that allow more freedom to women. As Gehena from the small North Indian town of Bhopal explained:

> There's still an information gap, like in Bhopal we don't have professional photographers, so to come here to Bombay [Mumbai] where a picture costs 35,000 rupees [seven hundred dollars], wow! I know you have to invest something if you want a return, like in clothes and a portfolio, but in a small town it just seems like so much money.

Gehena's candid admission that the standard rate for a portfolio seems exorbitant to someone from a small town points to the manifold ways in which geography and social class conspire to make it extremely difficult for most women to even think of entering Miss India. Family pressure not to participate was also a major concern for contestants from small towns; as Sharayu from Pune noted, "I had to brainwash my parents that Miss India is not a skin show."

Watching young women wait an entire day for two minutes onstage and a four-minute interview with the judges that would determine who would participate in the training program that could potentially change lives constantly reminded me of the problematic nature of evaluating women. Given the difficulties that many young women faced in transcending the boundaries of class and geography, it is not surprising that almost all of the young women selected for the training program were from urban areas. The standards set at the pageant are nearly impossible for most women to meet, and as such, the next chapter discusses how the pageant uses the rhetoric of national identity and representation in order to perform this highly selective version of India on a global stage.

# 6

# Miss India and National Identity

Anthropological approaches to power and globalization have often focused on the centrality of the experience of colonialism in constructing national identity. India became united as a nation only because of the trade networks and conquests of land that took place in the British colonial period and served to foster links between India and Western Europe that privileged European ways of being over Indian ones. Language and education were crucial to this process, as they provided a common "universe of ideas and structures of cultural exchange" (Naregal 2002, 58) necessary for social interaction between previously discrete social groups. Colonialism involved the use of "cultural technologies of rule" (Dirks 2001, 109) as much as the direct imposition of power, and such technologies under British administration included structures such as an English-language education system that continues to regulate class and status today.

Anthropological understandings of colonialism have directly impacted anthropological understandings of globalization, as India's colonial history is inherently embedded in the process of globalization. As Cohn (1996, 21) has meticulously documented, the production of grammars, translations, and concepts of knowledge about India under colonial rule served to "convert Indian forms of knowledge into European objects." Colonialism brought different ethnic and religious groups into closer contact than they had been before and served to make certain social forms and ways of being more prestigious than others. Postindependence Indian leadership was turned over to what quickly became a thinly veiled dynasty of ruling elites who employed an economic policy based upon

Soviet-style five-year plans aimed at making India a self-sufficient nation and alleviating poverty (Farinelli 1992, 28). This oddly echoed the broader British colonial strategy that aimed to "connect India to the universal processes of improvement as represented by Western technological, political and social achievements" (Gottlob 2002, 78).

This process is very much in action today, most notably in the form of rigid class divisions in which privileged forms of American and Western European knowledge serve as the entry passes to the upper strata of society. The way in which femininity and gender are constructed at Miss India is thus directly related to broader sociopolitical issues in the nation at large, especially in that Miss India contestants are so physically and culturally different from most women in India. The fact remains that India can be accurately described as an overpopulated agrarian nation in which poverty and deprivation are facts of life for hundreds of millions of people and the sort of lifestyle that the Miss India contestants led at the training program would be incomprehensible to most South Asians in its sheer extravagance.

In truth, the lifestyle that the training program entailed was sometimes incomprehensibly extravagant to me as well. India's endemic class inequality was impossible to ignore each time I stepped out of the training program's five-star hotel in which enormous white marble pools of fresh water were filled daily with hand-picked rose and jasmine blossoms to perfume the air. On the street outside, children without limbs begged for spare change as lepers pushed themselves along on hand-made wheeled carts. This enormous difference between class groups is of course a sensitive subject, and yet I felt it was necessary to ask the contestants what they felt they had in common with the rest of India. Although most of the young women were sympathetic to the fact that they constituted a privileged minority who are able to participate in Miss India, a few were even a bit defensive in response to this question, such as Shonali from Delhi who snapped, "Just because we listen to western music and don't wear saris every day doesn't mean that we're not Indian."

Other contestants were remarkably reflective in their abilities to make comparisons between their own lives and the lives of most Indian women. Hemangi from Mumbai felt that she shared willpower as a common trait with a woman from a village, "Because in a male-dominated country, you face so much discrimination that you need willpower just to survive." Anurithi from Bangalore said that being goal-oriented was something she shared with rural women, because "she may have certain goals, like mine is to go to Berkeley and study journalism, and she may have a goal of going to an urban area to improve herself." Hemangi and Anurithi's points of comparisons with rural women shed a bit of light on what it means to be Miss India in that their quick response may indicate that the thought of being asked such a question at Miss Universe or Miss World could be a distinct possibility. For this reason, each contestant had an immediate answer to what winning the title meant to her, such as Shruti from Delhi, who was clear that Miss India meant responsibility:

> Being Miss India means keeping my head on my shoulders although my life will be extraordinary and I'll have a lot of responsibility. I'm going to be idolized, so I have to be careful what I emote. Miss India, after all, is a status symbol.

Citing the amount of power that the pageant holds in urban popular culture, Shruti's statement references the self-policing that she perceives being Miss India will involve. Sunaina from Delhi echoed Shruti's insistence that Miss India has a responsibility to her country, and emphasized how Miss India serves as a role model to her peers throughout the nation:

> It's not only appearance, because you have to be a beautiful person and be able to make India proud with your grace and dignity. Every woman who watches Miss India, there's a spark that comes up within her that says "that could be me—I have that grace, I can speak that way."

Armed with the powerful assumption that millions of women are gazing at them in awe, thinking "that could be me", Miss India contestants can be certain of having made a social class transition by the end of the pageant.

Most contestants initially insisted that social class had nothing to do with their ability to participate but also tacitly admitted that the pageant has certain prerequisites that have everything to do with class. Introspective as always, Parvati was quick to note that "dreams are only given to people with the means to make them come true," thereby hinting that young women who are not financially or socially able to enter Miss India would not even be given the potential to think about such a thing. Discussions of dreams and life goals were never absent in the discourse at Miss India, and class-related issues proved to be no exception to this. Purva, the dental student from Pune, responded to my question as to whether a domestic servant has a fair chance of becoming Miss India by saying that

> a housemaid can't be Miss India, because you need to be able to converse on different topics, you can't just be stuck in your own community. A housemaid can't talk about issues and they can't talk about how they would change the world. If they had a perspective like that, then they wouldn't be doing a job like that. I am still wondering if people like that can dream.

Purva's mention of "people like that" questions the ability of the poor and marginalized to even imagine a better life for themselves, something that runs contrary to notions of equality and empowerment implicit in the pageant's focus on social mobility. This kind of double-speak was common at the pageant so that while contestants repeatedly voiced their conviction that anyone could be Miss India, they were equally emphatic that a poor or rural woman could never be.

This raises the important question of just who that "anyone" who can become Miss India is. Contestants ranged widely in their responses to the question of why a poor or rural woman could not compete at Miss India from derisive laughter to well-reasoned arguments that it takes some amount of money in order to even consider entering. Shonal from Calcutta noted that "a village girl can't do certain things like have a passport, so maybe not everyone can be Miss India." Shonal's insistence that a young woman from rural India is simply unable to fulfill basic entry requirements (such as a passport) for the pageant underscores the class divide that bars such women from competing at Miss India. Poonam from Mumbai more explicitly cited economic necessity as the primary reason why a poor woman could not enter Miss India, arguing that although such a woman could enter provided she "has charm, intelligence and grace, maybe she is too busy cleaning houses and can't leave her job."

Ami from Los Angeles was the most informed and sensitive in her response to my question, claiming that

> not any woman from the street can be Miss India, because you need some etiquette. The contestants here are all upper middle class, but that's because the education system here doesn't allow lower class women to have access to any education.

Ami's well-reasoned explanation for the class inequality at Miss India was the most honest I received, perhaps because she had grown accustomed to asking such questions of herself since relocating to India from the United States. There are numerous systems in place that preclude women who do not fit into a very narrow category of both beauty and class status from participating at Miss India, and some contestants also highlighted what Indian English terms "mentality" as a factor that precludes the entry of some young women. Particularly Indian in character, "mentality" refers to a constellation of behaviors and beliefs that often center on one's ethnic and religious background, so that speakers might describe "a Delhi mentality" as one that has an androcentric view of the world that prevents women from having equal access to public space. A similar statement such as "that's their Kashmiri mentality" might be used to describe a conservative outlook that most individuals who are ethnically from the state of Kashmir are perceived to share.

The word "mentality" can also be used to describe class groups, such as in Hemangi's use of the mentality metaphor in her explanation of why less-privileged young women cannot enter Miss India:

> It's a difference of mentality, that's why we're all from the same background, because people from the lower middle class don't allow their minds to progress enough to allow their daughters to enter.

Hemangi's insistence that it is the lack of mental "progress" on the part of poorer families that deters young women from entering is part of the discourse of modernity that was fairly consistent at the pageant. Only Kaveri from the small town of Nasik rather notably chose to observe that some young women are simply not interested in beauty pageants, using examples to extend the title of "Miss India" to include women from a variety of backgrounds:

> Miss India isn't just being onstage. Even Kiran Bedi [a famous female police officer] is Miss India because she excelled in a male field. All the pilots and female laborers can be seen as Miss Indias because of the way they work with men, they too are Miss Indias in their own respect. They don't get the opportunity to get ahead in life and enter Miss India, because a laborer's life revolves around her work and her children and she's satisfied with that, just like an IAS [Indian Administrative Service, a prestigious wing of the Government of India] officer is satisfied with her job.

Kaveri's description of Miss India seems to link the title directly with women's achievement in a sexist world. Although her view of female laborers as Miss India is perhaps not the best choice given the fact that such women could never participate in the pageant, Kaveri's insistence that being Miss India means being the best that one can be is indeed striking, as it reveals just how much status the pageant has in urban popular culture. Miss India has been a prestigious institution since its inception in 1959 but has been the consistent focus of an enormous amount of media attention only since 1994, when Miss India contestants won both the Miss Universe and Miss World titles. The next section discusses how Miss India has emerged as both a symbol of national achievement and a representation of a more "international" India following structural adjustment in 1991.

### *Femina*, the *Times of India*, and the Postliberalization Dilemma

In a country in which more than half of all women are illiterate and still more do not have access to basic health care, one might reasonably question the utility of a beauty pageant and a magazine that cater to the tiny minority who can afford the kinds of products they advertise. The postliberalization economy has generated so much media competition in the form of slickly produced American and Western European fashion magazines with offices in Mumbai that *Femina*'s publisher, the Times of India Group, decided to attract as many advertisers as possible in order to maximize revenue, a choice that made it perfectly suited to handle the Miss India pageant in its post-liberalization avatar. The *Times of India* is a formidable media machine and thus the perfect vehicle with which to create celebrities in the form of Miss Indias. A review of the *Times of India* archives from 1993 revealed a number of key trends surrounding the pageant, the first of which is the sheer amount of press coverage of the event, as it seems that everyone and anyone even remotely related to the pageant is given the authority to write about it in some capacity. Another is the focus on the pageant as sponsor-driven, so that even simple articles about the contestants are careful to document the presence of commodities, and sentences often read something to the effect of "Neha puts on her Regal shoes," in reference to the brand of footwear that sponsored the 2002 pageant.

Another interesting key theme in the *Times of India* coverage is the stress on how difficult life is as a beauty queen. As part of the rhetoric that beauty does not "just happen," but is the result of hard work and dedication, articles detail the sacrifices that contestants make in order to win, usually in terms of dietary restrictions and rigorous fitness regimens. The *Times* retains a focus on beauty as a group process in its coverage of the training program, so that the transformation of a tall but otherwise ordinary young woman into a potential Miss Universe is described as the result of the pageant process itself.

The *Times* also focuses on how pageants help to position India as "on par" with the rest of the world, and beauty queens are often credited with "putting India on the map." Miss Indias are seen as ambassadors and stars worthy of coverage in every way, and in the breathless language of the press winners seem ethereal in their beauty and unparalleled in their achievements. As the most powerful media house in the country, the Times of India Group is uniquely able to promote celebrities and sometimes the power that the group holds to create stars is rather frightening. A pageant official explained the benefits of joining the Times of India Group's modeling agency in very clear terms in a presentation to the contestants in the middle of the training program:

The Times Group is in the best position as a media house because it can select and promote girls in the best way. We'll promote you in film, advertising, modeling and events on a five year contract. We'll take 30 percent of what you earn, because we will invest a lot in you. We have the means of promoting you like no other agency can.

The Times of India Group was founded in 1838 and today has a composite monopoly over information in India, as it owns the *Times of India* with its circulation of 4.6 million readers and eight regional editions as well as the *Economic Times, Navbharat Times, Femina, Filmfare,* and the *Maharashtra Times.* The increased amount of competition that the postliberalization economy has brought to the Times of India Group provided an impetus for the *Times of India* to feature more coverage of popular culture in order to attract readers who might not otherwise buy a newspaper. *Times Sunday Review* editor Malavika Sanghvi described the newspaper's increased coverage of Indian and American celebrities as part of a "softening process" that has also meant that the *Times of India* now routinely features large lots for advertisers that occupy 25 percent of the front page alongside headlines about an actress's tumultuous love life and the ongoing conflict in Kashmir. It is surreal to pick up a copy of the newspaper with the largest circulation in the world and find one quarter of the front page taken up by an enormous advertisement for Pillsbury pizza dough, a product that the vast majority of Indians would not be able to identify. In a postliberalization world, the *Times* must negotiate the line between the commercial and the substantial, although it very often sways toward the former. It is this dilemma, which sometimes positions responsible journalism and advertising revenue as diametric opposites, that served at least in part to shape the Miss India pageant as it exists today.

**Selling Beauty, Selling Class, Selling Modernity**

The concept of using young women's bodies to sell products is by no means new, as beauty pageants reached their heyday in post–World War II America and Britain with the notion that the opportunity to admire and evaluate the bodies of young women would draw crowds of potential customers to

12. *Sponsors play a critical role by subsidizing the pageant in hopes of associating their brand with the beauty and glamour of Miss India.*

heavily advertised events. Beauty pageants provided yet another visually seductive means to advertise products as part of the postwar Euro-American commoditization of vast numbers of objects and experiences ranging from TV dinners to package vacations. The postwar economic boom and the resulting explosion of popular culture that the United States experienced closely mirror the postliberalization development of the same in India. Although I would not argue that the commoditization of women's bodies in the form of beauty pageants is part of some sort of progression toward a free market economy, there is definitely a link between commodity culture and the objectification of women's bodies.

Much has been made by a skeptical Indian public about the number of potential consumers that beauty pageants create for their sponsors, and Miss India is an exception only in terms of scale. Watching both the preliminaries, during which minor titles are awarded, and the final pageant, in which the winners who will go on to international pageants are decided, one cannot help but be amazed at the amount of sponsorship money that goes into the pageant. The two main sponsors for the 2003 pageant were Sunsilk, a popular Indian brand of shampoo, and Sahara Airlines. Pageant officials requested that I not divulge the amount of money sponsors contributed in 2003, so suffice it to note that it was an enormous amount. The Grand Maratha Sheraton, where the training program was held and rooms cost upward of $200 per night, provided accommodation for approximately fifty pageant-related individuals and contestants for thirty nights. Other hotels also provided rooms for pageant officials, contestants, and judges in Bangalore and Delhi during the selection rounds and semifinals. Given the sheer amount of money involved in sponsoring the pageant, it is not surprisingly that Sunsilk, the main sponsor, went out of its way to demonstrate philosophical connections between the Miss India pageant and their shampoo. Sunsilk is owned by Hindustan Lever, the Indian branch of the British corporation Unilever, and has been a popular brand of shampoo in India since 1964. The company has diversified its range of beauty products enormously since liberalization to include home hair color kits and a wider variety of shampoos and conditioners to suit different hair types.

Sunsilk official D. Shivkumar was quick to describe ideological traits the shampoo and the pageant share in our discussion of the dynamics of sponsorship, noting that "the shampoo brand represents the woman of today, one who is erudite, spirited and with the times, just like Miss India." He described Sunsilk's sponsor strategy by incorporating both the shampoo and the pageant into a discussion of female achievement:

> The spate of international winners in the last decade has excited the young Indian girl to try to achieve something for herself, to make a mark and be noticed for what she is. The desire is strong across the country, be it a small or a large town, and we believe that this will only grow in the coming years. An event like Miss India is the ideal platform for the realization of this ambition, hence the association with Sunsilk.

In linking international beauty pageants, female achievement and shampoo, Shivkumar presented an interesting, if spurious, claim to be working in the interests of the nation. Words such as "ambition" and "platform" speak more to female empowerment than to the corporate sponsorship of a beauty pageant, and yet it is precisely this masking of goals that makes the pageant and its sponsors seem interested in uplifting women rather than selling shampoo. Sunsilk already controlled 60 percent of the multi-billion dollar shampoo market in India at the time of the 2003 pageant, and so by associating the brand with beauty under the pretext of female empowerment, the company was able to position itself as a positive influence on women's lives, and on the creation of the new Indian woman, as Shivkumar describes below.

> Indian women are evolving and coming out to express their individuality. The core of Sunsilk is understanding and uniqueness. That is the core of any young girl today: the need to belong, yet stand out. This trend will stay and events such as Sunsilk *Femina* Miss India will actually make the women's ambition and aspiration flower.

Sunsilk chose to host the semifinals in Bangalore, a city symbolic of a newer, better India to many and best known for its gardens, the Indian software company Infosys, and numerous other multinational software firms. As A. P. Parigi insisted, "Market research has clearly demonstrated that there is only one city in the country, Bangalore, which is a city of innovation." This alone underscores the intimate connection between sponsoring Miss India and the postliberalization creation of a vastly expanded consumer culture in a new market economy.

Sunsilk's association with Miss India in 2003 was especially unique in that it was an alliance designed to make both the shampoo and the pageant better known across all of India. Rural and urban India are almost two different countries for advertisers, and rural women are not the targets of multinational cosmetics companies because they do not have the money or set of cultural norms about beauty that such products require. Rural women rely instead upon natural beauty products they prepare themselves, and so perhaps the greatest challenge that Sunsilk faced when trying to spread awareness of its product outside of cities and larger towns is the fact that rural women do not use shampoo. Instead, they use inexpensive yellow soap or an herbal powder called *śikākāī*, which they massage into the scalp about once a week in the form of a paste and then rinse out. Hair is a powerful index of female beauty and health in rural India and a host of natural remedies exist to care for it, the most common of which is the use of coconut oil as a leave-in conditioner to make hair shiny, straight, and soft even in the most remote regions of India.

Sunsilk representatives began an aggressive rural marketing campaign to combat this lack of need for shampoo in which they traveled from village to village in vans and met with women to explain the benefits of using shampoo rather than *śikākāī* or soap. Stylist and brand ambassador for Sunsilk shampoo Samantha Kocchar, who worked with L'Oreal brand ambassador Jawed Habib at Miss India 2003, was quick to point out that Sunsilk's penetration of rural markets was a positive thing for women. She noted that "when the vans go from village to village to teach them about how to use our free shampoo samples, they see how nice it feels when they use it."

This concise description of the creation of new markets in rural areas that previously had no need for products such as shampoo illustrates how the postliberalization economy of beauty works at multiple levels. Habib observed that "in villages, where girls only wash their hair once a week, Sunsilk is teaching them that's very unhygienic, and in urban areas they teach about style statements." By teaching village women that their habits are what Habib called "unhygienic," Sunsilk worked to create a discourse of shame and pollution for rural women from which only shampoo could redeem them. Rural India is consistently positioned as backward by numerous forces in popular culture; to be called "a villager," for example, is a supreme insult in an urban Indian context because it implies that the insulted party has none of the knowledge or sophistication that an urbanite does. Rural women are no doubt aware of this depiction of themselves as less beautiful and "modern" than their urban peers, and so the Sunsilk marketing strategy outside of urban areas was as much about selling class and modernity as it was about beauty products.

An executive at Sunsilk's parent company Hindustan Lever made it clear that beauty and self-esteem go hand in hand for urban women by noting that "just like a Mercedes gives a man a feeling that he's bigger than anyone else, Sunsilk will remove bad hair days from a woman's life and make her believe in herself, just like *Femina* Miss India." The executive's gendered evaluation of what gives an individual a feeling of power is notable in its contention that a Mercedes, a consummate South Asian mark of success, allows a man to assert his sense of masculine authority, whereas a woman's sense of self-worth centers on her beauty. He insisted that there is an enormous amount of overlap between ordinary women and Miss India, as "Miss India is not a plastic perfect beauty, but rather beauty with substance, like Sunsilk."

Sunsilk is regarded as a widespread and ordinary brand in an urban context in which imported American and Western European shampoos are seen as better quality despite their higher cost. Miss India is a much more prestigious name in an urban context than Sunsilk, even for those who can afford imported shampoo, because of its association with international events like Miss Universe and Miss World. The Sunsilk executive hoped that the shampoo's association with Miss India would prove mutually beneficial for both:

> In the three years in which they have a contract with us, Miss India will become known by the lowest of the population strata who already know about Sunsilk. People will remember us with Miss India in their first thought, and start associating us with beauty.

This joint goal of pan-Indian penetration on the part of Sunsilk and Miss India served as a business strategy that sought to simultaneously elevate a rather ordinary product in the eyes of urban women, who see international brands of shampoo as more alluring, and to also encourage rural women to buy a product for which they have no real use by making them aware of a pageant in which they could never compete. The Miss India contestants serve as living dolls of a sort in the midst of these corporate strategies, representative of the alluring face of cosmopolitan modernity. The pageant sponsors actively sought to position beauty as a vehicle through which women could attain "empowerment," a word used throughout the pageant to describe a set of characteristics that revolved around the central theme of women's independence. By redefining beauty as an agent of women's liberation rather than male hegemony, the sponsors rather cleverly positioned the pageant as an organization that worked toward the improvement of women's lives. This positioning is by no means accidental given that much is at stake in the production of the identity of the pageant, especially in terms of sales generated from advertising.

It was immediately clear to both Sunsilk and Miss India that the vastly different urban and rural Indian markets required equally dissimilar advertising campaigns, and so while Sunsilk sold the rural woman hygiene and modernity it simultaneously embarked upon a project of selling the urban woman the most elusive commodity of all: confidence. This process was couched in the language of "international standards," which invoked hierarchies not only of beauty but also of national identity.

### *Femina* and the Creation of the "New Indian Woman"

Former Editor Vimla Patel described the creation of *Femina* magazine in 1959, just over a decade after India's independence from British rule in 1947, as a tool to help create a homogenous Indian woman who would transcend the boundaries of caste and ethnicity to unite the nation. Patel drew a strong parallel between India's struggle for independence and the creation of the magazine in observing that when *Femina* was started, "women in India at that time needed a direction—they needed to know where to go, which way to go, how to accept new things but not give up old things—how to find their place in a newly independent India."

Describing the years following independence as "the most fundamental and most productive in terms of defining women's status in India," Patel was adamant that it was a period which was instrumental in the creation of both a new version of womanhood and national identity. Patel linked the creation of *Femina* with the enormous legislative changes in women's rights that followed independence, including the 1950 Indian Constitution's guarantee of equal rights of citizenship to women, followed by the passage of the 1956 Hindu Code Bill that gave women the right to divorce, and the Hindu Succession Act, which made women equal recipients of family inheritance.

*Femina* has consistently focused on women's self-improvement via its self help and advice columns, recipes, fashion features, and articles that focus on social issues such as poverty and public health. The magazine addresses its average reader as a total woman who is a wife and a mother as well as a citizen and consumer, a woman who is Indian rather than regional in identity and is also fluent in English. The magazine even created a name for this woman in the form of the "woman of substance," which remained its slogan until 1991. It was with sentiments such as these about national identity and womanhood that the Miss India pageant was born. By showcasing what Indian women should be in the form of a single woman, Miss India became emblematic of the entire *Femina* project. According to Patel:

> The aims were to get an Indian woman, so that applied to textiles, which were the most important industry in India. And the women who were our future leaders were in college, and to build up our readership we started staging college pageants. . . . So by getting them together, and making them understand that they were a national identity rather than a regional identity, they would make up the future Woman of India.

It is perhaps not surprising that although *Femina* magazine was ready for young women to embody the nation in the form of a beauty pageant, the rest of India was not. Patel described in detail the problems that the pageant faced from activists who decried the existence of beauty pageants as "un-Indian," and it was because of this that the Miss India pageant switched its focus in the 1960s to a forum that showcased Indian textiles in order to appeal to a wider audience early in its existence. Patel described how the pageant rented a train and traveled throughout the country with the Miss India contestants showing off the textiles of each region, a pattern that continued when Prime Minister Indira Gandhi encouraged the Miss India pageant to do over three thousand shows promoting handloom textiles in international locations from Fiji to Brazil.

*Femina* remains actively involved in addressing issues relevant to numerous facets of women's lives and is divided into four main strengths: relationships, food, fashion, and beauty. Editor Sathya Saran mentioned that she "works to channel women's wherewithal and India's raw materials into a fashion consciousness, which we as a country are in desperate need of right now." Saran noted that while both rural and urban women have "great fashion consciousness," the first of which comes from what

13. *At least part of each Miss India pageant is dedicated to the display of Indian textiles, such as this red Rajasthani batik sari.*

she called "tradition" and the second from "international exposure," the urban middle class "commits a lot of kitsch in the process of trying to be modern." Statements such as these are almost offensive in the context of real social problems such as poverty and illiteracy that could be more appropriately characterized by Saran's reference to India's "desperate need," and yet they also reveal much about the cultural framework in which Miss India operates.

If *Femina* represents a new way of thinking for urban Indian women, then the Miss India pageant is the idealized form of such women and embodies national identity on a global scale in the form of the Miss Universe and Miss World pageants. Miss India truly represents the culmination of the *Femina* goal of creating an image of Indian womanhood, a "woman of substance," whom Saran described as an achiever who is never satisfied with her life.

> The *Femina* woman wants to do everything. She wants to take holidays, she wants to be a mother, she wants to work, she wants great sex, she wants everything. So she switches gears all the time. The *Femina* lifestyle is very aspirational—you reach point A, you want to go to point A1, you want to go even higher. So there is an upwardly mobile philosophy at work here, and it's not just economic or financial. It's emotional. It's like, oh, I have a great rapport with my husband, I want a great rapport with my children. I have a great rapport with both of them, I want to have the best of friends. I have a great rapport there, I want my in-laws to love me. And it never stops, it's never really satisfied.

This rhetoric has permeated the lives of urban women to such an extent that contestants expressed it throughout the course of the pageant. When asked what it means to be Miss India at the selection round, Kaveri from Nasik said that "a Miss India should be able to take care of family, ramp modeling, everything around her." It is no accident that Kaveri's estimation of what it means to be Miss India was almost identical to Saran's. This underscores just how homogenous and iconic the figure of Miss India is; although she is the representation of the nation, she is also something of a carbon copy of previous Miss India winners and *Femina* press releases.

Judges and pageant officials throughout the entire pageant process pressed what they perceived to be the critical importance of representing India at Miss Universe or Miss World. Contestants were repeatedly told that they were the best that India had to offer and that this status conferred upon them a responsibility to represent the nation on a global platform, a notion that became deeply embedded in the minds of many of the young women. Miss India 2002 Neha Dhupia told me before her departure to compete in the Miss Universe pageant, "I'll have a billion eyes on me," which is a gross overestimation given that the majority of Indians do not have access to the television networks that broadcast Miss Universe or the English language skills to understand it. Nevertheless, the fact remains that young women who participate firmly believe that being Miss India entails a serious amount of responsibility, as former Miss Universe Lara Dutta observed:

> At Miss India, you have a sash that says your name on it, but at Miss Universe you have a sash that says your country's name on it, so you are "India." That's what you embody and that's what you represent. So there's a lot more pressure on you, because you've got a billion people who want you to go out there and win. That's on your shoulders. You represent everything your country has ever stood for—its culture, its traditions and its way of thinking, what the modern Indian woman is like, where we're headed.

Dutta's assertion that Miss India actually is "India" at the Miss Universe pageant highlights how important and weighty that role is felt to be by many young women, although the idea of representing "everything your country has ever stood for" is a heady proposition that hardly reflects the reality that beauty queens spend most of their time as spokespeople for commercial products and sufficiently apolitical causes. The rhetoric of representation used at Miss India is less about the real responsibilities that contestants have than it is about the comparative *lack* of responsibilities that their peers have, as it is precisely because little is expected of most young women in India that being a beauty queen is seen as such an important distinction. With the characteristically emphatic language that public figures tend to use with the Indian press, former Miss India Nafisa Joseph said, "India is part of a global system, and it's important for our patriarchal society to provide equal opportunities, so that we continue to excel in all spheres."

Women throughout the world are forced to negotiate patriarchal spaces that allow them only limited representation in areas deemed sufficiently unthreatening to established gender norms. The sort of representation that being Miss India or Miss Universe provides is one that reinforces patriarchy

14. *Although the responsibility of the relatively privileged contestants to help the less fortunate is frequently espoused at beauty pageants, visits to orphanages such as this one by Aishwarya Rai are secondary to contestants' aspirations for media stardom.*

while simultaneously situating women's performances of gender-approved behaviors in a rhetoric of female achievement. This seemingly contradictory combination is the result of a particularly interesting point in history in which what it means to be Indian, female and above all, a member of an increasingly interconnected world, are all deeply in question.

## Performing India

What is at issue is the performative nature of differential identities: the regulation and negotiation of those spaces that are continually, contingently, "opening out," remaking the boundaries, exposing the limits of any claim to a singular or autonomous sign of difference. (Bhabha 1994, 219)

*Miss India ke rāj se pahlē uta bhārătīyă sundărīyā ka ghūmghaṭ* [The Miss India crown is the first to lift the veil from Indian beauty] ("*Miss India*" 2002)

Using the metaphor of the *ghūmghaṭ*, a large piece of cloth that village women wear in some parts of India to hide their faces, the Hindi language *Navbharat Times* suggested that Miss India led the way in (quite literally) unveiling the beautiful women of India to the world. The 2003 pageant carefully orchestrated exactly who these Indian woman were via the training program and the format of the pageant itself, so that contestants were constantly reminded that the performance of nationality and femininity requires a great deal of work. The task that the majority of contestants found most difficult was a series of lessons in how to walk in a sari, the garment worn by most mature Hindu women that many of the young women had never tried on before. Saris consist of six yards of cloth worn wrapped around the body and are not considered convenient or "modern" garments by most urban young women, who wear them only at ceremonial occasions such as weddings and often prefer jeans and other garments that global popular culture dictates as fashionable, another notable way in which their lives are in sharp contrast to their sari-wearing village counterparts.

The sari round of the 2003 pageant was added as part of the focus on "international standards" as a localized form of the national costume competitions that are part of both Miss Universe and Miss World. In a somewhat bizarre enactment of a national identity that they do not embrace in their everyday lives, contestants played at being "Indian" in a way that was more suggestive of a performance than an actual representation of who they were as urban Indian women. Sari designer Ritu Kumar was exasperated with the contestants as they struggled to walk in saris during the training program, because none of the young women were comfortable wearing the garment and changed into it only when it was absolutely necessary for rehearsals. Many of the young women were professional models, and yet it was an enormous effort for them to sashay down a catwalk in the heavily embroidered saris that they had been asked to wear, and many of them tripped as they walked.

Much to choreographer Anu Ahuja's chagrin, only three contestants had brought saris with them to the pageant, which meant that the other twenty-three attended their afternoon ramp walk sessions in their normal attire of miniskirts and tank tops. "Please," she pleaded with Nupur, who wore an Italian leather miniskirt, "at least walk as if you're wearing a sari!" Nupur responded by reducing her miniskirt-clad stride into the slower shuffle that a sari demands in order to avoid loosening its folds. Ahuja was frustrated with this poor performance of national identity and advised the contestants to send one of the chaperones out to buy an inexpensive sari in which to practice; when the contestants were silent in response, she moaned, "Please, girls! You can throw it away afterward!" In the meantime, however, contestants shared a few saris between them, grudgingly wrapping the six yards of cloth around their bodies in front of everyone by using the waists of their miniskirts and low-rise jeans to hold the saris in place.

This reluctance on the part of contestants to be "sufficiently Indian" in wearing saris draws attention to the disjuncture between Miss India and the reality of actually being a Miss India contestant. Although Miss India as a representative of Indian national identity wears saris that are considered extremely glamorous and exotic at international pageants, Miss India contestants as individual young women were uncomfortable with what they saw as a relic of a more conservative India that was not relevant to their preferences and aspirations. Contestants seemed to feel that to wear a sari as Miss Universe or Miss World was elegant because of the way in which it celebrated difference vis-à-vis less spectacular national costumes, but to wear one as a Miss India contestant seemed prosaic and conservative.

Nonetheless, the contestants did eventually learn how to walk in saris, as the 2003 pageant itself was about presenting what were effectively old ideas about national identity in new ways. From the slogan of *strī śakti* to each contestant's brief speech at the semifinals about womanhood in India, the entire process was filled with references to Indian national identity. Ami from Los Angeles introduced herself onstage at the semifinals by saying, "Tonight, *bhārat mātā* [Mother India] stands proud!" The audience was thrilled with this statement, and responded to it with resounding applause. The concept of *bhārat mātā* means much more than "motherland" or even "Mother India," as it is a complex amalgamation of ideas that combine religion, femininity, and power in a single phrase that has emotional associations including the perceived responsibility of men to protect women and the near-sacred connections between motherhood and sacrifice. *Bhārat mātā* is often invoked as both a powerful force and a cause to defend in the speeches of Hindu fundamentalist leaders, especially in reference to the perceived Muslim male threat most often represented in the form of Pakistan. The notion of *bhārat mātā* proudly embodied in the form of Miss India connects beauty and the nation in a fundamental way that mirrors numerous instances cross-culturally of the use of women's bodies as sites for the contestation of national identity. From the female genital cutting campaigns led during the Mau Mau Rebellion in Kenya to the use of rape as a tool of war by Serb soldiers in Bosnia, femininity is a locus within which the dynamics of nationalism and what it means to belong to a particular geographical space are routinely questioned and reaffirmed.

What twenty-six young women were doing onstage throughout both the semifinals and the final pageant was essentially about embodying national identity. Performing India in the saris they had taken great pains to learn to wear, they served as paragons of Indian femininity, a fact that was routinely alluded to throughout the course of the training program. Hair consultant for the pageant Apoorva Shah mentioned, "This is *Bhārat Darśan* [seeing India], a great medium of national integration." His statement positions the concept of *Bhārat Darśan*, of gazing at India in an almost reverential way, as a means to link the diverse groups that make up the subcontinent.

The semifinals made a consistent effort to at least present a superficial sense of the Miss India pageant as an accurate representation of the entire subcontinent. In a concerted attempt at integrating relatively marginalized South India with the more powerful North, the semifinals were held in the software capital of India, Bangalore. This choice was clearly the result of A. P. Parigi's decision to spread a message of Miss India's accessibility throughout the country. The semifinals featured a South Indian film star named Prema as a judge as part of this attempt at national unification, and it was absolutely fascinating to watch how the local press virtually ignored the other celebrity judges, some of whom were Hindi film stars, in favor of surrounding Prema with the nonstop glow of flashbulbs throughout the pageant.

15. As "India's ambassador to the world," Miss India is often
shown performing ordinary activities, such as sitting on the floor
and eating with her right hand, to demonstrate her respect for
Indian cultural norms despite her international success. Pictured
are Aishwarya Rai and her mother.

There are enormous cultural differences between North and South
India that include cinema and popular culture, and so the Bangalore audience was thrilled when Parvati from Hindi-speaking Delhi greeted them
in the local language of Kannada. The second time that the relatively quiet
South Indian audience became involved in the performance by clapping
was during a singing competition between South Indian star Vasundra
and Hindi language singer Sunidhi Chauhan. In a fascinating effort at

national integration onstage that delighted the audience, the two switched languages midway through the performance so that Vasundra began to sing in Hindi and Chauhan in Kannada. The entire event was televised on January 26, the day in 1950 that India officially became a sovereign state, as part of the association of Miss India with the patriotic construction of national identity and yet also featured a number of performances that made it sufficiently "modern" and "international," including a dance troupe from the United Kingdom.

The final pageant was held on January 31 and constituted a similar effort at performing India. As hostess and sex symbol Malaika Arora Khan announced, "We welcome you to a night of power—women power!" all twenty-six contestants appeared in saris that had been designed especially for the pageant. The contestants paraded onto a revolving stage in the saris they had taken so long to learn how to wear as European techno-pop played in the background. The young women smiled at the audience as Khan began a running commentary on how the design of the saris worn by contestants had been inspired "by the magic of Khajuraho," the North Indian Hindu temples that make use of a religious space to depict the female body in various states of erotic undress and sexual pleasure.

The connection of the contestants' bodies onstage to the sacred sexuality of Khajuraho may have been a conscious decision on the part of organizers to culturally legitimize the display that is inherent in a beauty pageant. The obvious parallels between the two sites aside, the use of Khajuraho as an integral theme of the final pageant drew a direct correlation between a "traditional" India of temples and saris and a "global" India in the form of beauty queens and techno-pop. This line of reasoning was consistent with the opening performance of the pageant in which a woman dressed as an Indian classical dancer in the tradition known as *bhārat natyam* performed rather aggressively to a Goan trance remix that combined North Indian classical music with a techno beat.

Performing India is also about negotiating an India that does not conform to the standards and norms in place at the pageant, and this was especially evident when the contestants went to the Amby Valley luxury resort for their first press conference. Transported in minibuses through the urban sprawl that characterizes most highways outside urban areas in India, the contestants could only stop once to use the bathroom on the three-hour trip, as there were no suitable places for twenty-six scantily clad young women to use the toilets other than the McDonald's on the highway immediately outside of the Mumbai city limits.

Even inside the sparklingly clean space of the highway McDonald's, the contestants created quite a sensation as everyone in the restaurant stopped what they were doing and stared at the long line of potential Miss Indias standing outside the bathroom, which only had two stalls. The message from the stares the contestants received at McDonald's revealed just how distinctive and anomalous they appeared in any space except the Miss India pageant itself, although once we arrived in the enclosed Amby Valley the young women no longer seemed provocatively dressed. When the bus pulled into the complex, one contestant exclaimed, "It's so beautiful, it doesn't look like India anymore!" as several others chimed in with similar thoughts. Indeed, with its enormous golf course, lush meadows full of European wildflowers, green grass, and wooden houses, the Amby Valley had much more in common with Gstaad, Switzerland, than with the rest of India.

Fifty men dressed as Rajasthani villagers beating drums lined up on either side of the road to welcome the contestants, who were garlanded as an expression of respect and then led to meet the press. In this performance of national identity, the contestants were welcomed as the very representation of India. This was further enforced by the first group photograph of the contestants at the Amby Valley, which was taken in front of a fifty-foot high statue of *bhārat mātā* that featured her commanding a chariot pulled by tigers with a huge Indian flag flowing in the background. The message was unmistakable.

# ⊘ 7 ⊘

## Conclusion

### *Miss India in the Postliberalization Candy Store*

It's like the first time you go into a superstore, you want to buy everything, because all the chocolates are within your reach, you can touch
them. It's only after you've been going there for a year that can go and
buy what you want and leave.

This rather concise description of making sense of postliberalization
urban India's consumer culture comes from interior designer Kareem
Furniturewallah, who described how difficult it was for his affluent clients to
choose between the enormous numbers of styles that had become available
to them in the decade following structural adjustment. Using the metaphor
of the superstore, which became a popular phenomenon in urban India following liberalization, he highlighted the way in which the new postliberalization India requires some degree of negotiation and self-restraint.

The sheer variety of images and commodities from American and
Western European markets that urban Indians now have to contend with
and choose from is rather overwhelming and not unlike Furniturewallah's very vivid image of entering a superstore for the first time. The phenomenon of Miss India can be firmly situated within the same cultural
logic as the superstore because it only grew to a state of national obsession after structural adjustment. The kind of fantasy space that structural
adjustment programs created for privileged urban Indians is remarkable;
within a single decade India's media and corporate capital of Mumbai
grew from a city with one nightclub in a five-star hotel into a metropolis

in which one could go out every night for a month without visiting the same establishment twice. People who could afford to partake in the new experiences that urban India offered after liberalization were often reminiscent of people in a candy store experimenting with as many types of food, fashion, and sexuality as they possibly could.

The prime example of this candy store phenomenon was "A Walk in the Clouds" an event sponsored by the Indian champagne house Chateau Indage. Billed as "a place where Indian culture and wine culture blend together, creating harmony between the two traditions in a festive atmosphere," the event celebrated the culmination of the year's grape harvest. Chateau Indage spared no expense in the construction of the event, with French experts from Burgundy available to help educate participants about wine and chefs who created innovative fusion foods with a wine-based theme.

Complete with fire eaters, dance troupes, tattoo artists, magicians, palmists, and copious quantities of complimentary alcohol, the event sought to mimic the vineyard harvest celebrations of Europe. Chateau Indage made no secret of its desire to do so and proudly emphasized how invitees could "dance in a tub full of grapes the way village virgins in ancient France have traditionally welcomed the first harvest." "A Walk in the Clouds" and its myriad references to sybaritic pleasure is extremely representative of the candy store phenomenon that pervades postliberalization urban India.

Indeed, the entire concept of the postliberalization candy store closely corresponds to Ritzer's concept of the phantasmagoria, which

> implies a cornucopia of goods and services that offer the possibility of satisfying people's wildest fantasies. The dream here . . . is to be immersed in a world filled with everything one could imagine, with all of these things there for the taking. It is akin to the childhood dream of finding oneself in a land in which everything is made of candy and all of it within reach. (2001, 21)

Like "A Walk in the Clouds," the Miss India pageant offers the same world made of candy ready for consumption by visitors. Although it is partially an empty promise, the idea of being able to embody the national ideal and by extension be accorded the title of the most beautiful woman in the universe grants urban middle-class young women an opportunity to participate in this candy store world that is otherwise only open to the extremely privileged.

If Miss India can teach us anything, it is that beauty and femininity are cultural performances that are learned as part of broader sociocultural processes. Although Miss India does offer a great number of possibilities to the twenty-six contestants who are given access to the training program each year, these young women are drawn primarily from the same urban middle class and predominantly North Indian backgrounds. Although this is partially masked by the rhetoric of evolution and transformation, the fact remains that these young women already fit into a mold of what is considered beautiful in India.

This book seeks to open a dialogue about different ways of seeing both India and the world. By following a methodology that placed me at the center of the sometimes confusing barrage of images surrounding the pageant, I was as much a part of the gaze through my interactions with pageant officials as I was subject to it via my participation in the Miss India training program. Although this no doubt influenced the conclusions presented here, there would have been no other way to gather such a rich body of data. This book could have taken a variety of stances ranging from an all-too-simplistic critique of the exploitative, classist, and sexist nature of pageants to a wholesale embrace of the opportunities that the institution of Miss India provides to young women who are lucky enough to participate in it. I honestly considered writing from both perspectives, before I decided that each would inadequately describe the cultural institution of the Miss India pageant. Instead, I chose to carefully examine what being Miss India means to a host of individuals, and what I found was that participating in the pageant allowed young women a form of social mobility that they otherwise would not have had. Although this mobility came at the price of modifying their bodies and, to some degree, their very selves, I was consistently impressed by the way twenty-six young women were willing to work so hard for the chance to be someone called "Miss India."

Women who participate in Miss India are not simply victims of oppression as a result of life in a patriarchal society. They are women with

16. *Miss World Diana Hayden returns to India amid great fanfare and is almost certainly assured celebrity status for years to come.*

hopes and dreams for their futures who understand that because they are not part of the classed social networks that control Indian media, they often have to play certain games of which Miss India is the most socially respectable. On some levels, Miss India is no different than any number of other sexist social structures and institutions that women have historically been forced to negotiate in order to attain social mobility, but it is also unique in the complex connections it draws between national identity, women's bodies, and the rapidly expanding consumer culture of post-structural adjustment India. After spending over a year of my life both formally and informally immersed in the world of the Miss India pageant, I contend that certain feminist schools of thought that regard beauty pageants as the misogynist commoditization of women's bodies are fundamentally flawed in that they deny women the agency, intelligence, and creativity to survive in a system designed to work against them.

Since 1994, India has been absorbed by the success of Miss India contestants at international beauty pageants. It may not be right or desirable that many urban Indians find validation in a young woman from a poor country winning a title that deems her the most beautiful woman in the universe, but the fact remains that a huge number of Indian people do feel that their beauty queens are a source of pride. A photograph of a young woman from a place often called "the third world" smiling and wearing a sash that reads "Miss Universe" is inherently problematic in that it raises a number of questions about economic inequality, ethnicity, and national identity. To the young woman in the photograph, however, her ability to be awarded such a title represents social mobility and immense national pride in a new urban India. There are no easy answers to these questions, as in the end the Miss India pageant reveals much less about what a privileged urban minority has access to than it does about what the majority of Indians are denied.

# GLOSSARY

# WORKS CITED

# INDEX

# Glossary

**bahinjī:** sister (honorific) respectful term used when addressing unrelated women

**bahut:** much, a great deal

**baiṭhī hūī hain:** sitting, to be sitting

**bhārătīyă:** Indian

**bhārat mātā:** Mother India, motherland

**bhārat natyam:** a form of North Indian classical dance

**bekarī:** poverty

**būdīyā:** old ladies

**burī nazar:** bad intentions transmitted visually, a bad look, the "evil eye"

**calō:** come on, let's go

**caukīdār:** security guard, gatekeeper

**darśan:** to gaze, to look

**dekhō:** look

**duśman:** enemy

**ek-hī:** only one; each

**farq:** difference

**gajrāvālī:** female street vendor who sells strands of jasmine to adorn women's hair

**ghūmghaṭ:** a thin, broad cloth worn over women's faces to demonstrate modesty

**hain:** are

**hindutvă:** Hindu nationalism

**itnī patlī:** so thin or emaciated, extremely thin or emaciated

**izzat:** honor, dignity (often used specifically to refer to men or male-headed households)

**jaan:** life (literally), also a term of endearment used by men for women

**janta:** people (literally), crowd, "the common people"

**jay hind:** long live India, victory to India

**ka:** of

**kacrā:** garbage, waste

**kahān gāya:** to where (as in, "where has he gone?")

**ke līyē:** for

**khadī:** homespun cotton cloth associated with the movement for Indian Independence

**khūbsūratī:** beauty (usually female beauty)

**koī:** someone

**lagatī:** to seem or appear

**laṛkī:** girl, unmarried young woman

**log:** people

**māliśvālī:** female masseuse

**mazdūr:** manual laborer

**meṅ:** in

**merē:** my (form used with plurals or adjectives)

**meri saheli:** my female friend, used by women to refer to other women

**nahi:** no

**naśā:** intoxication

**pahlē uta:** to have lifted for the first time

**palaṅg:** bed

**par:** on

**pardā:** curtain (literally), social seclusion of women from unrelated men

**pūrā din:** entire day

**rāj:** rule, crown

**sab:** all

**sabse baṛai:** the biggest, most formidable

**sāhab:** sir, an expression of respect for a man of higher status

**salwar kameez:** a North Indian garment consisting of a long tunic and scarf worn over pajama pants

**śikākāī:** an herbal cleanser used instead of shampoo in villages

**strī śakti:** woman power

**sundǎrīyā:** beauty

**tv dekh rāhē hain:** watching television

**umrao:** rich or sumptuous, also a woman's name

# Works Cited

Abu-Lughod, Lila. 1986. *Veiled Sentiments: Honor and Poetry in a Bedouin Society.* Berkeley: Univ. of California Press.

Allison, Anne. 1994. *Nightwork: Sexuality, Pleasure and Corporate Masculinity in a Tokyo Hostess Club.* Chicago: Univ. of Chicago Press.

Appadurai, Arjun. 1996. *Modernity at Large: Cultural Dimensions of Globalization.* Chicago: Univ. of Chicago Press.

———. 1988. *The Social Life of Things: Commodities in Cultural Perspective.* Cambridge: Cambridge Univ. Press.

Banet-Weiser, Sarah. 1999. *The Most Beautiful Girl in the World: Beauty Pageants and National Identity.* Berkeley: Univ. of California Press.

Bartky, Sandra. 1990. "Foucault, Femininity and the Modernization of Patriarchal Power." In *Feminism and Foucault: Paths of Resistance,* edited by Lee Quinby and Irene Diamond, 61–86. Chicago: Northeastern Univ. Press.

Baudrillard, Jean. 1998. *The Consumer Society: Myths and Structures.* New York: Sage Publications.

Behar, Ruth. 1995. "Writing in My Father's Name: A Diary of *Translated Woman*'s First Year." In *Women Writing Culture,* edited by Ruth Behar and Deborah Gordon, 65–84. Berkeley: Univ. of California Press.

Bhabha, Homi. 1994. *The Location of Culture.* London: Routledge.

Bhatia, Tej. 2000. *Advertising in Rural India.* Tokyo: Institute for the Study of Languages and Cultures of Asia and Africa.

Bordo, Susan. 1993. *Unbearable Weight: Feminism, Western Culture and the Body.* Berkeley: Univ. of California Press.

Brumberg, Joan Jacobs. 1988. *Fasting Girls: The Emergence of Anorexia Nervosa as a Modern Disease.* Cambridge, Mass.: Harvard Univ. Press.

Bryan, Dominic. 2000. *Orange Parades: The Politics of Ritual, Tradition and Control.* Herendon, Va.: Pluto Press.

— Buck-Morss, Susan. 1996. "The Dialectics of Seeing." In *The Senses Still,* edited by C. Nadia Serematakis, 45–62. Chicago: Univ. of Chicago Press.

Burke, Timothy. 1996. *Lifebuoy Men, Lux Women: Commodification, Consumption and Cleanliness in Modern Zimbabwe.* Durham: Duke Univ. Press.

Butler, Judith. 1993. *Bodies That Matter: On the Discursive Limits of Sex.* New York: Routledge.

— Cannell, Fernando. 1993. "The Power of Appearances: Beauty, Mimicry and Transformation." In *Discrepant Histories: Translocal Essays on Filipino Cultures,* edited by Vincente Rafael, 43–63. Philadelphia: Temple Univ. Press.

Chopra, Ajai, Charles Collins, Richard Hemming, Karen Parker, Woosik Chu, and Oliver Fratzscher. 1995. *India: Economic Reforms and Growth.* International Monetary Fund Occasional Paper 134. Washington, D.C.: International Monetary Fund.

Cohen, Colleen, Wilk, Richard, and Beverly Stoeltje, eds. 1995. *Beauty Queens on the Global Stage: Gender, Contests and Power.* New York: Routledge.

Cohn, Bernard. 1996. *Colonialism and Its Forms of Knowledge: The British in India.* Princeton, N.J.: Princeton Univ. Press.

Cole, Sally. 1991. *Women of the Praia: Work and Lives in a Portuguese Coastal Community.* Princeton, N.J.: Princeton Univ. Press.

✳ Davis, Kathy. 1995. *Reshaping the Female Body: The Dilemma of Cosmetic Surgery.* New York: Routledge.

De, Shobhaa. 1999. "Designer Charity Is Here to Stay." *Times of India.* Jan. 6.

Dickey, Sara. 1993. *Cinema and the Urban Poor in South India.* Cambridge: Cambridge Univ. Press.

di Leonardo, Micaela. 2000. *Exotics at Home: Anthropologists, Others, American Modernity.* Chicago: Univ. of Chicago Press.

Dirks, Nicholas. 2001. *Castes of Mind: Colonialism and the Making of Modern India.* Princeton, N.J.: Princeton Univ. Press.

Douglas, Mary. 2003. "In Defense of Shopping." In *The Shopping Experience,* edited by Pasi Falk and Colin Campbell, 15–29. London: Sage Publications.

Dwyer, Rachel. 2000. *All You Want Is Money, All You Need Is Love: Sex and Romance in Modern India.* London: Cassell.

———. 2001. "Shooting Stars: The Indian Film Magazine *Stardust.*" In *Pleasure and the Nation: The History, Politics and Consumption of Popular Culture in India,* edited by Rachel Dwyer and Christopher Pinney, 247–85. London: School of African and Oriental Studies.

Eck, Diana. 1998. *Darshan: Seeing the Divine Image in India.* New York: Columbia Univ. Press.

Faludi, Susan. 1988. "Miss Teen Covina's Revenge" *Mother Jones* 13 (3): 32.

Farinelli, Franco. 1992. *Capitalist Forms of Production in South Asia: Consequences of British Policies.* Delhi: Manohar Books.

Farquhar, Judith. 2002. *Appetites: Food and Sex in Post-Maoist China.* Durham: Duke.

"The Fear of Freedom." 2003. *Femina Girl,* February, 12–16.

Fisher, William. 1997. "Doing Good? The Politics and Anti-Politics of NGO Practices." *Annual Review of Anthropology* 26:439–64.

Foucault, Michel. 1995. *Discipline and Punish: The Birth of the Prison,* second edition. New York: Vintage.

———. 1980. *Power/Knowledge: Selected Interviews and Other Writings, 1972–1977.* New York: Pantheon.

Freedman, Rita. 1988. *Beauty Bound.* London: Columbus Books.

Furman, Frida. 1997. *Facing the Mirror: Older Women and Beauty Shop Culture.* New York: Routledge.

Ganti, Tejaswini. 2000. "Casting Culture: The Social Life of Hindi Film Production in Contemporary India." PhD diss., New York Univ.

Gell, Alfred. 1998. *Art and Agency: An Anthropological Theory.* Oxford: Oxford Univ. Press.

Gerke, Solvay. 2000. "Global Lifestyles under Local Conditions." In *Consumption in Asia: Lifestyles and Identities,* edited by Chua Beng-Huat, 131–48. London: Routledge.

Gill, Leslie. 1995. "Examining Power, Serving the State: Anthropology, Congress and the Invasion of Panama." *Human Organization* 54:318–24.

Gillespie, Marie. 2001. *Television, Ethnicity and Cultural Change.* London: Routledge.

Gledhill, John. 2000. *Power and Its Disguises: Anthropological Perspectives on Politics.* Herndon, Va.: Pluto Press.

Gold, Ann. 1994. "Sexuality, Fertility and Erotic Imagination in Rajasthani Women's Songs." In *Listening to the Heron's Words: Reimagining Gender and Kinship in North India,* edited by Ann Grodzins Gold and Gloria Goodwin Raheja, 30–72. Berkeley: Univ. of California Press.

Gottlob, Jon. 2002. "India's Connection to History: The Discipline and the Relation Between Center and Periphery." In *Across Cultural Borders: Historiography in*

*Global Perspective,* edited by Eckhardt Fuchs and Benedikt Stuchtey, 34–52. New York: Rowman and Littlefield.

Goodwin, Andrew. 1992. *Dancing in the Distraction Factory: Music Television and Popular Culture.* Minneapolis: Univ. of Minnesota Press.

Grosz, Elizabeth. 1999. "Psychoanalysis and the Body." In *Feminist Theory and the Body,* edited by Janet Price and Margrit Schildrick, 120–43. Edinburgh: Edinburgh Univ. Press.

Gupta, Akhil. 1998. *Post-Colonial Developments: Agriculture and the Making of Modern India.* Delhi: Oxford Univ. Press.

Gupta, Nilanjana. 1998. *Switching Channels: Ideologies of TV in India.* Delhi: Oxford Univ. Press.

Hammonds, Evelynn. 1999. "Towards a Genealogy of Black Female Sexuality." In *Feminist Theory and the Body,* edited by Janet Price and Margrit Schildrick, 93–104. Edinburgh: Edinburgh Univ. Press.

Handelman, Dan. 1990. *Models and Mirrors: Towards an Anthropology of Public Events.* Cambridge: Cambridge Univ. Press.

— Haraway, Donna. 1999. "The Biopolitics of Postmodern Bodies." In *Feminist Theory and the Body,* edited by Janet Price and Margrit Schildrick, 203–14. Edinburgh: Edinburgh Univ. Press.

Hejaiej, Monia. 1996. *Behind Closed Doors: Women's Oral Narratives in Tunis.* New Brunswick, N.J.: Rutgers Univ. Press.

— Hutnyk, John. 2000. *Critique of Exotica: Music, Politics and the Culture Industry.* London: Pluto Press.

Jewell, K. Sue. 1993. *From Mammy to Miss America and Beyond: Cultural Images and the Shaping of US Social Policy.* London: Taylor and Francis.

Johnson, Mark. 1997. *Beauty and Power: Transgendering and Cultural Transformation in the Southern Philippines.* London: Berg Publications.

Jones, Carla. 2003. "Dress for Sukses: Fashioning Femininity and Nationality in Urban Indonesia." In *Re-Orienting Fashion: The Globalization of Asian Dress,* edited by Sandra Niessen, Ann Marie Leshkowich, and Carla Jones, 185–213. New York: Berg.

Kemper, Steven. 2001. *Buying and Believing: Sri Lankan Advertisers and Consumers in a Transnational World.* Chicago: Univ. of Chicago Press.

Kobkidsuksakul, Supatra. 1988. "Miss Thailand, 1934–1987." Master's thesis, History Department, Thammasat Univ., Bangkok, Thailand.

Kuhn, Annette. 1985. *The Power of the Image: Essays in Representation and Sexuality.* London: Routledge and Kegan Paul.

Kulshreshtra, Manisha. 2000. "Dūnīyā kī sabse khūbsūrat aurat aishwarya rai." *Merī Sahelī* (October): 1.

Liechty, Mark. 2002. *Suitably Modern: Making Middle Class Culture in a New Consumer Society*. Princeton: Princeton Univ. Press.

Maayang, Lazarus Dempsey. 1990. "Miss Ghana Pageants: A Perilous Venture into History." *UHURU Magazine* 2:23–29.

"Making Miss World: Ingredients." 1996. *Times of India* 12 (27): 5.

Mankekar, Purnima. 1999. *Screening Culture, Viewing Politics: An Ethnography of Television, Womanhood and Nation in India*. Durham, N.C.: Duke Univ. Press.

Mathews, Gordon. 2000. *Global Culture/Individual Identity: Searching for Home in the Cultural Supermarket*. New York: Routledge.

McVeigh, Brian. 1995. "The Feminization of Body, Behavior and Belief: The Cultivation Of 'Office Flowers' at a Japanese Women's Junior College." *American Asian Review* 13 (2): 29–67.

Mernissi, Fatima. 1985. *Beyond the Veil: Male-Female Dynamics in a Modern Muslim Society*. London: Saqi Books.

"Miss India ke rāj se pahlē uta bhāratīyă sundărīyă ka ghūmghat." 2002. *Navbharat Times* 12 (6): 1.

Mulvey, Laura. 1989. *Visual and Other Pleasures*. London: Palgrave Macmillan.

Naregal, Veena. 2002. *Language Politics, Elites and the Public Sphere: Western India Under Colonialism*. London: Anthem.

Orlove, Benjamin, ed. 1997. *The Allure of the Foreign: Imported Goods in Post-Colonial Latin America*. Ann Arbor: Univ. of Michigan Press.

Paul, Bimal. 1992. "Female Activity Space in Rural Bangladesh." *Geographical Review* (January): 1–12.

Pels, Peter. 1997. "The Anthropology of Colonialism: Culture, History and the Emergence of Western Governmentality." *Annual Review of Anthropology* 26:163–83.

Perlmutter, Dawn. 2000. "Miss America: Whose Ideal?" In *Beauty Matters*, edited by Peg Zeglin Brand, 155–68. Bloomington: Indiana Univ. Press.

Pitman, Joanna. 2004. *On Blondes*. New York: Bloomsbury.

Rangarajan, Chakravarti. 1994. "India's Balance of Payments: The Emerging Dimensions." Shri Govind Ballabh Memorial Lecture. *Reserve Bank of India Bulletin*. Delhi.

Raut, Ujjwala. 2002. "Ujjwala in Paris." *Femina Girl* (August): 15.

Ring, Laura. 2003. "Agents of Shame: Narratives of Love and Longing in Karachi." Paper Presentation, Univ. of Wisconsin at Madison South Asia Conference.

Ritzer, George. 2001. *Explorations in the Sociology of Consumption: Fast Food, Credit Cards and Casinos.* London: Sage Publications.

Riverol, Armando. 1992. *Live from Atlantic City: The History of Miss America Before, After and in Spite of Television.* Bowling Green, Ohio: Bowling Green Popular Press.

Saran, Sathya. 1997. "Femina Announces the Look of the Year." *Femina* (April): 22.

Segalen, Martine, and Josselyne Chamarat. 1983. "La Rosiére et la 'Miss': Les 'Reines' des Fêtes Populaires." *Histoire* 53:44–55.

Siddiqui, Imam. 1997. "So You Want to Be a Model?" *Femina* (March): 15–18.

Tarlo, Emma. 1996. *Clothing Matters: Dress and Identity in India.* Chicago: University of Chicago Press.

Virilio, Paul. 1994. *The Vision Machine.* Bloomington: Indiana Univ. Press.

Wadley, Susan. 1994. *Struggling With Destiny in Karimpur: 1925–1984.* Berkeley: Univ. of California Press.

Walker, John Albert. 2003. *Art and Celebrity.* London: Pluto Press.

Wolf, Eric. 1999. *Envisioning Power: Ideologies of Dominance and Crisis.* Berkeley: Univ. of California Press.

# Index

Italic page number denotes illustration.

Other titles in Gender and Globalization